m 1st Earl of Warwick   Margaret Russell *d.1616* m George Clifford *Earl of Cumberland*   John Russell *d.1584* m Elizabeth Cooke

1584-1657   Ann Clifford *1590-1676* m Philip Herbert *4th Earl of Pembroke*   Anne Russell *d.1584* m Henry Somerset *1st Marquis of Worcester*

Margaret Russell *1681-1676* m James *3rd Earl of Carlisle*   Edward Russell *d.1665* m Penelope Brooke

Diana Russell *1642-1695* m Francis *1st Viscount of Newport*   Ann Russell *d.young*   Margaret Russell m Admiral Edward Russell *d.1727 Lord Orford*

Wriothesley Russell *1680-1711 2nd Duke of Bedford* m 1695 Elizabeth Howland *d.1724 daughter of John Howland & Elizabeth Child*

710-1771 4th Duke of Bedford m 1: 1731 Diana Spencer *1710-1735*   Elizabeth Russell *1711-1784* m William Capel *1697-1743 3rd Earl of Essex*
m 2: 1737 Gertrude Leveson Gower *1715-1794*

Caroline Russell *1743-1811* m 1762 George Spencer *4th Duke of Marlborough*

William Russell *1767-1840 murdered by his valet*

m 2: Georgina Gordon *1781-1853*

.1874   Lord John Russell *1792-1878*   Rev. Wriothesley *1804-1886*   Admiral Edward *1805-1887*   Charles *1807-1894*   Francis *1808-1869*

Arthur Russell *1825-1892*   Odo Russell *1829-1884*   Georgiana *1810-1867*   Louisa *1812-1805*   Henry *1816-1842*

Herbrand Russell *1858-1940 11th Duke of Bedford* m 1888 Mary Tribe *d.1937*   Cosmo *1817-1875*   Alexander *1821-1907*

Hastings Russell *1888-1953 12th Duke of Bedford* m Louisa Crommelin Whitwell *d.1960*

John Ian Russell *1917-2002 13th Duke of Bedford*   Rachel *1826-1898*

m 2: 1945 Lydia Yarde-Buller *d.1960*   m 3: Nicole Millinaire *d.2012*

Francis Russell *b.1950*

5 m Dawn Alexander

Leo Russell *b.2013*

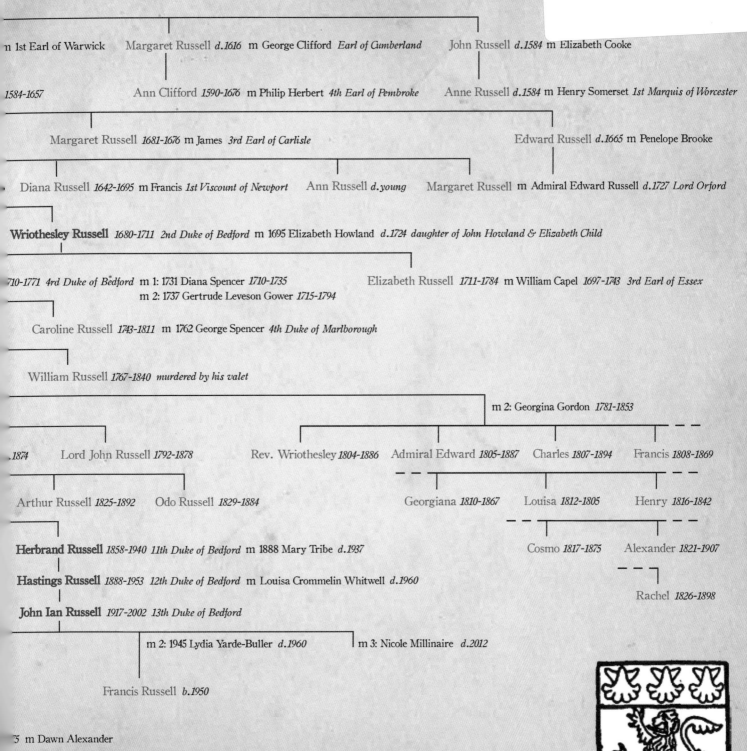

The Earldom & Duchy of Bedford

not all the children from every generation are included

WOBURN
ABBEY

THE PARK & GARDENS

WOBURN ABBEY

THE PARK & GARDENS

KEIR DAVIDSON

FOREWORD BY
HER GRACE, THE DUCHESS OF BEDFORD

PIMPERNEL
PRESS LTD
www.pimpernelpress.com

Pimpernel Press Ltd
www.pimpernelpress.com

Woburn Abbey: The Park and Gardens
Copyright © Pimpernel Press Ltd 2016
Text © Keir Davidson 2016
Photographs © see page 240

Special photography by Bridget Davey
Designed by Becky Clarke

A catalogue record for this book is available from the
British Library

ISBN 978-1-910258-13-2
Printed and bound in China
9 8 7 6 5 4 3 2 1

PAGE 1 H. W. Burgess, *View in the Evergreens*
(showing the 'Arch' and 'Colonnade'), 1837.

PAGES 2–3 Humphry Repton, 'The Dressed
Garden', Red Book for Woburn, Plate XXVII,
1805.

THIS PAGE Humphry Repton, 'View to the West'
(after), Red Book for Woburn, Plate VIb, 1805.

CONTENTS

FOREWORD

Her Grace, The Duchess of Bedford

Andrew and I were married in October 2000 and came to live at Woburn. I remember at the time being transfixed by the park and house, and being welcomed by everyone who helped on the estate. When I first moved in it was very daunting to think how I could contribute. I had always been interested in gardening and spoke with Andrew about landscaping the forty-two acres behind the Abbey.

My passion for gardens led me to find in the library Humphry Repton's Red Book, where I discovered Repton's proposals for Woburn and realized we didn't need a landscape designer as we already had one. This is when we came up with the plan to reinstate his designs, since much of Repton's work had disappeared under lawn and trees. Working with a series of five-year plans devised with Martin Towsey, our Gardens Manager for the Abbey, we started slowly restoring the structures of Repton's gardens.

Repton's belief that without animation we tire of any view has encouraged our family's interest in wild animals and conservation. The Camellia House lake has been cleared and original views towards the church revealed. The cone-roofed pavilion, where the family viewed the wildlife with protection from the expanse of water, has also been restored (we hope to encourage back exotic birds and wildlife from around the world). At the start of the project, there was no trace of Repton's Cone House, his idea for a Chinese pavilion on top of the Rockery, the Aviary or his children's garden, and now all of these have been restored. In addition to this work, features added to the gardens by Jeffry Wyatville after Repton left have also been restored, including his shell grotto, the small 'temple' dedicated to the 5th Duke of Bedford, and his garden seat.

It has been a very exciting journey, and I could not have done it without the amazing team that we have here. Their passion, drive and enthusiasm have made the garden what it is today. I am also very excited about the publication of this book, something that I feel will not only tell the story of how the successive generations of the family have sought to develop the park and the gardens, but also set the landscape in which the Abbey sits into the wider context of English landscaping. I hope, too, that the book will help visitors to the Abbey gardens today identify what is old and what is new in the view around them, to make its history more visible and comprehensible. My thanks, therefore, also go to Keir, whose dedication to this book has been enlightening.

I hope Repton would be proud!

Louise Bedford

INTRODUCTION

'No one could have placed a gentleman's house in a better situation'

(Anon., Inventory for Berwick Manor House, Dorset, 1583)

The small village of Swyre sits amongst the gently rolling forms of an ancient agricultural landscape that runs off the Dorset Downs to meet the long curve of Chesil Beach. It is a landscape of open downland, fields and clumps of woodland, with narrow lanes linking scattered houses and villages, and is as peaceful today as it must always have been – except perhaps on those dark nights when the smugglers' boats were run up on to the shingle and their cargoes hastened into hiding in barns and cellars. It is a place slow to change, steeped in its own long traditions, local identity and sense of place, and just to the north of the village itself stands Berwick Manor, a settlement that dates back to the time when these traditions and sense of identity were first being formed in the wake of the Norman Conquest. We do not know exactly how many times the buildings have been altered, but in a brief survey dated 1583 the manor was described as follows:

John B. Knight, *Berwick Farmhouse*, 1850. A nineteenth-century image of the quadrangle at Berwick Manor, its basic form still surviving and recognizable from the description in the inventory of 1583.

> The house is built as a quadrangle. It is of stone. Near by is a great barn and a dove-house. Around it are gardens, 3 orchards and a grove of ash trees. Beyond this are pasture and arable land to the extent of 500 acres. The situation is pleasing, delectable and healthy. No one could have placed a gentleman's house in a better situation. There is no moorland or dampish ground near it, but a rising of the ground to the north protects the house from the cold winds. Besides this 'rising of the ground', the house is guarded from wind and weather by elms of a very great height.[1]

There is something timeless about this description of the house, and it takes us to the very heart of what house and home have meant through the ages.[2] At the centre of everything lies a 'quadrangle', the protected inner space that in castles had provided, amongst other things, for communal recreational activity in the open air, that in monastic buildings had been the location for the cloisters – a deep, silent focal point for spiritual reflection – and that in houses became the location of gardens, which, in a way, represent

a combination of the two. An inner space is defended by the house, which 'is of stone', and beyond these stones which formed the quadrangle itself lie those of the garden walls, the barns and the dove-house, all 'guarded' in turn by a carefully managed grove of trees, and beyond that 500 acres of rolling land: everything necessary to sustain the family and the community into which it was woven.

Yet, as this description leads us steadily out from that inner space, from the house itself, to gardens and the surrounding buildings, past the orchards and the grove of trees to the wider landscape beyond, we start to form an impression of a building in its wider context, set deep into and protected by its surroundings, a settlement which – in the same way as the patterns of life around it – has developed slowly, steadily changing and adapting in response to the changing needs of the community that occupied it. The house and its farm buildings have evolved to become as similar and as different from the original manor as the house that stands there today is from the one described in 1583. Today, there may no longer be a quadrangle, and the outlines of

the house may have changed, but its odd windows and unequal elevations suggest a building that has been modified rather than rebuilt, different but recognizable, as are the farm buildings and cottages that surround it.

Berwick Manor is of interest to us now because it was in this house, and against this background, that one John Russell was born *c.*1485. While his ascent to an earldom may have changed the family's status for ever, following that family through the history of the places in which they subsequently lived, we find aspects of this house, the spaces it contained and the way of life it represents threaded through the story, surfacing again and again over the centuries like echoes, repeating as they also fade. These threads provide the continuity that will enable us, amidst the confusion of fads, fashions and theories, and the ever-changing cast of designers and theorists that make up the surface history of English landscaping, to make sense of what happened and to link Woburn Abbey as we know it today with this humble house in distant Dorset. In addition, understanding how those within the family sought to pick up these threads helps us to distinguish the original contributions of individual countesses and duchesses, each with their own unique experiences and sense of place, in the development of the landscapes – contributions, like those of some of the children, which are often overlooked in the story of their husbands, the earls and dukes of Bedford, whose interests and activities inevitably dominate the historical record.

Woburn Abbey, which became the Russell family's principal home, stands today at the centre of gardens and parklands that developed from the remains of an older monastic estate. The structure of the Abbey itself is now diminished by demolitions in the 1950s, but at the pinnacle of its development in the late eighteenth and early nineteenth centuries, the Abbey had emerged as a larger and grander house than that at Berwick, but one that was also, in the words of the survey, 'built as a quadrangle . . . of stone'. Today, it too is still surrounded by 'pasture and arable land', there is 'no moorland or dampish ground near it', and the 'situation is pleasing, delectable and healthy'. Throughout a long history, those who sought to preserve and develop it shared a vision of what made it not just a ducal seat, but also a home of the kind which would be recognizable to those who lived at Berwick Manor many years ago. A place guarded by trees, where the rising of the ground protects the house from the cold winds. This continuity, despite the family's changing circumstances and different individual interests, persists and provides the basis for the story of this book,

The Abbey is seen here nestled in its landscape, against the background of the woodland of the pleasure grounds and framed by the trees on either side of the line of the 2nd Duke of Bedford's Great Avenue of *c.*1710. The avenue ran from the Abbey, round the Bason Pond in the rear middle distance, over the London road in the near middle distance and up the slope of Wayn Close. The isolated tree in the right middle distance may be a survivor of the old avenue plantings.

which, as we will see, began on a wind-swept day over 500 years ago. It is a family story, but also one which features input from a succession of the designers, gardeners and architects who drove the story of English landscaping, including (in chronological order) Inigo Jones, Isaac de Caus, John Field, George London, Henry Wise, Stephen Switzer, Charles Bridgeman, Philip Miller, Peter Collinson, John Sanderson, Henry Flitcroft, William Chambers, Henry Holland, Humphry Repton, Jeffry Wyatville, and there was even a visit by Lancelot 'Capability' Brown.

Life changed rapidly and radically for John Russell in the spring of 1506 when, following a particularly severe storm in the Channel, a ship carrying Archduke Philip of Austria, his wife and retinue from the Netherlands to Spain was blown ashore near Weymouth. Amidst the hasty confusion of greetings and protocol, Russell acted as translator for the local authorities in dealing with their unexpected guests, and he then accompanied the party when the king, Henry VII, invited them to Windsor. In the course of the visit, the archduke was 'delighted to find so excellent a translator and spoke of Mr Russell to the king, as a young man of the most promising endowments . . . The commendation excited Henry's curiosity [and] Russell was appointed to the Privy Chamber.'[3] In his new role at court, Russell soon came into contact with the future king, Prince Henry, then aged 15, and the two young men clearly became close, sharing interests and perhaps an education, as Henry's tutors at Greenwich Palace introduced him to the arts and sciences, and to the new and exciting world of the Italian Renaissance.

Certainly, by 1509, when the young prince became Henry VIII, John Russell found himself at the heart of the new royal court, an intimate of the king's inner circle as a trusted advisor, diplomat, military commander and witness to the meeting of Henry and the French King Francis at the Field of Cloth of Gold. With his position came a knighthood in 1522 and active service on the Continent between 1522 and 1524, during the course of which he was to lose his right eye; in 1540 he was raised to Baron Russell of Chenies on his appointment as 'Lord President of the Council of the West', a role in which, at the head of a considerable army, he was required to keep the peace and order in an area that included Cornwall, Devon, Dorset and Somerset.

Russell's position at the court had been consolidated by his knighthood, but perhaps the biggest change in his material circumstances at this time came with his marriage in 1526 to the widow Anne Sapcote. Anne was an

English School, *John Russell, 1st Earl of Bedford* (*c*.1485–1555), *c*.1555.

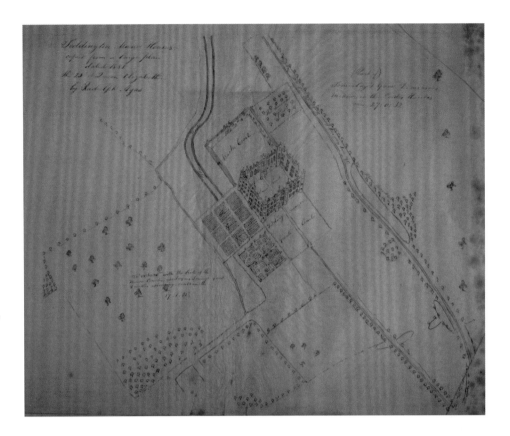

Ralph Agas, *Toddington Manor*, 1581. Standing some six miles from Woburn Abbey, the house and gardens at Toddington are shown as developed by Henry Cheney from 1560 onwards. It is not clear how it looked some fifty-five years earlier when it had come into the Russell family with Anne Sapcote, but the quadrangular house, approached along a tree-lined axial avenue and surrounded by a landscape of gated courts, formal gardens, walks and orchards, illustrates exactly the kind of development during Elizabeth's reign which did not happen at Woburn. It was to be another fifty years before the first such gardens began the transformation of the old abbey.

interesting woman who had lived for some time in France, where Russell will have originally met her when her previous husband held a diplomatic post in Tournai, and who, as a lady-in-waiting to the queen, had also been present at the Field of Cloth of Gold. She was also twice widowed and therefore owned considerable properties, including, from her own family, estates at Thornhaugh and Wansford, Northamptonshire, and Chenies Manor House, Buckinghamshire, which she had occupied since 1510, as well as Toddington Manor, Bedfordshire, from her first husband.

Toddington Manor House, to judge from a surviving plan, was evidently a substantial property, a large courtyard structure surrounded by formal gardens and parkland, but when it came to Sir John Russell and his wife it may not have been this developed. Sited not far from Woburn Abbey, it appears Toddington might have been an ideal home for the well-established courtier and his family, but for some reason the Russells seem never to have occupied it; it could be that Sir John considered it beyond his means at this time. On the other hand, the Thornhaugh estate, though considerable, was far more distant from the court, being located in the north-eastern corner of Northamptonshire, west of Peterborough. Perhaps this was the reason why, although it also included a house, parkland and gardens, as well as the large hunting park in the ancient woodland of the Bedford Purlieus and other extensive acreages, it too was not occupied as the main family residence. Instead of either of these two properties, the Russells chose to

Anon., *Chenies Manor House.* This picture, looking across the central court towards the south range, is undated but indicates that the court had become a garden setting. The battlements of the original west range peeping over the trees give us a flavour of the history of Chenies, where the old fortified manor house was developed by the Russells into a grand home capable of playing host to both Henry VIII and Queen Elizabeth.

settle at Chenies Manor House, which was closest to London, but perhaps also because it had been Anne's home, and it is here that we see the first development of a new house and garden by the Russell family. The original manor house at Chenies is thought to date from the 1460s, but had been significantly altered by the time the Russells lived there.

With the manor came two hunting parks, but the old buildings themselves needed considerable renovation and additions by John to host a visit from Henry VIII in 1534. This work included substantial rebuilding of the existing west range, the addition of the south range and, perhaps a little later, what John Leland was to describe in 1544 as 'fair lodgings . . . newly erected in the garden'. Such were the changes, in fact, that John Leland noted in his *Itinerary*: 'The old house of Cheynies is so translated by my Lord Russell that little or nothing of it in a manner remaineth untranslated: and a great deal of the house has been newly set up made of brick and timber: and fair lodgings be newly erected in the garden. The house is within diverse places richly painted with antique works of black and white.'[4]

Further changes were made to the house with the creation of the north range, which, together with a substantial wall down the east side, completed the enclosure of the quadrangular courtyard, updating the whole look of the complex in the prevailing style. Wessex Archaeology believes that the 'fair lodgings . . . erected in the garden' may in fact refer to the alterations made to what was possibly part of an original gatehouse across the Privy Garden to the west of the main house.[5] Here, the two-storey L-shaped building now known as the Old Nursery was upgraded with rooms on both floors, and there are suggestions that this may have served as a banqueting house overlooking the Privy Garden. In addition, a much grander formal layout

Possible reconstruction of the original Cistercian abbey at Woburn (north is to the left).
This reimagining shows the lost church along the north side of the buildings, the south wall of which was incorporated into the 4th Earl's new north range in the 1630s. Beside this wall lie the cloisters, while the chapter house and monks' quarters form the east range. The west range facing the gatehouse provided quarters for the lay members of the community and various service rooms, while the south range of the cloisters contained the kitchens and refectory. Beyond this lay an open courtyard surrounded by offices, stores, the still room and brew house. The overall footprint of the abbey buildings, minus the church, is still largely recognizable on the mid-eighteenth-century maps.

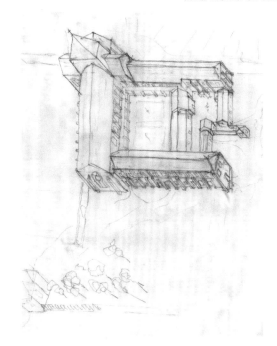

filled the extensive terraced area to the north of the house, and these gardens attracted what may have been the final phase of construction undertaken by John and Anne Russell, when a series of bay windows were inserted into the north wall of the north range looking out over them.

By the time the work at Chenies was completed, further properties had come to Russell: first, the lands and estates of the dissolved monastic house at Tavistock Abbey, Devon, and then Corney House, on the Thames at Chiswick, was conveyed to him from the Bishop of Rochester. These additions, particularly that of the Tavistock estate, all substantially increased his wealth, but on the death of Henry VIII in 1547 Russell's fortune was enormously enlarged and finally secured. As a long-time trusted member of Henry's inner circle, Sir John was one of those rewarded for his service on the death of the king with substantial additional grants of land, and the properties that came to him included the old Cistercian monastery at Woburn Abbey, a monastic estate at Thorney Abbey in the Cambridgeshire Fens east of Peterborough, and some open fields north of the Strand in London which had belonged to a convent associated with Westminster Abbey and were known as the 'Convent Gardens'.

At this point, however, the property at Woburn was not the great prize it was later to become: the old abbey and its gatehouse stood empty and abandoned in open undeveloped grounds, with the woodlands of a 'Rookery' behind on the rising ground to the east, and the medieval fishponds (or Stews) strung out along the stream course in front. Much of the land that became the park and gardens was still intricately divided up into small fields let out to a number of tenant farmers, but at this stage little of this land, and none of the large estates beyond, were included in the grant. The value of the grant to Russell was further diminished by the fact that the abbey building itself was semi-derelict following a major fire. It was not until his son the 2nd Earl's time that the leases on the wider abbey lands reverted to the Russells, but even then the family showed little interest in the rather sad and neglected remnant of Cistercian splendour.

Apart from Woburn Abbey, further properties came to Sir John: first, in 1549, he was granted the remains of the old Dominican abbey in Exeter, where he went on to rebuild part of the monastic buildings as Bedford House; and second, in 1550, the year in which the elderly baron was created 1st Earl of Bedford by Edward VI, came an additional grant of a house and seven acres of land beside the Thames on the Strand. Renamed Russell House, this became the family's first major home in central London. Nevertheless, in spite of presiding over this most extraordinary accumulation of land and assets, the earl seems to have been content with the type of house he had known growing up in Dorset, and although he died at Russell House, he largely lived and was eventually buried amidst the tranquil landscapes of the manor house at Chenies in a special chapel built in the church by his widow, Anne, where she (along with his many successors) was interred beside him. Following his death in 1555, of the estates he had accumulated, those at Chenies, Thornhaugh, Thorney and Wanstead, Covent Garden in London, and Tavistock Abbey in Devon remained at the core of the Russell inheritance, while other important properties came to the family through marriage, notably Southampton House on the Bloomsbury estate in London and Stratton Park, Hampshire, both in 1669. All of these had some influence on and play a role in the development of what turned out to be the most important of all, Woburn Abbey.

Woburn's ascendancy was, in fact, by no means certain. Largely left to itself by Francis, 2nd Earl, who spent most of his military career away from his estates, it was almost sold by Edward, 3rd Earl, and it was not until the 1620s that Francis, 4th Earl, chose it to be his primary family home. Since that time it has survived further impulses to sell it in the eighteenth, nineteenth and twentieth centuries, faced challenges from other favoured properties and suffered periodic neglect, but remains today the most important of John Russell's acquisitions and the repository of rich layers of family history. While the rural estates in Northamptonshire, Cambridgeshire and Devon remained a consistent source of both income and, before the home farm at Woburn was developed in the late eighteenth century, farm produce for the Abbey, it was the development of gardens at both Bedford House on the north side of the Strand and Southampton House in Bloomsbury (Bedford House after the 1730s), and of a parkland landscape at Stratton Park, that help explain developments at Woburn as it became a faint, but perhaps still recognizable, version of the old manor at Swyre.

To start uncovering the history of the development of the park and gardens at Woburn, in Chapter 1 we look initially at the period between 1627 and 1632, when Francis Russell, 4th Earl of Bedford, and his wife, Katherine, became the first generation of the family to make the Abbey their principal home. Once there, working with Isaac de Caus, they partially rebuilt the old monastic structure, including its unique extant grotto chamber, and laid out the first recorded formal walled gardens on three sides of the building. In addition, at much the same time, working with Inigo Jones, assisted by de Caus, they also created Covent Garden church and piazza, the first such planned urban space in London, in conjunction with new gardens and the enlargement of Bedford House, which stood next door.

Moving on to the years 1641–1700 we follow William Russell, 5th Earl, as he developed what his father had created both at Woburn and in London. Living through the difficult years of the Civil War, William was nevertheless responsible for further work on the Abbey as well as expanding the gardens and orchards out into the parkland beyond. Once a world enclosed by its

Map of England showing the locations of the Russell family's main properties. See page 31 for a map showing houses in Greater London.

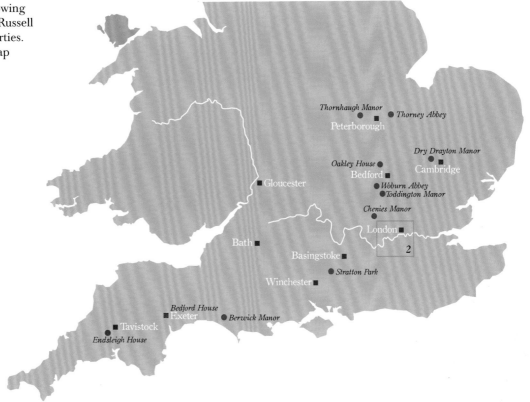

paling fences, the sole preserve of deer hunts and horse riding, the layout of the park contiguous with the gardens starts to become focused on the Abbey, providing a setting for the house and a place of recreation for the whole family. In this section we also discover the influence of other properties such as Stratton Park in Hampshire and Wanstead House outside London on the work at Woburn and find the earl raised to become the 1st Duke of Bedford.

In Chapter 2 we see William's grandson Wriothesley inherit as 2nd Duke in 1700 and embark on ambitious plans to create a new, axially aligned layout of ponds, avenues and gardens. Influenced by the homes of family relatives at Wanstead, Badminton and Chatsworth, the 2nd Duke worked with the designers George London and Henry Wise to create the initial phase of a much grander setting for the Abbey. Unfortunately, the duke's early death in 1711 meant that this was never realized to its full extent, and no plan survives (if one ever existed), leaving only the designs shown on an estate map of 1738, some tantalizing traces of which are still visible in the park today.

After a period of uncertainty during the 3rd Duke's short life, developments at Woburn began again when his younger brother John Russell became 4th Duke. In the second part of Chapter 2 we follow the story as John initially continued the development of Stratton Park into a home, before turning his attention to Woburn on inheriting the dukedom in 1732. Here, working over a period of time with the designers Charles Bridgeman, Henry Holland and Sir William Chambers, the duke was responsible for major changes to the Abbey and its service buildings, an entirely new set of formal gardens, including the new 'Pleasure Grounds', new rides and ponds in the park, and the first plantings of what became a major feature of the park to this day, 'The Evergreens'.

Chapter 3 covers the period between 1787 and 1839, some fifty years that saw an unprecedented surge of activity at Woburn as the brothers Francis, 5th Duke, and John, 6th Duke, initiated sustained programmes of development. Both had been raised at the Abbey amidst the splendour of their grandfather the 4th Duke's house, park and pleasure grounds, and both were determined to build on the legacy left them. Their interests covered almost every aspect of the estate, from rebuilding large parts of the Abbey to laying out new roads, creating new gardens and plantations, as well as introducing new standards of agriculture, forestry and horticulture.

In this chapter we follow their story, one which, on the one hand, was intensely practical, such as the 5th Duke's commissioning of Henry Holland to rebuild the south and east wings of the Abbey, his enclosure of a larger park, his creation of a state of the art model farm and an annual agricultural show, and his demolition of Bedford House, Bloomsbury, and development of the estate into lucrative housing. On the other hand, it was also the time when the highly decorative, picturesque aesthetic was integrated into both the park and gardens by his younger brother John, 6th Duke, and Duchess Georgina. Using such designers as Humphry Repton (four of whose Red Books of designs feature in this story) and Sir Jeffry Wyatville (from 1802 until John's death in 1839), this era witnessed the creation of much of what we see at Woburn today and has provided the designs which lie at the heart of the programme of restoration currently transforming the gardens. In the course of this chapter, we also follow further influences from Stourhead and Longleat, as well as the creation of the magical picturesque *cottage orné* and its grounds at Endsleigh in Devon.

Following this period of sustained expenditure, the next thirty years were a time of retrenchment as Francis, the 7th Duke, sought to rationalize costs, consolidate what had been achieved and ensure the long-term viability of Woburn and the wider Bedford estates by investing not in new projects but in essential infrastructure. In Chapter 4 we follow the story initially from 1839 until 1940, through the lives of the 7th, 9th and 11th dukes and duchesses, a period which perhaps represents the heyday of life at Woburn Abbey, when the carefully managed estates produced enormous wealth for a series of dukes and their families whose royal connections and political achievements placed Woburn and its inhabitants at the heart of Victorian and Edwardian society. It is the story of life at the Abbey from the pageantry and splendour of Queen Victoria's visit in 1841 on her honeymoon to the dark days of the Second World War, when the continuity of family life was broken. As the nineteenth century wore on, and the dukes and their families pursued their personal interests amidst the splendour of the landscapes created by their predecessors, the park became home to an unprecedented collection of deer species, wild animals from musk ox to giraffes, and exotic game birds and wildfowl. At the same time the gardens, under a succession of duchesses, became a showpiece of formal display beds for flowers and shrubs. Individual contributions, such as the estate cottages of the 7th Duke and Duchess Anna Maria's flower gardens, the aviaries of the 9th Duke and the expansive parterre gardens of his wife, Elizabeth Sackville-West, and the aeroplane hanger, landing strip and seasonal ice rink of the 'Flying Duchess', Mary, wife of the 11th Duke, all added to the variety and interest of the wider landscape. This period lasted until the death of the 11th Duke in the Abbey in 1940, at which point the house was requisitioned by the secret services and the park by the Air Ministry, as world events brought this long twilight of Edwardian splendour to an abrupt end.

Wartime occupation was to last from 1940 to 1948, and left the Abbey stripped bare, its contents stored in dusty rooms full of boxes, the gardens shut down, and large swaths of the park altered for ever by its use as a Satellite Landing Ground for the fighter planes and bombers of the RAF, but today Woburn is a place transformed. By the 1950s circumstances required drastic measures to keep the house and parkland viable. Hastings, the 12th Duke, oversaw the demolition of a large section of the Abbey, and, desperate to save what remained from demolition or sale, his son John, the 13th Duke, opened the remaining house, gardens and parts of the park to the public. Today, after continued efforts by his son Robin, the 14th Duke, and now his grandson Andrew, the 15th Duke, the Abbey, the gardens, the Safari Park and the wider estate combine to form a thriving enterprise catering to large numbers of visitors with a wide variety of interests every year. This part of the chapter tells the stories of all the changes this new reality has brought to the look and uses of the park and gardens, the people who made it happen, and the restoration of the historic landscape that funds from this success have made possible.

It is hoped that this book will help to identify and explain all the layers of accumulated history, both to record what has been lost and to enable the modern visitor to locate the forms and fragments that have survived, and make it possible to read this history in the landscape that can be seen at Woburn Abbey today. It is hoped, too, that the extensive 'Notes and References' section will enable those interested to follow up on specific aspects of the story as it unfolds.

CHAPTER ONE

*'... there are three large Gardens full of fruit ... the walks
are one above another with stone steps'*

(Celia Fiennes, 1697)

FRANCIS RUSSELL, 4TH EARL, AND WILLIAM RUSSELL, 5TH EARL AND 1ST DUKE

The year 1627 was pivotal in the history of Woburn Abbey, since it was with the inheritance of Francis Russell as 4th Earl that, after some eighty years, the old abbey finally became the principal family residence, and it has remained so with a few exceptions until the present day. It is the point at which the Russell family became fully engaged with the house and the landscape in which it sits – a landscape they were to modify steadily in response to their interests, needs and outside events – and this landscape sits at the heart of our story. In 1661, some forty years after Francis and his wife, Katherine Brydges, came to live at Woburn, Jonas Moore drew up a 'survey' of the Woburn estate, and even though some changes had occurred by this time, the map gives us a fascinating glimpse of how it would have looked when Francis and Katherine arrived.

Clearly visible is a network of roads which had probably not altered substantially for generations, and which is still largely recognizable today. From the south-west corner two roads run in towards the village of Woburn from the old Roman road of Watling Street, while further round to the south the 'London Lane' runs north from Dunstable and Hockcliffe to the village, and from the north-west the road runs in from Woburn Sands. These roads all meet at the market square in the centre of Woburn, and from this crossroads a further road, known then as 'Abbey Lane', runs east before dividing in two, the northern branch heading off towards Luton, the southern branch passing north of the Abbey on its way to Froxfield. To the south-east of the village lies the Abbey itself, recognizable still as a medieval structure complete with separate gatehouse (by now a farmhouse), and

FAR LEFT Sir Anthony van Dyck, *Francis Russell, 4th Earl of Bedford (1593–1641)*.

LEFT Marcus Gheeraerts the Younger, *Katherine Brydges, Countess of Bedford (c.1582–1657)*.

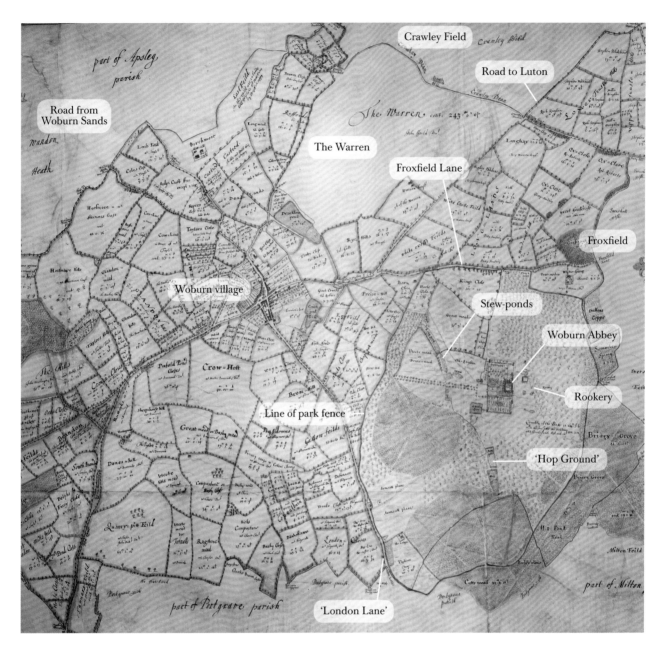

Crawley Field

Road to Luton

Road from
Woburn Sands

The Warren

Froxfield Lane

Froxfield

Woburn village

Stew-ponds

Woburn Abbey

Rookery

Line of park fence

'Hop Ground'

'London Lane'

Moore's 1661 map of the
Woburn estate, overview.

described by Moore as 'a very faire large building fitted for the habitation'.[1]
Enclosed behind a 'high brickwall', it looked down over the old monastic
fishponds set amongst the low-lying, well-watered level ground of the Old
Leighton and Utcote hay meads. On the gently sloping land to the north
of the ponds are the fields belonging to the Abbey enclosed within a paling
fence – Horse Close, King's Close, Great Meadow and Dove House Close –
running up to Froxfield Lane, while behind the Abbey, on rising ground to
the north and east, the dense woodland includes the all important Rookery.
Similarly important was the Dove House or Dove Cote, a key element of the
life and economy of the Abbey. Keeping doves or pigeons meant not just

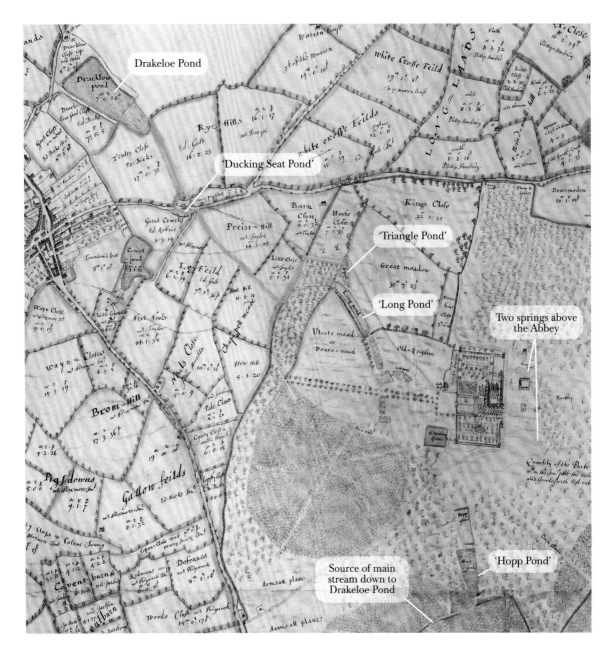

Drakeloe Pond

'Ducking Seat Pond'

'Triangle Pond'

'Long Pond'

Two springs above the Abbey

Source of main stream down to Drakeloe Pond

'Hopp Pond'

Moore's 1661 map, detail of ponds and streams.

meat, eggs and guano, a valuable fertilizer; birds could also be released for sporting purposes as targets for falcons. Moore tells us that the Dove Cote once stood on the south side of the gatehouse, and by the mid-seventeenth century this is likely to have been a stone circular or rectangular structure capable of housing hundreds, if not thousands, of birds.

To the south of the Abbey the woodland of the park, cut through by hunting rides, spreads out past the pond above the old 'Hop Ground' to the access road to the rear of the Abbey from the London road, and round to the meads in front of the Abbey, while to the north of the roads to Froxfield and Luton, we see a large open area occupying the high ground which slopes sharply down to Drakeloe Pond labeled 'The Warren'. The rabbits of the Warren and the gamekeeper who guarded them from all comers were another crucial part of the estate economy from the earliest times, and this large area retained its importance well into the eighteenth century. And then, beyond the Warren, lies another traditional part of the rural fabric, the open spaces of 'Crawley Field'. Also called Crawley Heath and Crawley Common, this was the common land on which local villagers had ancient rights to grazing, pasturage, foraging and the collection of fuel, in this case peat and underbrush. This common, with others like it, was to be the location of a bitter struggle in the late eighteenth and early nineteenth centuries as the 5th and 6th Dukes of Bedford enlarged the park at Woburn by enclosing this land and extending the park wall to include it. Enclosure ended free access and the commoners' traditional rights to its resources, developments that provoked unprecedented confrontation and the use of the local militia, and created the first sustained tension in the traditional relationship between the Woburn estate and those who lived on and around it.

Also visible on this map are the two ponds which mark the springs emerging above the Abbey to the east, and the stream which runs north off the ridge, filling first the 'Hopp Pond' reservoir and then the seven fishponds, before finding its way round the field boundaries to the 'Ducking Seat Pond' beside Abbey Lane, and from there into 'Dracklow Pond'. These various springs and streams provided the Abbey with a generally reliable source of water, although by the mid-eighteenth century the massively increased demands of the great house – by then well supplied with baths and water-closets, and its gardens full of water features – required drastic measures to be taken to ease seasonal water shortages. These springs and their limitations were to have an influence on the way the landscaped park and the pleasure gardens that were created around the Abbey were developed, the first of which is indicated on Moore's map – although the details of the walled gardens he shows need to be approached with caution.

The reason we need to approach Moore's rendering of the house and garden with caution is that the real purpose of this survey can be found just beyond the immediate lands of the Abbey, where we see, crowding right up to the boundary paling fences, the small fields and pastures of the tenant farmers, all carefully outlined in green on the map and annotated with their acreage and the names of the individual tenants. This map was drawn up not to display the Abbey and its fine park and gardens, as so many later maps were, but rather to enable the 5th Earl and his steward to accurately assess and understand who his tenants were, the acreage each leased, and the type and value of the different plots. It was a management tool, and this is important to understand because, although the 'agricultural' information may be accurate, the representations of the Abbey and its garden certainly are not. As Dianne Duggan points out: 'One must be a little cautious here . . . as it is completely possible that

Moore's 1661 map, detail of tenanted fields and park paling.

The main purpose of this map was to register the fields beyond the park, the name of the tenants and the acreage of each; highlighted are those tenanted by a Mr Taylor and called Priest Hill, Barn Close and Little Close. This particular Mr Taylor is likely to have been Dixy Taylor, who was personal attendant to the 5th Earl and his wife, and whose family served the Russells for a number of generations at Woburn. While Taylor had considerable responsibilities within the household, he was also a major tenant of the estate. Within the park fence the fields, including Horse Close, King's Close, Great Meadow and Dove House Close, were fenced off from the deer and accessed through a number of gates, while the two hay meads, Utcote and Old Leighton, lie on either side of the stew-ponds in front of the Abbey.

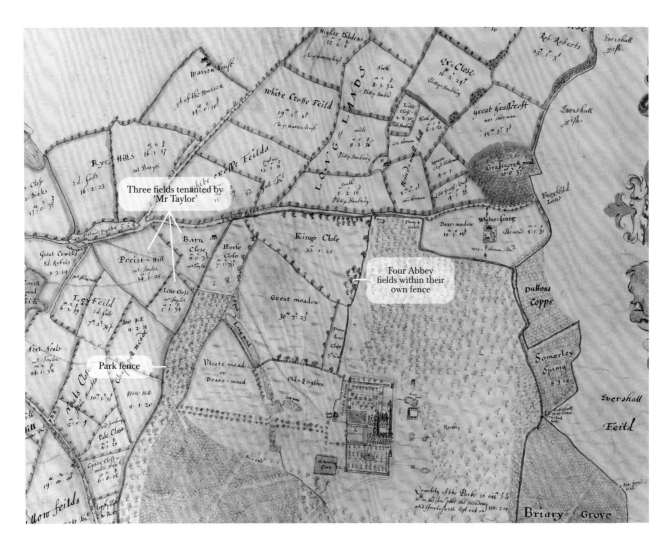

Moore used as much artistic licence in depicting the garden design as he did with the architectural features of the house.'[2]

If the map cannot tell us exactly how the house and gardens looked, what it can do, however, is to give us a glimpse of the world into which Francis and Katherine moved when they brought their growing family of six children to occupy the run-down Abbey. An agricultural landscape spread around it, including an extensive kitchen garden beside the gatehouse, the Dove Cote, Rookery and Warren, an intricate chain of stew-ponds, which also supported a population of wildfowl, the Hop Ground and its associated brewhouse, orchards and, of course, venison readily available in the park – a rural world essentially unchanged from what the monks had known. Indeed, the Abbey will have still seemed as remote and tucked away as it had done to the monks. The lane from the London road ran across the park through the open spaces of Armsall Plane before crossing the stream, following the sloping ground through the trees, and arriving at the stables and coach house at the rear of the Abbey. In its turn, the lane in from Woburn left the Froxfield road just after the Ducking Seat Pond, first cut across Priest Hill and Barn Close, before passing through the gate in the palisade fence, along the side of a wood, round the pointed end of the 'Triangle Pond'. From here it headed across the slope of the Great Meadow, and through another gate in the fence, before crossing 'Old Leighton' mead to arrive at the old gatehouse. Alternatively, the family, returning from Woburn, could stay on the Froxfield road until they came to the gate into King's Close and take the track running up the hill to the woods, pass through another gate and follow the fence down the side of Dove House Close to arrive at the stables.

Inside the Abbey itself, the old cloisters remained an open court, the south range of which retained its functions as kitchen, bakehouse and scullery (although the monks' refectory had become the servants' hall). The footprint and much of the original fabric of the east range survived: the old monks' quarters had become the stables, while the chapter house and the vestry and south transept of the lost church had become a coach house, parlour and wash house. Although the 2nd Earl may have done some work on the apartments in the south and west wings of the Abbey, particularly when Queen Elizabeth visited in 1572, it is clear when we look at this plan that the Abbey had not undergone the development typical of her reign that saw old monastic buildings turned into grand houses, approached along axial avenues flanked by lines of trees that arrived at a series of symmetrically aligned courtyards. Woburn Abbey was still essentially a medieval monastic fabric set in a late medieval monastic agricultural landscape.[3]

Francis Russell, 4th Earl of Bedford, born in 1593, was the only child of Lord William Russell, 1st Baron of Thornhaugh, and his wife, Elizabeth Long. He had spent much of his early childhood at his father's estate at Thornhaugh, Northamptonshire, but following his marriage in 1608 to Katherine Brydges, the couple lived at Nyn Hall in Hertfordshire, which came to him through his aunt the Countess of Warwick, and at his father's property Corney House, Chiswick. As soon as Francis took over responsibility for the Bedford estates c.1618, however, he and his wife seem to have had no hesitation in choosing to make Woburn Abbey their principal home, and were living there certainly from 1621, if not a few years before.[4]

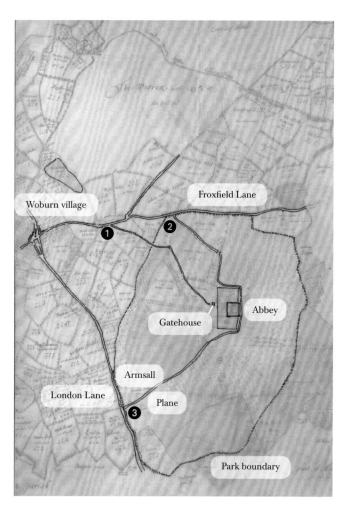

Plan of park, access roads and entrance gates. Froxfield Lane: Gate 1 'just after the Ducking Seat Pond'; Gate 2 'gate into King's Close'. London Lane: Gate 3 'lane across park over Armsall Plane'.

Reconstruction of the monastery ground plan from surviving features. This simplified plan aims to give some idea of what the original abbey layout may have looked like and where the main buildings may have been.

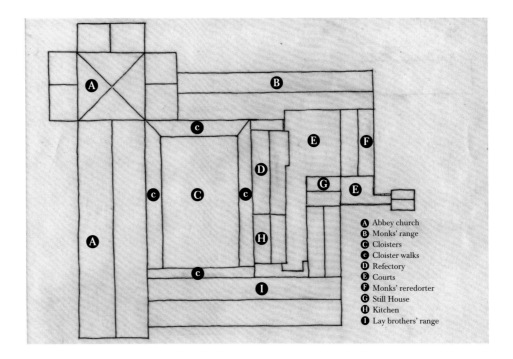

Ⓐ Abbey church
Ⓑ Monks' range
Ⓒ Cloisters
ⓒ Cloister walks
Ⓓ Refectory
Ⓔ Courts
Ⓕ Monks' reredorter
Ⓖ Still House
Ⓗ Kitchen
Ⓘ Lay brothers' range

Nyn Hall was another property like Chenies Manor where a new house was created by additions to a much older medieval fabric.[5] Before the dissolution of the monasteries, Nyn Hall had been a large farm owned by the abbey of St Albans. By the 1540s Sir William Cavendish had taken possession, and created a new domestic range. By 1576, the house had come to Ambrose Dudley, Earl of Warwick and husband of Anne Russell, Francis's aunt; their main contribution to the house was to enclose the surrounding 'common ground', allowing them to create what John Norden describes in 1598 as 'delightful gardens and walkes with sundrie other pleasant and necessary devices'. Nyn Hall offered to its various owners the attractions not only of proximity to both London and the great house at Theobolds, a firm royal favourite, but also the opportunities for hunting that were presented by its extensive landholdings.

By the time couple arrived at Woburn, they were familiar with the processes of adapting old buildings, changing land use and developing gardens. Even apart from their experience at Nyn Hall, with its converted buildings, 'delightful gardens' and hunting park, Francis had grown up amongst his father's development of the old house at Thornhaugh and the creation of gardens there, while Katherine's childhood had been spent at Sudeley Castle, Gloucestershire, where her father had refurbished the mid-Tudor house and gardens between 1572 and 1580 in anticipation of a visit from Queen Elizabeth. Katherine would also have been very familiar with the grand Jacobean parterre gardens, probably complete with grotto, laid out at Sudeley between 1602 and 1610 by her cousin Grey Brydges, 5th Baron Chandos (a courtier whose lavish lifestyle led to the nickname 'King of the Cotswolds').

THORNHAUGH MANOR

ABOVE Thomas Eayre, 'The old house of the first Russell that was Baron of Thornhaugh, now a farmhouse belonging to the Duke of Bedford', 1721.[6] Eayre's drawing of the house seems to have been done for Bridges's *History of Northamptonshire*, and is one of two he did of the area; the other shows Lord William Russell's tomb in the parish church.

ABOVE Marcus Gheeraerts the Younger, *Lord William Russell, 1st Baron of Thornhaugh* (*c*.1557–1613).

Lord William inherited Thornhaugh following his elder brother's early death. He was a noted soldier, fighting with Sir Philip Sidney in the Netherlands, before becoming Lord Deputy of Ireland where he fought in a number of campaigns. He became one of Queen Elizabeth's leading generals and served as Commander of the West, overseeing the defence of the south-west in the face of possible Spanish invasion. At Thornhaugh he initiated the drainage of fens in Cambridgeshire, and played an important role in dissuading his nephew Edward, 3rd Earl of Bedford, from selling off family properties and in securing the inheritance of his own son Francis as 4th Earl.

The manor at Thornhaugh was an estate of over 1,000 acres, including the extant woodland of the 'Bedford Purlieus', and after coming into the Russell family with Anne Sapcote, wife of the 1st Earl, it passed in 1572 to her grandson Lord William following the death of his elder brother Lord Edward. From that time it remained in the family until sold in 1931 'at very low reserves'.[7] In 1723 John Bridges reported that the house was 'An old stone manor house . . . about a quarter of a mile from the church, and is embattled all round, with a small embattled hexagonal tower. Part of the gatehouse, which is also embattled, is still standing. On the south side is a porch, inhabited by a tenant . . . To the east of the house is a little mount; and beyond a rivulet, which encircles the north part of it, are marks of fishponds. The woods and whole estate, are free-hay, and called Bedford Purlieus.'[8]

It remains unclear, however, exactly where this manor house stood, and the 'Map of the Manor of Thornhaugh with Wansford', surveyed in 1729,[9] indicates two possible locations 'a quarter of a mile' from the church, both beside the lane that runs up the west side of the 'Church Park'. The first, on the corner, includes a 'homestead', a 'garden' and a field called 'The Steward's Piece', while further up the lane we find a second, more substantial 'homestead' which includes an 'Orchard', a 'Hop Ground' and a 'Meadow', and in addition fronts on to a large piece of land called 'Whittering Park'.

'Map of the Manor of Thornhaugh with Wansford', 1729, detail showing possible locations for manor house, as described by Bridges in 1723.

English School, *Lord Edward Russell* (d.1572), *c*.1570.

These details would suggest that if either of these is the old manor house, it is more likely to be the latter, especially given its proximity to the rivulet encircling it to the north, with the former, the location of the existing 'Manor Farm', being the steward's house and offices.

Although neither of these properties would seem to match the likely footprint of the house shown in Eayre's drawing, perhaps because the details of the map are representative rather than representational, together the drawing and the map give us a good idea of the surroundings in which Francis Russell grew up. The 'Park', 'Orchard', 'Hop Ground', 'fishponds' and 'little mount' all suggest a substantial landscape at the larger property, and, intriguingly, a portrait of Lord Edward Russell, who occupied Thornhaugh Manor before his early death, includes a small allegorical scene with the motto 'Fata Viam Invenient' (Fate will find the Way). In the scene a figure stands at the centre of a garden maze at the centre of a garden, beyond which we see what could well be a 'little mount' amongst the trees. Beyond its allegorical content, this scene also provides a glimpse of the kind of garden Lord William might have laid out in association with the little mount at Thornhaugh – the gardens amongst which Francis spent his childhood.

Following the 3rd Duke's death in 1732, however, family interest in Thornhaugh waned until the mid-nineteenth century when, as we will see, the 6th and 7th Dukes took an interest in the estate again. By that time all traces of the old house above the Church Park were gone, but a new property a few miles away, at what is now New Farm, had been built.[10] At this site the 7th Duke was to build a series of cottages, and the existing house bears a striking resemblance to that shown in Eayres's image of 1721. Who built it and when, since there is no trace of it on the 1729 map, is unclear, but by the nineteenth century this site was known as Thornhaugh Manor.[11]

New Farm, Thornhaugh, 2014.

In London, the first property with which Francis and Katherine became associated was Corney House in Chiswick, inherited from his father, and Francis may well have been present as a 9-year-old at the grand occasion in 1602 when the family entertained the elderly Queen Elizabeth at the house,[12] witnessing all the pageantry of the royal barge arriving and the queen making her way through the gardens to the house. As it turned out, following visits by Henry VIII to Chenies and Elizabeth to both Chenies and Woburn during the 2nd Earl's time, this was to be the last occasion on which the Russells could honour the royal family who had been responsible for their great fortunes over the last sixty-two years.

It is not clear who created the gardens at the house that can be seen in Jacob Knyff's painting *Chiswick from the River* (*c*.1670), since by the time the painting was done Corney House had been sold, but we see that at some point the original river margins, 'marshy riverside land described as an island',[13] had been embanked and a garden laid out between the house and the river. Such a reclamation is the kind of project his father had been interested in, as was Francis himself, since both were involved in similar work in the Fens, and the gardens are very much of their period.

In Knyff's image we see the double gabled house and walled gardens running towards the river, the latter featuring four parterres with low hedges divided by gravel walks, espaliered fruit trees set against sunny walls, and the interior space shaded by two or three trees. On the main axis from the house, a conical roofed pavilion projects out over the river from the high brick wall of the embankment, which in turn curves elegantly up towards the corners and may have had a raised terrace running along the inside.

Jacob Knyff, *Chiswick from the River*, *c*.1670.

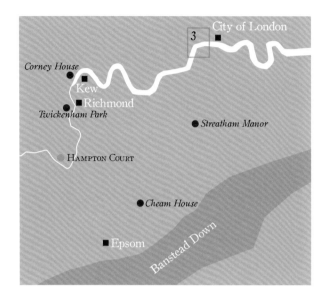

ABOVE Russell family houses in Greater London. See page 35 for a map showing houses in central London.

RIGHT Marcus Gheeraerts the Younger, *Edward Russell, 3rd Earl of Bedford* (1572–1627).
Something of the sadness of Edward's life is captured in this portrait. Physically frail after his riding accident, his arm still in a sling, he also appears overwhelmed by the glorious hangings and the oversized chair on which he is perched, his feet barely touching the floor. Compared to the towering figure of his uncle William, 1st Baron of Thornhaugh, or indeed that of his cousin Francis, who succeeded him as duke, Edward appears as a diminutive figure for whom the responsibility of rank proved a burden. Not for the last time, Woburn Abbey was to find itself on the brink of being sold.

In one corner a gateway beside another pavilion permits access from the river, while further downriver beyond the property we can see the kind of marshy river margins that these gardens had replaced. Perhaps the gardens had been laid out for Queen Elizabeth to enjoy, or perhaps they were added by Francis and Katherine: certainly, there are elements here of the gardens the couple were soon to build at Bedford House and Woburn.

Although Edward, the 3rd Earl, had ceded control of the Bedford estates to his cousin Francis *c.*1618, Bedford House had been leased back to him for life, though from the time he and his wife moved to the estate at Moor Park in Hertfordshire *c.*1617 he seems to have taken no more interest in it or any of the other family properties. Equally, although his wife, Lucy Harrington (also spelled Harington), became well known for her gardens at Twickenham and Moor Park, it seems that the Russell properties never caught her imagination or engaged her interest. Lucy, the daughter of

31

Sir John Harrington, had been brought up at the two family homes in Rutland, Burley-on-the-Hill and Exton, and as a precocious, charismatic and highly educated young woman who was equally comfortable speaking English, French, Spanish or Italian, she soon made her mark after 1603 at the new Stuart court. Indeed, it was her position as a Lady of the Bedchamber and confidante of Queen Anna (to use Anne of Denmark's Danish name), and her role as a leading artistic and literary patron, that made her an influential figure in the early Stuart period. Quite apart from participating in at least eleven of the court masques created between 1605 and 1611 for the queen, she was also active in promoting the careers of musicians and poets, including John Donne.

Yet in spite of her popularity and Edward's position, he fell from favour following his disputed involvement in the Earl of Essex's doomed uprising against Queen Elizabeth and her administration in 1601. Edward was to claim that he had no idea why he had been invited to Essex House that morning, but knowledgeable or not about what was going on, he marched forth towards Whitehall behind Essex's banners, was promptly arrested, imprisoned, heavily fined and released into house arrest at Bedford House.

John de Critz, *Lucy Harrington, Countess of Bedford* (c.1581–1627), c.1610.
This charming portrait shows Lucy in what may have been one of her favourite roles – as a participant in the elaborate fantasies of court masques. One can imagine her processing around the extraordinary garden at Twickenham Park in just such a costume, poets and admirers trailing in her wake.

Eventually, he was allowed to 'exile' himself at his childhood home of Chenies, a period of banishment which lasted until the death of the queen in 1603. While such a period of retirement may have suited his increasing dissatisfaction with public and social life, the heavy fine was catastrophic for the Bedfords' already difficult financial situation, and during this period he saw financial salvation in a plan to fell and sell the timber in the park at Woburn. He may also have been considering selling the property altogether; either way, his plans were only dropped after considerable pressure from his uncle Lord William of Thornhaugh, and the property survived.

Yet while Edward was content to lead a reclusive life, and one of increasing ill health following a serious riding accident in 1612 which left him with partial paralysis and a stammer, Lucy was participating fully in court life in London and Hampton Court, and to facilitate this she took the lease on a property at Twickenham Park in 1608. Here she went on to adapt the old hunting lodge and to utilize the elaborate 'symbolic' garden to one side.[14] This garden epitomized contemporary cultural and artistic preoccupations,

Robert Smythson, *Plan of Twickenham Park*, 1609.

and was recorded in 1609 in architect Robert Smythson's plan of the house and courts, which are dominated by the enormous walled enclosure containing the garden.

It is not entirely clear who created this garden – whether it was laid out by Lucy, or whether she inherited an earlier garden from the previous owner Francis Bacon and perhaps went on to develop it[15] – but what is so interesting about the complexity of this precise and highly contrived garden is that it was designed to provide something more than the simple recreational amusements of a maze, labyrinth or flower garden. Looking at the plan one is struck by the fact that the garden not only dwarfs the house itself, but is entirely separated and cut off from it; inside the garden, the size of the surrounding terraces and the widths of its paths, between 11 and 18 feet, seem to suggest that it was designed to make it possible for large numbers of people to move through it at once, or for it to host masque-style processions, watched by spectators on the surrounding terraces. This was a self-contained, complex world, not one designed as a decorative setting for the house. Its purpose was to act as a catalyst for metaphysical, artistic and poetic contemplation and inspiration; it was capable of becoming a 'true paradise' where, 'blasted with sighs, and surrounded with tears', John Donne in his poem 'Twickenham Garden' comes to receive 'such balms as else cure every thing', an ineffable place of which he seeks to become but a 'senseless piece'. Like the garden in which Lord Edward stands bemused at the centre of his maze, Lucy Harrington's garden expresses the contemporary vision of the potential of these places, and the grottoes they so often contained, to facilitate transcendence beyond our basic everyday existence, to transform for a moment those who enter them. It was designed not to display plants, or purely for relaxation or amusement, but for contemplation of our existence and its place in the wider setting of the universe beyond – and possibly also as the setting for the kind of elaborate masques through which the king and queen and their court sought to express their sense of place within this wider context.

No other family member was to be associated with anything like this garden, and it remains Lucy Harrington's unique legacy to the rich story of landscaping associated with the Russell family. It expressed the complex expectations that lay behind the idea of a garden during this period, and provided – with those of his father at Thornhaugh and her family at Sudeley – the context and background against which Francis and Katherine started to build the first important gardens at the Russell family homes of Bedford House and Woburn Abbey.

Due to the prior arrangement with his cousin the 3rd Earl, it was not until Francis inherited as 4th Earl in 1627 that Bedford House came to them, and when it did, as at Woburn, the condition of the house must have been a matter of great concern. Although they may already have had plans for Woburn, it would seem that work actually started in London first, since the accounts indicate that in 1628 they began to restore and refurbish the dilapidated and empty buildings of Bedford House, and to create new gardens for it. The exact sequence of events here is not entirely clear because at much the same time, and using a number of the same people, Francis carried out an ambitious development of the fields of Covent Garden immediately to the north. Work on Bedford House, its gardens and Covent Garden ran largely concurrently between 1628 and 1632, work on one leading to developments on the other. This work, and that which followed immediately at Woburn, indicate that for Francis and Katherine, after the difficulties of his cousin Edward's time, the main priority was to finally create houses and gardens for the family which reflected their status – and to do so in a way which also reflected the new Renaissance-inspired culture of Stuart Britain as embraced by members of Queen Anna's circle such as Lucy Harrington.

Russell House had passed out of the family with the death of the 2nd Earl in 1585, at which point Bedford House was built for Edward, 3rd Earl, on the other side of the Strand. Here the open fields spread out to the north, while the new house lay at right angles to the Strand beside its courtyard, accessed through a gatehouse. The layout was dominated by the neighbouring gardens of Essex House with their pavilions and banqueting houses lined up along the wall.[16] The full extent of what Francis was to achieve over the four to five years of work is clear from Wenceslas Hollar's bird's-eye view of the area drawn *c*.1658–60, in which we see that almost everything has changed.

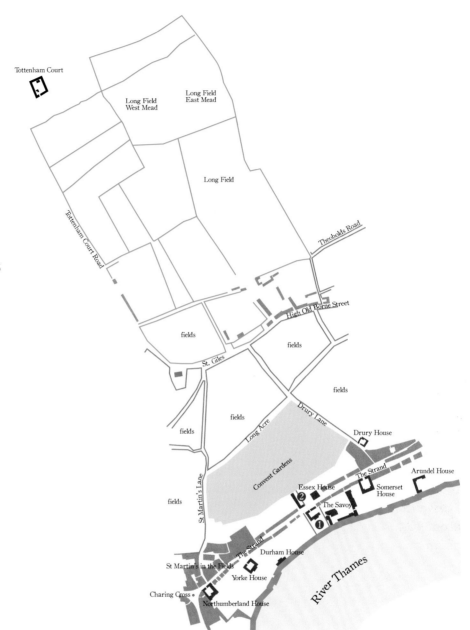

Central London properties of
the Russell family, 1550–1632.

1 Russell House, 1550–85
2 Bedford House, built *c.*1585

All the open fields are gone, and now immediately to the north lies the
open space of the new Covent Garden Piazza surrounded on two sides
by new terraces of houses, on a third by the new church of St Paul's,
and on the fourth by the north wall of the new gardens of Bedford
House. The house itself has also been enlarged, running alongside the
gardens beyond its courtyard leading off the Strand. An unrecognizably
rural London has become suddenly more familiar with the first planned
development of an open urban space, the forerunner of all the glorious
squares that were to come.

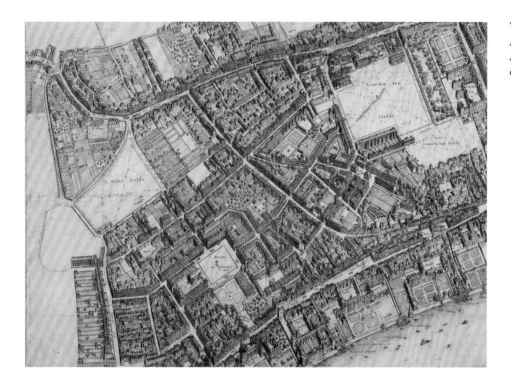

Wenceslas Hollar, *Bird's-Eye View of the West Central District of London,* *c.*1658–60.

Work on this great undertaking at Covent Garden began in 1628 with the restoration of the house itself. That year the paving was replaced, new stone floors laid and the steps at the front door rebuilt,[17] but by the next year a much more ambitious plan was under way. At about this time Charles I had complained about the state of the roads running around the earl's Covent Garden property, especially Long Acre (his route out of London from Westminster to Theobolds), and this intervention provided the earl with the opportunity to get rare royal permission to develop the entire area of the fields. Work on the plans for this started in 1629 and building work the next year.

Our first hint as to what was to come at Bedford House during this time appears in an 'annotated plan' by Isaac de Caus of the Covent Garden proposals drawn *c.*1629.[18] This plan shows the basic layout of the Piazza, balanced with the new church of St Paul's, its churchyard and the blocks of housing which surrounded it. On the south side, the Piazza is closed off by a raised terrace which will divide it from the gardens and stables of Bedford House, which have yet to be designed. Duggan points out that de Caus's pencilled notes on the plan indicate that the management of surface water in the area and 'the collection of the large amount of water required for the fountain . . . and for water features in the grotto' were early considerations.[19] As the Piazza and church were built between 1603 and 1637, so work also seems to have gone on in the gardens, creating the raised terrace which separated them from the public space, the pavilions at either end and the grotto underneath, but not until Wenceslas Hollar publishes his view of Covent Garden some ten years after work was completed is it possible to see the whole garden design.

Attributed to Isaac de Caus, *Grotto Design,* seventeenth century.

In Hollar's image we see the layout of the garden's main parterre, with quartered grass areas divided by paths, featuring signature cut-away corners framing a central fountain, and looking almost identical to the gardens laid out at Somerset House also shown in the Hollar view and also created at much the same time by de Caus. Beside the main parterre at Bedford House, we see a smaller rectangular 'wilderness' of densely planted trees, the raised terrace dividing the garden from the Piazza – with the entrance to a grotto beneath the steps up to it, accessed from the central path of the parterre – and a banqueting house at either end. To the east of the garden we also see the new stable yard and dormered stable buildings, accessed by a pathway along the south side of the wilderness. We cannot be sure that Hollar's image shows the gardens as first laid out, but it would seem unlikely that the 5th Earl altered the gardens significantly during the period of the Civil War.

The Piazza itself appears in Hollar's view, and it provides us with a clear image of how, in an echo of the Italian style that lay at the heart of Inigo Jones's architecture, the buildings and garden space outside were related through the use of arched arcading running along the ground floor. The Piazza garden in the centre is then fenced off, with path entrances at each corner and two others on each side, with barriers to prevent horse riders entering, the paths linking side to side to create a basic grid. Here under the watchful eye of the earl's terrace and Jones's austere chapel, the tenants of the square and their visitors could parade, gather to gossip and enjoy this groundbreaking development. It is such a different scene from that which was to follow as the Piazza was developed to become one of London's most important markets.

Unfortunately, the grotto de Caus built under the terrace at Bedford House was demolished with the rest of the house and gardens in 1705, but just before this happened its footprint was recorded on a plan[20] which in turn provided enough corroborating detail for it to be possible to identify an anonymous coloured drawing of a grotto in the Victoria and Albert Museum as being by de Caus and of the lost grotto at Bedford House. This picture shows, amongst other details, that 'at the apex of the vault . . . are four winged cherubs, surrounded by clouds and holding a raised heraldic coronet. A display of rank inside a grotto was unusual, and indicates the earl's mind-set, particularly in the period immediately following his succession to the earldom.'[21] The picture itself is, of course, a little misleading since the grotto interior will never have looked as light and airy as the image suggests. Entered through a doorway under the stairs, this was a dark windowless space, a total contrast to the garden parterre outside, and will have felt full of mystery and supernatural excitement as the mother-of-pearl, the shells, the gilding and gemstones of the walls and vaulted ceiling flashed and sparkled in the flickering candlelight, and the water splashing into the basins filled the room with an insistent, echoing background of sound. Perhaps this grotto was simply used as a drinking den, as James I's seems to have been in the basement of the banqueting house built by de Caus a few years earlier, but the fact that it, and the one built soon afterwards at Woburn, were both such central elements of the designs of the houses and gardens suggests that they played a much more important role in the imagination of both Francis and Katherine. Indeed, the survival of the Woburn grotto until the present day suggests that it retained some significance for subsequent generations of the Russell family.

With work under way in London, the earl and countess turned their attention to Woburn Abbey, the family's home since c.1618–19, and they were now in a position to make it habitable. No doubt encouraged by the success of their schemes in London and having exactly the right people working for them, the Russells conceived an ambitious plan that called for the old building to be extensively remodelled and new gardens laid out to

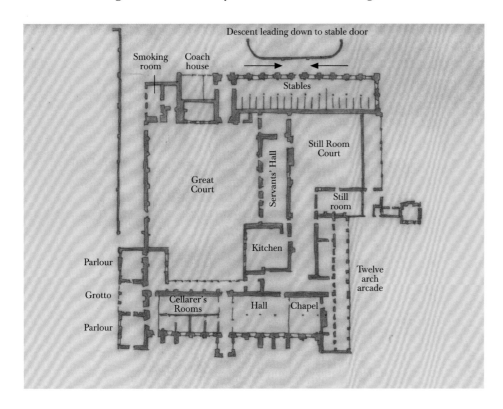

Annotated drawing of John Sanderson, 'record ground plan' of Woburn Abbey, 1733 (north is to the left).

Comparison of suggested reconstruction of monastic layout (see page 27) and Sanderson's record ground plan of 1733.

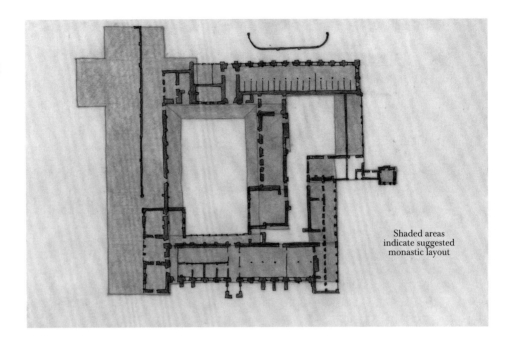

Shaded areas indicate suggested monastic layout

create a suitably grand setting; this marks the moment when the Abbey emerges from the shadows of history and takes its place as one of England's great houses.

Comparing John Sanderson's ground plan of the Abbey of 1733 with the possible layout of the old monastery, it becomes clear that the building work executed in 1631–2 by Francis and Katherine added to, altered or simply repaired various parts of the old structure. First, there was the addition of the completely new north range, built within the footprint of the lost church[22] and utilizing an original section of its south wall. Second, the west range of the monastery was heavily altered on its southern end and in its interior layout to create a hall and chapel, and the south range was altered to accommodate these changes. Finally, the south cloister range and the east range were repaired but, with minor alterations, seem to have largely retained their original interior layouts. The exception here was the ground floor of the large southern space of the east range, which was converted into stables. As Sanderson's plan makes clear, all of this work was directed to making the buildings a home, with the addition of comfortable family bedrooms and parlours in the new north range, the creation of large reception rooms and a long gallery in the west range, with its grand porch, and the rationalization of the cloister, south and east ranges to provide all the domestic service spaces necessary for such a large household.

The earliest image we have of the gardens that were built at this time comes, as we have seen, in Moore's 1661 estate plan, but since it was drawn up some thirty years after they were built, just how accurately they depict what Isaac de Caus may have created for the 4th Earl is not clear. Some of what is shown may have been added by the 5th Earl, but equally, since

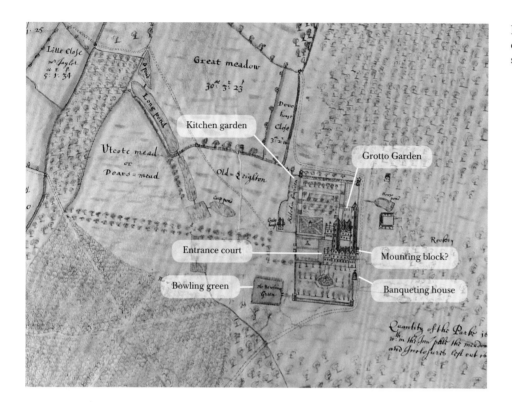

Moore's map of 1661, detail of gardens surrounding the Abbey.

Moore's map is not accurate in its depiction of the Abbey itself, when it comes to the detail of the gardens it may not be either. Concentrating on his commission to clarify the estate tenancies and landholdings, Moore may well have rendered the house and gardens at the centre of it all in an 'artistic' fashion, to convey the impression of a grand contemporary home, but making everything look more finished, tidy and regular than it actually was. Certainly, this is the case with the image of the house, and looking at both the house and gardens in the wider context of the map, they are represented as a neat, self-contained rectangle of order, offering a strong contrast to the random disorder of the arrangement of ponds and blocks of woodland in the park, and the irregularities of the patchwork of ancient field boundaries beyond. And yet, there is a logic to what is shown around the Abbey, suggesting that Moore was referencing what existed, even if he did embellish the details. To start with, on the east side of the Abbey, even though he may have truncated its east–west dimensions, his depiction of the layout beyond may well be largely accurate, with the road running down the length of the building and the horse-mounting blocks marking the door to the stables, and beyond this a scatter of agricultural buildings and two ponds occupying the open space beside the Rookery and woodlands of the park. Not directly related to any of the new building work, or the new facades, the area seems to have remained largely undeveloped.

Following this, on the other three sides, Moore indicates that a complex of gardens was created, and looking at these closely, one can perhaps find credible reasons for what is shown in the general layout, if not in the specific details or the dimensions. The sloping land north of the Abbey was utilized to create an elegant terraced garden, accessed by a series of steps climbing up past pools and fruit trees to a raised terrace at the top from which one could look back down over the garden, a rural version of the arrangement of terrace, parterres and wilderness that had been created at Bedford House. Below this, the small formal wilderness, with diagonal paths and a small building at the centre of it, was then separated from the new entrance courtyard by a wall with a door in it. Beyond this in turn lay the entrance court, a paved area from which a path between two grassed areas leads to the gate to which the road has been diverted from the gatehouse.

In the position of this courtyard we see the first phase of the alignment which was to dominate the landscape on the west side of the house until the present day: a path leading from the building, across the garden, through a new axially aligned gateway and out along an avenue leading down past the fishponds and across the undulating meads beyond. It is not clear if this avenue was contemporary with the gardens of the 1630s or added by the 5th Earl, but the new courtyard, unrelated to the old gatehouse, indicates a new sense of the centre of the building and its relationship to the landscape beyond. South of this entrance court, through an arched doorway and lying along the south side of the building, is a large rectangular garden, with a central fountain and what has been identified as a small banqueting house in the eastern wall.[23]

Other than these gardens there are two further enclosures, very sketchy in their details, laid out north of the buildings, running up the slope within the boundary walls and beside, but clearly separate from, the terraced gardens. One other point of interest here is the feature shown in the centre of the northern grassed area. Indistinct in Moore's rendering, although its form suggests a column topped by a cross mounted on a stepped base, it is not mentioned in any accounts, diaries or letters, and would pass for a contemporary ornamental feature were it not for the fact that it is shown again on Browne's survey of 1738. In the latter, however, it stands alone in the sweep of grass that has long replaced all the gardens, suggesting perhaps that it was something of more lasting importance than simply a garden feature and dated, perhaps, from monastic times. What it was, and why it was retained, remain a puzzle, but it was gone by the end of the eighteenth century.

While the general style of gardens may reflect contemporary fashions, more revealing of the Bedfords' individual taste are the two architectural elements of designs for the house which, as Duggan points out, were 'closely related to garden settings'. These elements repeated the kind of linkage between the building and outside space that we saw used in the residential terraces fronting the Covent Garden Piazza. Looking closely at Sanderson's 1733 record of the ground plan, we can see two arched arcades were built into the Abbey, one on the north side consisting of three arches, and one on the south side consisting of twelve, and the accompanying elevations indicate that these were all built in a similar style of rusticated stonework.

On the north side the three arches open into a small room positioned between two parlours on the ground floor of the north wing, while on the south the twelve arches open into a loggia running along the ground floor of the western end of the south range, as shown in elevation on Moore's map of 1661, which also indicates that both arcades open directly on to a

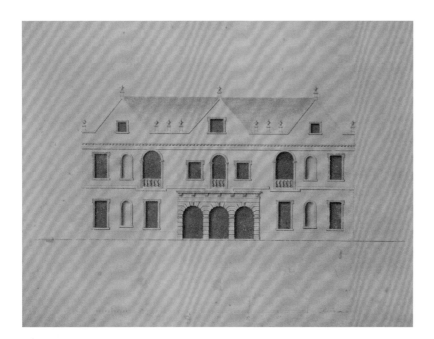

LEFT John Sanderson, north elevation of the Abbey, 1733.
In Sanderson's drawing we see the six rooms of the north range, with the grotto at the centre of the ground floor, and the parlours on either side. On the floor above we see what may have been an open gallery for the display of sculpture, connecting two bedrooms.

BELOW John Sanderson, south elevation of the Abbey, 1733.
Sanderson's drawing shows the twelve-arch arcade as built, with a further proposal for developing the south range to link up with the stables. This work was not carried out.

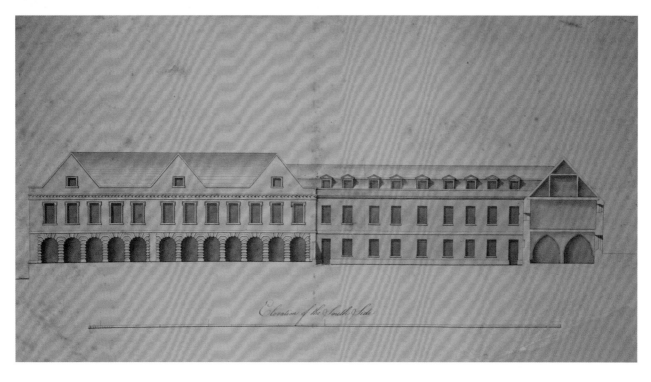

Elevation of the South Side.

ABOVE Circle of Sir Godfrey Kneller, detail of portrait of Joseph Willoughby showing the grotto at Woburn Abbey. The heavily rusticated stonework of de Caus's grotto exterior can be seen on the left.

garden space. While all this would seem to suggest that Francis and Katherine simply fitted comfortably into the prevailing tastes of the Stuart court, they actually emerge as both interestingly individual and innovative, not just in the groundbreaking creation of the urban piazza at Covent Garden, but also in details of their arcades at Woburn. Most interesting of all, perhaps, was the fact that behind the three arches of the north front was not a loggia, or indeed a parlour, but an elaborate grotto similar in many ways to the one de Caus had built tucked away in its more conventional location under the raised terrace running across the garden.

To include the grotto actually within the fabric of the house rather than out in the garden – and as an integral part of the family's suite of reception rooms – was most unusual and tells us much about the couple's sensibilities and interests.

As interesting and absorbing as the interior of the grotto will have been, and is today, of equal interest to us is the enclosed garden space shown on Moore's map located immediately outside the grotto. This piece of land slopes up to the north, and although there are no detailed plans or pictures specifically of the garden itself from any era, some consistent features are identifiable over time on estate maps and later photographs. First of all, Moore shows what appears to be a walled enclosure separated from the elaborately detailed hillside terraces and 'wilderness' garden to the west. Although all these walls have long been removed, this enclosure covers an area of similar size that was still known as the 'Grotto Garden' as late as the 1879–81 Ordnance Survey map and that has remained a discrete space until the present day.

Second, the other feature that shows on plans across the whole period, in the Ordnance Survey map and twentieth-century photographs is a path running straight up the hill and aligned on the central arch of the grotto. The continued survival of this discrete area and its central path might suggest that although overgrown at some points in their history, we are looking at two of the original features of this garden. In addition, on Moore's map the area is elaborated

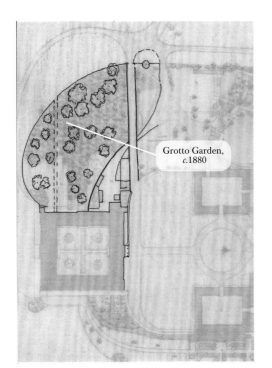

Grotto Garden, c.1880

LEFT 'Grotto Garden', c.1880.
This drawing indicates the 'Grotto Garden' in the late nineteenth century, shown against the garden as seen in Wyatville's plan of the 1830s. By this time the formal gardens here have been removed and the woodland no longer covers the area; rather it has thinned down to single trees. The central path, however, is still in place and has been extended right up to the garden fence. It seems clear that the nineteenth-century dukes and duchesses had little interest in this area, or the grotto itself, and did not add to them.

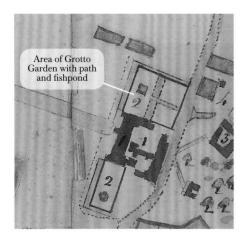

ABOVE 'Grotto Garden', *c.*1755, from Anon. 1738 map (see note 44, page 227). Although all the gardens have gone from the west side of the Abbey, the area of the Grotto Garden has remained intact. The grass-covered slope rises up in front of the grotto and the 'Gold Fish Pond' has been created half-way up. The slight depression left when this pond was eventually filled in is still visible on the slope today.

ABOVE 'Grotto Garden', detail of plan of the pleasure grounds by Sir Jeffry Wyatville, *c.*1830s. The next map to show any detail of the Grotto Garden is Wyatville's plan, and in this image we see that the fishpond is gone and the gravel path runs up the slope into dense woodland.

with a series of short vertical lines in a distinct pattern, and these may provide us with a glimpse of the contents of this garden, since they seem to suggest the kind of pencil cypress tree that was so popular in the Italian originals and in the Italian-style gardens in England during this time. This would give us an open grassed garden with gravelled paths running between lines of thin cypresses, a garden directly related to the interior spaces and one which would have added greatly to the atmosphere of the grotto itself and enriched the experience of those in it.[24]

The other garden space related to the arcading lay on the south side of the house. Here Moore is considerably more specific, indicating a large rectangular garden divided into four grassed areas by paths lined with trees leading to a central fountain. Half of this garden is aligned on the arcade, which would have provided both a viewing point and access to the garden and the banqueting house on the east wall. Thus, the garden is strongly reminiscent of the layout of Covent Garden, and has echoes of the Corney House garden with its parterre and banqueting house, indicating a consistency of inspiration and design that helps to give Moore's image some credibility.

If the plans help us understand what the gardens looked like, we can perhaps gain a little insight into their purpose, beyond being simply a physical setting for the house, from the contemporary writings of Sir Henry Wotton in his *Elements of Architecture* (1624), a book the 4th Earl is known to have read. Wotton describes the physical layout of a garden he admires: 'I have seen a Garden . . . into which the first Access was a high walk like a Terrace, from whence might be taken a general view of the whole Plot below but rather in a delightful confusion, than in any plain distinction of the pieces.'[25] This echoes the layout of contemporary gardens such as those at Somerset House, Bedford House, Wilton House in Wiltshire, and The Durdans near Epsom in Surrey, as well, of course, as that at Twickenham Park. With this comment in mind, we can imagine Francis, Katherine and their guests making their way up the flights of steps to look down over the 'whole Plot below', the terrace gardens, the 'wilderness' and out to the park beyond, and admiring the 'delightful confusion'. This expression indicates a change of priorities and in this context represents a new idea: that of providing interesting and stimulating contrasts within the organized regularity of the symmetrical garden layouts. Those walking around the new gardens at Woburn and Bedford House were seeking the intellectual stimulation and aesthetic pleasure generated by what Wotton describes as 'wilde Regularitie', a key new ingredient which was seen to allow the garden to open up the viewers to 'various entertainments' as they pass through it. We are strongly reminded of Lucy Harrington's garden at Twickenham Park, and Wotton goes on: 'From this the Beholder descending many steps, was afterwards conveyed again . . . to various entertainments of his scent and sight . . . [and] every one of these diversities, was as if he had been *Magically* transported into a new Garden.'[26] The gardens and increasingly the orchards, rather than simply providing a suitable setting for a house, were now expected not just to entertain but also to transport and stimulate the viewer – to provide within the garden walls the same sense of transformation and magic that lay at the heart of the grotto experience.

At this time, however, such expectation stopped at the garden walls, since the parkland beyond was perceived as integral to something different: the everyday, practical worlds of timber, deer herds, hunting and other recreational and sporting activities. Out there the rides, or 'walks', were kept clear for carriages and horses and deer hunting. As Celia Fiennes writes, 'the parke is fine with visto's of walks cut through and across, a great many which delights the rider and walker being so shady with lofty trees,'[27] while the ponds were managed for fishing, netting wildfowl and, on occasion, boat races. Other than this, the open spaces of the park were the venue for falconry, archery, hare coursing, the increasingly fashionable sport of horse racing, and all kinds of 'faire and pleasant field-games', many endorsed by James I's *Book of Sports* (c.1616),[28] including wrestling, running and 'leaping', and games such as bowling and croquet. All of these were enormously popular, along with the extravagant gambling which accompanied most of them, and were pursued with renewed vigour after the Restoration. In his map of 1661, Moore shows this parkland in some detail, where both the 4th and 5th Earls indulged their passion for hawking and falconry; occupying pride of place just outside the gardens

Robert Peake the Elder, *Francis, 4th Earl of Bedford as a Child.*

The importance of the parkland as a venue for hunting and other outdoor activities for the family is illustrated by this image of Francis, the 4th Earl, as a child. He is shown with his favourite falcon, having just removed its hood, and his pair of dogs.

is the 'Bowling Green', protected from the deer and rabbits by a ditch and paling fence, and accessed from a door in the south garden wall. The Bowling Green is likely to have been added during the 4th Earl's time, along with the new gardens, and features in the accounts throughout the rest of the seventeenth and eighteenth centuries before being replaced *c.*1759 by a fashionably new 'Nine Pin' bowling alley in the Abbey's pleasure grounds by the John, the 4th Duke.

Following all this work, Francis and Katherine were finally able to take up full-time residence at the Abbey sometime in 1632–3, and other than his interest in pursuing his father's pioneering project to drain sections of the Fens in Cambridgeshire, where land grants were received from the Crown in exchange for private investment in the project, the earl was able to concentrate on an increasingly challenging political career. After his marriage, the 4th Earl became an active member of Parliament and by 1640 was one of its leading figures. As Lord High Treasurer he sought to resolve the increasing tension developing around the issue of royal expenditure and revenue raising, but his inability to mediate a solution with Charles I led him steadily into opposition with the royal position. There is some doubt as to what exactly his stance would have been when the war between the king and Parliament finally broke out, and the complexity of the situation is reflected in Edward Hyde, 1st Earl of Clarendon's comment when he wrote that the earl 'would have proposed and advised moderate courses, but was not incapable, for want of resolution, of being carried into violent ones'.[29] In the event, his sudden death in 1641 came just before war broke out, and it was left to his son William to navigate the treacherous waters of the Civil War, the Commonwealth, the Restoration of the Stuarts, and the arrival of William and Mary in 1688: the long and difficult years of uncertainty between 1642 and 1688.

William Russell, the 5th Earl, was born in 1616, the fourth child of Francis and Katherine, and the first head of the Russell family to be born and raised at Woburn Abbey. His association with the Abbey remained central throughout his life, and it was to the Abbey that he returned to pass the years when he was periodically caught out on the wrong side of the rapidly changing political scene. Indeed, with his inheritance in 1641, Woburn entered a prolonged period of consolidation and development, part of the earl's tireless efforts that not just stabilized the family finances and consolidated their position in the lucrative East India trade, but also saw the Russells raised to the rank of dukes of Bedford. As the old family home at Chenies Manor fell into a long decline, so Woburn developed to match any of the great houses in England.

William had grown up amidst the great building works of his father and mother at Bedford House, Covent Garden and Woburn, but rather than making radical changes to what were relatively new properties, he concentrated his efforts on developing and improving what his parents had created.

THE GROTTO, WOBURN ABBEY

The grotto, due to its survival intact to the present day, is one of the most fascinating features of the Abbey. Clearly a variation of that built a few years earlier at Bedford House by Isaac de Caus, there is some agreement that he also designed and built this one. What makes the Woburn grotto particularly unusual is that fact that, rather than being constructed out in the garden, it was included within the fabric of the house.

Today it appears largely as an anomaly, an odd, if pretty, interlude within the sedate sequence of richly furnished rooms elsewhere in the house, and

Interior of the Woburn grotto, 2014.
This modern photograph of the grotto catches something of both the detail and the atmosphere of this magical room. The statuary in the niches and central fountain bason are not original. The pipework for the various water features decayed within the walls of the structure, and no attempts have been made to undertake the difficult job of replacing it. Miraculously, however, the intricate decoration of the walls and ceiling have remained largely intact.

Grotto and Grotto Garden. View from inside the grotto indicating the original connection between the interior and exterior spaces.

one which, largely because of its extraordinary state of preservation, gives little hint of its age or uniqueness. Although water no longer runs – slipping, falling, dripping and splashing down the jagged stone and tufa work of the central niche, filling the room with sound, sparkling and shimmering in candlelight – the intricate swirling detail formed on the walls and ceiling by such materials as tufa, mother-of-pearl, pearls, real shells of ormer, cockles and black mussels, as well as shells carved from stone and cast in plaster, is still capable of transporting the visitor to another world.

Figures pass by, riding the waves in seashells drawn by dolphins above an underwater world inhabited by the gods and spirits of mythology, and looking up from the depths the 'ceiling' above undulates and sparkles like the surface of the sea lit up by pinpoints of sunlight. This grotto, like that at Bedford House before it, is a place of transformation and magic, a powerful space created by a 'collaboration of nature's art and the artist's imitation of nature . . . supplied with imagery from classical myth'.[30]

Although the grotto has survived intact, its uses have clearly changed over the centuries, and this is illustrated in the early twentieth-century photograph which shows shelves nailed to the grotto walls for the display of china. Clearly, by this time, the grotto had completely lost its function as a place of entertainment or interest in itself, and has simply become a useful place to display chinaware: a curio to be lived with and for which other uses had to be found.

Accounts from the 1650s, however, help to answer an intriguing question about the grotto, since glaziers' bills of this period for 'the replacement of "squares" of glass in the "gratoe"' raise the suggestion that it always had some sort of protection from the elements'.[31] If Duggan is right, it seems likely that the location of the grotto on the north side of the building, traditional in sunny Italy but not so suited to English weather, meant that the rusticated arches were never open but always had some kind of glazing. By the late twentieth century there were 'wire-grilled glass doors' fitted into the arches, which, in turn, were replaced by plate glass windows.

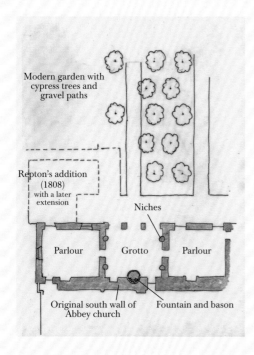

Plan of the grotto and garden area.
This plan shows the interior of the grotto and its relationship to the modern garden.

Grotto interior in the early twentieth century.

RIGHT Sir Peter Lely, *William Russell, 5th Earl/1st Duke of Bedford* (1616–1700), 1678. Something of the wealth and rank which came to the family at this time is caught in Lely's portrait, in which, with a simple gesture, William appears to be drawing our attention to the great family estates stretching out into the distance.

FAR RIGHT Sir Anthony van Dyck, *Anne Carr, Countess of Bedford* (1615–1684), 1637. Although posed against a similar backdrop to her husband, Anne's portrait has a very different feel, facing inwards, her back to the view, and storm clouds filling the sky. Van Dyck has perhaps caught here something of Anne's troubled family life, her mother being confined to the Tower for murder, William's parents' opposition to the marriage, and her devout Protestant faith during troubled religious times; even her little dog looks up at her with an anxious look.

Household and garden accounts record William's activities right up until his death in 1700: stocking the park and gardens, creating new orchards and kitchen gardens, improving water management, roads and buildings, and repairing the Abbey. In addition to all this, he patronized and encouraged some of the most important nurserymen and gardeners of the seventeenth century.

In 1637 William returned from a trip to Europe and married Anne Carr, daughter of the Earl of Somerset. The couple had met as children, the two families being neighbours in Chiswick and – in spite of his parents' initial opposition[32] – had a long and happy marriage, sharing interests and a committed Presbyterian faith.[33] Having started the war firmly on the side of Parliament and fighting with their forces at Edgehill, Russell soon found himself alienated from the more radical elements and joined the 'peace party' advocating a settlement with the king. When their proposals to negotiate a peace were rejected by Parliament, William's disapproval led him to join the king's armies at Oxford, following which he was subsequently pardoned by the king and fought with the Royalist army at Gloucester and Newbury.[34] The immediate cost of his actions was that in 1643 Bedford House was seized by Parliament and its contents sold to pay an £800 fine for delinquency.

Yet, in spite of his commitment on the battlefield and his substantial loss of property, it was not enough to convince the king's advisors of his new-found loyalty, and he found himself isolated and excluded from the royal circle. Feeling that the king was being manipulated by his enemies, William sought to return to Parliament in December 1643, but was immediately refused permission to take his seat in the Lords; his apparent lack of commitment had cost him the trust of both sides. His predicament, similar to that his father was likely to have faced had he not died, was summed up in a wonderful remark by a cousin, Anne Clifford, Baroness de Clifford: 'The trouble with the Russells was that they disapproved at one and the same time of the character of the Stuarts and the politics of Cromwell.'[35] She may well have been right, but the complexity of these times is also clear when we realize that the loyalties of his brothers and his sisters and their husbands during this period of national and family divisions were split right down the middle.[36]

By 1644, William found himself marginalized and out of favour on all sides, leading to a period of some sixteen years – between 1644 and 1660 – when he effectively withdrew from public life. Bedford House, though lacking many of its previous contents, appears to have been restored to William by the end of the war, but after 1644 much of his time was spent at Woburn, where the family shared the house with his mother, the Dowager Countess Katherine, and his youngest sister, Diana, until the latter's marriage. Following the coronation of Charles II in 1660, William resumed his seat in the House of Lords, and although never close to the king or the court circle, he was appointed Governor of Plymouth and made Knight of the Garter in 1671.

The years between 1682 and 1688 saw the Russells fall spectacularly out of royal favour and then back in again. First, in 1682, William supported the attempt to exclude the Catholic Duke of York, the king's brother James, from the throne, an action which led to the withdrawal of the royal charter for the market at Tavistock in that year. This loss of income was one thing, but things rapidly got more serious the next year when his son and heir, Lord William Russell, was arrested and subsequently executed for his part in the Rye House Plot, an attempt to assassinate both Charles and James on a visit to Newmarket. In the wake of his son's execution, William was forced once again to withdraw from public life for the rest of Charles's reign and that of James II, but circumstances suddenly changed again in 1688 with the earl's appointment to the Privy Council under the new monarchs, William and Mary.

GARDENS AT THE DURDANS, SURREY (1634–5)

If Moore's image of the gardens de Caus built at Woburn is sketchy and possibly unreliable, another contemporary garden, at The Durdans, Epsom, Surrey, can help us form a more detailed picture of the kind of garden that was built at Woburn, and maybe also tell us something about its function. The Durdans is particularly interesting because it features in a highly detailed painting by Jacob Knyff (1639–1681), and if John Harris is right, the gardens may also have been built by Isaac de Caus at much the same time as he was working at Woburn.[37] The house was inherited c.1632 by Theophilia Berkeley and her husband, Sir Robert Coke, Lord Chief Justice, who together modernized it to include a new 'Great New Hall' in the style of Inigo Jones, walled formal gardens and, above these, a 'Grove' or woodland through which paths ran to an ornamental pavilion overlooking parkland beyond.

In the walled garden we see a large parterre laid out in front of the house's main reception rooms, no doubt with doors opening out on to the wide gravel path. Beyond this lie four squares of grass, neatly outlined with low plants and separated by cross paths, all surrounding a central circular pool with a fountain statue. The inner corners of the grass squares are cut away in a style identical to those at Bedford House, Somerset House and the south garden at Woburn, giving the whole layout a familiar look. Beyond the parterre centrally placed steps lead up through two levels of terrace and out, through a gate, into the dense woodland beyond, while the brick walls running along either side of the garden flow up these level changes in gentle curves. The raised terraces and the walls containing them look, in turn, very like those at Woburn and, indeed, at Corney House. Two of the parterre spaces also feature a centrally placed statue, while the central axis running from the house to the raised terrace is accentuated by pencil-shaped cypresses of the kind that may well have featured in the Grotto Garden at Woburn. Espaliered fruit trees line the inside faces of the brick walls, while two doors in them provide access

Jacob Knyff, *The Durdans, Surrey*, 1679.
Note to the left of the image the sunlight shining down the path that leads into the woods, the 'Grove', from the top of the raised terrace. And to the right of the house the rectangular 'Great New Hall'.

to an orchard on one side and an open field on the other. All these features are familiar to us from the work in the gardens at Woburn and Bedford House.

The function of all of the new features at The Durdans – the new hall, the formal garden and the 'Grove' beyond – was largely to provide the Cokes with interesting indoor and outdoor spaces where they could entertain parties of guests for social gatherings centred on the race meetings that were being held on nearby Epsom Downs.[38] Indeed, the gardens appear to have retained this function as late as 1701, when we hear of 'the Colonel' who is reported to have 'this day set forward for Epsom, to trifle away two or three days amongst the citizens' wives. He expects to meet a great deal of company, for on Monday in the Grove at Durdans there are to be illuminations after the Roman fashion, and a concert of vocal and instrumental music.'[39]

The extent of the 'Grove' and the pavilion at the other end of the path from the garden and overlooking the park beyond are shown in John Talman's watercolour of 1702, although by this date the house and the pavilion structure were newly built. It is also interesting to note in Knyff's image the sportsman shooting at game birds in the field in front of the gardens, something that almost certainly would have been happening at Woburn as well.

While the colonel may have been seeking something slightly different during the evenings in the gardens and 'Grove' at Durdans to the Russells in their gardens, there is no doubt that it was in this spirit of entertainment that the gardens at Bedford House and Woburn were developed during the seventeenth and early eighteenth centuries.

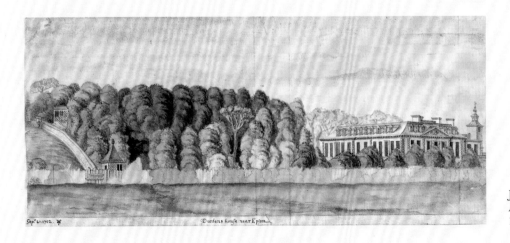

John Talman, *Durdans House near Epsom*, 1702.

This change in fortune was then followed by another when, in recognition of what was seen as his family's great sacrifice in the loss of his executed son, the earl was raised to become Duke of Bedford and Marquis of Tavistock in 1694 by the new king and queen, and the preamble to the Letters Patent creating him a duke stated that the earl received this step in peerage by reason 'that he was the father of Lord Russell the ornament to his age, whose merit it was not enough to transmit by history to posterity'.[40] The family's fortunes were then further secured when in 1695 William, now the 1st Duke of Bedford, managed to arrange the marriage of his grandson and new heir apparent, Wriothesley Russell, to Elizabeth Howland, daughter of one of London's wealthiest businessmen and property owners, John Howland, and his wife, Elizabeth Child, daughter of Sir Josiah Child of the East India Company. It was an alliance of interests which brought the Russell family into the heart of London's booming property and commercial worlds. Five years later the elderly duke, who had been widowed since 1684, died at Bedford House, becoming, as it was to turn out, the last of the family ever to occupy the old family house on the Strand.

As if his public and business commitments had not been enough, William had also pursued what may actually have been his favourite life, that of a country gentleman, to the full; it was in that role, and in a typically practical way, that he oversaw the further development of the

ABOVE LEFT John Riley, *Lord William Russell* (1639–executed 1683).

ABOVE RIGHT Sir Peter Lely, *Lady Rachel Wriothesley* (*c.*1636–1723).
The daughter of Thomas Wriothesley, 4th Earl of Southampton, Rachel married Lord William Russell in 1669. In her somewhat resigned expression we catch a glimpse of the sadness that was to dominate her life after her husband's execution. In widowhood she helped arrange the marriage of her youngest child, Wriothesley, now heir, to Elizabeth Howland, and after the death of her father-in-law, William, 1st Duke of Bedford, in 1700, she ran the estates as Dowager Duchess. Her astute business dealings with Elizabeth's family and their interests in the East India Company helped secure the family finances.

John Sanderson, elevation of west front of the Abbey: upper floor of porch as altered by William, 5th Earl, 1733.
Sanderson's drawing of the west front shows the building largely unchanged since the 4th Earl altered the north and south corner towers. The mixture of styles visible in the windows and doors indicates a building that has been altered to suit changing needs rather than carefully rebuilt. Whether the upper floor of the old porch was in need of repair, or whether the 1st Duke simply had a new idea, is not clear, but the new design rather dominates the old doorway below. Either way, the new windows will have provided a lovely view of the fishponds and the avenue stretching beyond.

park and gardens at Woburn. Part of this development, of course, was the commissioning of Moore's estate map in 1661, but while that is the last image we have of the estate at Woburn until the third decade of the eighteenth century, the 5th Earl's insistence on methodical bookkeeping means that there is a lot of information about what was going on. Through these accounts we get some hint, perhaps, of what is to come with the appearance of John Comines, the first known 'gardener' to be appointed at Woburn. Comines, who submits his bills between 1641 and 1656, was followed by George Bradford 1657–8, Mr Rowse 1658–63, and finally John Field between 1663 and his death in 1684. During this period Bedford House also had its own gardener, a post held for twenty-four years by Thomas Gilbank (1660–84), when he was succeeded by Thomas Todd.

In the case of Comines, Bradford and Rowse, the accounts suggest a period when the head gardeners – plus a team, at one point, of six labourers, three men and three 'widdos' – were keeping the flower beds well stocked, ordering seeds and plants, buying supplies, replacing tools and carrying out routine maintenance. At the same time, various repairs and alterations were being made to the Abbey – the new glass for the grotto in 1654, repairs to its cistern and water pipes in 1656, rebuilding the upper floor in the west porch that is visible in Sanderson's elevation of the west front from 1733. Between 1671 and 1672 three men were employed to transport stone and repair the grotto.

The family appear to have lived at the Abbey most of the time during these years, and only one cloud appeared at this time to cast a shadow over their enjoyment of the park and gardens. This came in 1657 when tragedy struck as William and Anne's 7-year-old daughter, Lady Anne, died after eating some berries she found while playing with her younger sister Diana in the park. The tragedy of this incident aside, the fact that Lady Anne and her sister were out in the park indicates to us that it had come to be included in whole family's use of the landscape around the Abbey. It was no longer the preserve simply of the huntsmen and sportsmen, and from this time

S. Verelst, *Lady Anne Russell* (d.1657), *c*.1657.
It is interesting that this lovely portrait of William and Anne's young daughter Lady Anne should be set against a view of landscape beyond the house and gardens. It was in just such a place, roaming the park at Woburn, that Anne was to meet her untimely death.

onward things develop from routine maintenance of the flower beds, fruit trees, paths and lawns of the gardens, to activity on a much larger scale. For the first few years after the arrival of John Field in 1663, work centres on maintaining the existing gardens.[41] A receipt from 1672 'To John Field for keeping his Garden, Orchard, Courts, Hop grounds and Bowling Green'[42] confirms that much of his time was spent on features that predate Moore's 1661 map, but it is clear that new plans for further developments were being made, and in the late 1660s we see the preparatory work for a wider programme of improvements out in the park.

In 1669, for example, vouchers detail the work of five labourers, working in September and October cleaning out ponds and springs in the park, carting away the mud, and digging new ditches to improve drainage. Then in 1670 work begins on 'levelling, digging and fencing a piece of ground to make a [kitchen] garden', planting and staking trees, and the erection of 'palisade pales' to protect them from the deer. This latter invoice is interesting because it specifies the location – 'palisade pales . . . in the park next to the Mount Walk', and for the first time we get a glimpse of named places in the park or gardens that are not captioned on Moore's map.[43]

Since there is no other image of the park or gardens until Browne's 'Survey' map of 1738,[44] it is only through these named places that we can keep track of what was being added, added to, or remained in use, in the park. The 'Mount Walk', for example, makes further appearances in the accounts, in a 1673 invoice for labourers' hours digging a 'new ditch being called The Mount', and in 1681 in an invoice for 'the destruction of Wasp's Nests . . . in the backside of The Mount'. It is not clear exactly what this term meant or where this feature was, but it is likely by this date that, rather than being a conical structure such as those we saw at Twickenham Park, it was a linear raised terrace, and perhaps was the name of that which ran along the top of the terraced gardens between the corner towers on Moore's 1661 map. Some confirmation of this suggestion comes from Celia Fiennes, who used the same term, 'mount', to describe the double terrace she saw at The Durdans *c*.1712: 'this garden is gravell'd round, the two middle walks run up to a double mount.'[45]

As work continued on the new kitchen gardens which, to judge from Browne's 1738 estate map, were relocated to a site which later became Park Farm, another interesting new development is documented between May and June of 1671. First, in May there is a bill submitted by the Bedford House gardener Thomas Gilbank for a visit to Woburn Abbey, and, second, in June a bill for £3 from Philip Moore 'owing for my journey to Woburn Abbey to survey the Garden and Orchard there'. It appears that Gilbank was not only responsible for the gardens at Bedford House, but also acted as the earl's London agent, purchasing trees, shrubs and flowers for Woburn as well, while Philip Moore, referred to variously as a 'surveyor', 'gardener' and 'nurseryman', was possibly a son of Sir Jonas Moore, who made the 1661 map. He may also be the same Philip Moore who was, in May 1671, working for Charles II as part of the team refurbishing St James's Park, where he was responsible for 'directing the levelling of the ground of the Pond by the Horse-ground and the ground by the Canall side'.[46] The arrival of these two at Woburn clearly indicates that now the kitchen garden had been moved, the parkland cleared and drained, the ponds cleaned and new fences put up, the earl was contemplating new projects and called in Gilbank and Moore to work with Field in drawing up plans. The result was that the gardens and orchards were to be redesigned 'into a new model according to the design agreed upon by his lordship',[47] which also included work being done on the 'Geat House' (gatehouse).[48]

In 1671–2, the biggest single bundle of accounts for any one year in the garden is accumulated and work is focused almost entirely on the redevelopment of the 'old' orchard and laying out and planting a new cherry orchard. During this period a team of labourers of between ten and twenty-four men were 'working in the Orchard', largely levelling the ground, digging, sifting and carting gravel for the new paths, 'making foundations', firing bricks and building buttresses and walls. This is followed by fitting coping stones, setting up door casings in the walls, laying stepping stones (which in this case refers to creating flights of steps), and invoices for work done to 'mend and repairing the Stone Steps and Coping Stones that were at fault in the Old Orchard' and 'Coping stones laid over the Arch and buttresses in the Court'. In addition, there are accounts for 'work done in the Orchard about filling in of 2 old ponds and making 2 new ponds', and 'Setting in of the sludge into the new pond'.[49] Help in understanding where this work went on comes a little later, in 1697, when Celia Fiennes visited Woburn and left an account of what she found there:

there are 3 large gardens, fine gravell walks and full of fruite . . . the walks are one above another with stone steps; in the square just by the dineing room window is all sorts of pots of flowers and curious greens fine orange cittron and lemon trees . . . on the side of this pass under an arch into a Cherry garden, in the midst of which stands a figure of stone resembling an old weeder woman used in the garden, and my Lord would have her Effigie which is done so like and her clothes so well that at first I took it to be a real living body; on the other side of the house is another large Garden severall gravel walks one above another, and on the flatts are fish ponds the whole length of the walke; above that in the next flat is 2 fish ponds, here are dwarf trees of a great bigness.[50]

Moore's 1661 map, detail of gardens as described by Celia Fiennes in 1697.

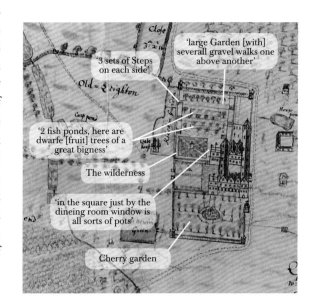

'large Garden [with] severall gravel walks one above another'

'3 sets of Steps on each side'

'2 fish ponds, here are dwarfe [fruit] trees of a great bigness'

The wilderness

'in the square just by the dineing room window is all sorts of pots'

Cherry garden

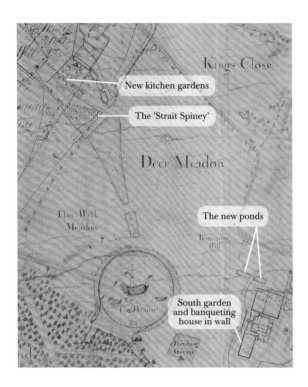

Browne's 1738 map, detail of kitchen gardens and 'The Straits'.
Moore's map of 1661 provided our last look at the formal gardens before the 2nd Duke, working with George London, removed most of the layout. We have to turn to Browne's map of 1738 to see the further developments by William, 5th Earl in the park itself and identify the location of the new kitchen gardens and plantations.

The alterations that the duke, John Field and Philip Moore have made to Francis and Katherine's Renaissance-inspired gardens of the 1630s are both interesting and reflective of the times. The impression we gain from Celia's description is one of the switch from the purely decorative 'wilde Regularitie' to the productive and practical, from the primacy of flower gardens to that of fruit orchards, from ornamental pools to useful fishponds, from celebrating the gods of Greek and Roman mythologies to celebrating the hard-working and, therefore, worthy 'old weeder woman'. The sole survivors from earlier times appear to be the dwarf fruit trees planted along the terraces of the upper garden, by now impressively large and highly productive.

Work also continued at this time on the new kitchen garden, where two men are employed to 'mark up the bank and ditch about the new kitchen garden' and 'Stake up bushes in the Strait'.[51] Following the work to create the new orchards, and as part of the process of restocking the old gardens, in the spring of 1672 large numbers of fruit trees – one delivery consisted of 200 trees: a mixed batch of pears, dwarf cherries, dwarf apples, plums and apricots – start to arrive at the Abbey.

Additional work mentioned in the accounts illustrates the extent to which the earl's 'new model' for the gardens was designed to develop their capacity to entertain, as at The Durdans, 'a great deal of company'. While alterations were being made to the ponds on the terrace gardens beside the Grotto Garden, other work was focused on the big south garden, or 'Cherry orchard', beside the entrance court. Here the twelve-arched rustic arcade provided a generous space where parties could gather to sit and enjoy the prospect of the garden on the sunny side of the house but remain in the shade, a critical requirement at this time. This also provided access to the banqueting house, to the 'good gravell and grass walks'[52] leading round the garden and past the central fountain, now joined by the realistic 'weeder woman', to the summer houses built into the corners, and to the door in the wall that led out to the Bowling Green beyond. As at The Durdans, this parterre garden was the main focal point for strolling in company and other group entertainments, and the accounts tell us that at this time joiners were refurbishing the banqueting house, the fountain was repaired, and new trees were added to the plantings.[53] Just beyond the walls of, but connected to, this parterre garden was the Bowling Green, sitting out in the park within its protective fence and ditch.

Located on a slight rise with wide views out across the park, the Bowling Green was described by Celia Fiennes in 1697: 'there is a large bowling-green with 8 arbors kept cut neatly, and seates in each, there is a seate up in a high tree that ascends from the green in 50 steps, that commands the whole parke round to see the Deer hunted, as also a large prospect of the Country.'[54] Built to provide non-participants with a vantage point from which to watch the progress of a hunt or the flight of falcons chasing doves or pigeons, these stands or 'standings' were common features of parks such as Woburn's through the sixteenth and seventeenth centuries. The fact that the 5th Earl had the Woburn Great Stand substantially rebuilt at this time serves to emphasize the communal nature of his 'new model'; here was a place, outside the usual confines of the house, arcades and walled gardens, to which the women, children and, perhaps, elderly of the household could easily walk, sit in the shady arbours or ascend the Great Stand, making an afternoon's bowling or hunting a more communal experience. There is a sense by this date, illustrated perhaps by young Lady Anne's tragic berry picking, of the family as a whole moving out beyond the walled gardens to experience and embrace the landscape of parkland beyond, a 'fine parke full of deer and wood, and some of the trees are kept cut in works and the shape of severall beasts'.[55]

Looking back over the accounts for this period, it is interesting to note that all this work was carried out by local labour drawn from the tenants of estate farms and their families, and that the bulk of it was carried out in two clearly defined periods of time, specifically from late winter until spring and then late autumn into winter. This pattern gives us a vivid picture of the 5th Earl's work set within the constraints of the agricultural year; as July turns to August the accounts go on to detail not landscaping work but jobs of high summer, particularly harvest time, then the fruit harvests, quickly followed by brewing and the lengthy task of carting dung to the fields.

This sense of Woburn beyond the house and gardens, as first and foremost an agricultural estate, becomes increasingly evident as the seventeenth century draws on. We get the impression that the vision of the 5th Earl was to update, add to and enhance the estate left to him by his father: not so much a grand vision of landscaping as a cultural statement, but improvements to create a prosperous, well-run, smoothly working country estate, an ethos very much in tune with the times. Thoughtfully organized and practical layouts created to maximize the efficiency of the estate and the orderly rows of trees in the avenue past the ponds to the west of the house, along with the new timber plantations and fruit orchards, all became a source of aesthetic pleasure in their own right, a pleasure not yet found in the indulgence of landscaping for its own sake.

Besides working on Woburn during this busy period, the earl rebuilt the house at Thorney Abbey near Peterborough in Cambridgeshire and laid out new gardens and orchards there in 1662, and by 1671 was in the process of updating Bedford House; but beyond the properties themselves, he was also looking towards future business investments. It was some forty years since

Central London properties of
the Russell family, 1632–1705.

❷ Bedford House, rebuilt 1632,
demolished 1705
❸ Covent Garden, laid out
  c.1632
❹ Southampton House, built
  by the Earl of Southampton
  1657, passed to the Russell
  family 1669
❺ Bloomsbury Square, laid out
  c.1660

Covent Garden Piazza had been created and times were changing; many
of the original tenants had moved on, as had London itself since the Great
Fire of 1666. In the booming city of the post-Restoration period, the earl saw
new opportunities for the Piazza, and in 1671 he 'asked for and received,
at a price, the royal patent of licence to hold a market "within the Piazza
at Covent Garden"'.[56] The coming of the market changed the atmosphere
of the Piazza: families of 'quality' who had not already left did so at this
time, and it comes as no surprise that the earl was the last of the Russell
family to occupy Bedford House. Over the garden wall there was no longer
the tranquil scene of the grassed Piazza and families promenading, but one
dominated by the sights and sounds, not to mention the smells, of one of
London's busiest markets.

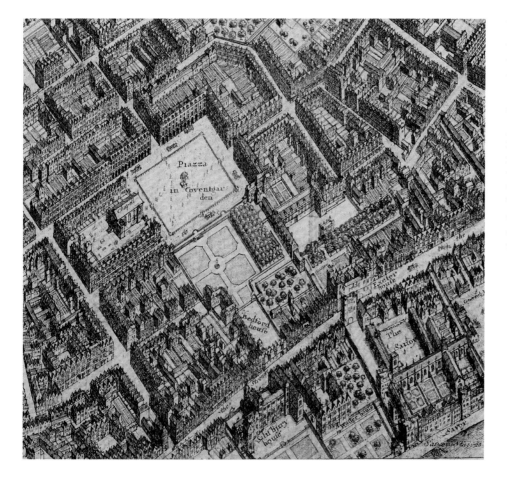

Wenceslas Hollar, *Bird's-Eye View of the West Central District of London*, detail of gardens at Bedford House, *c.*1658–60.
Hollar's map of Westminster shows the gardens of Bedford House in some detail, with the main parterre to the left, the wilderness next to it with the orchard below. The path from the house to the stable block and courtyard runs between these last two.

Because there are so few contemporary images of the gardens and estate at Woburn during these times, the development of the gardens at Bedford House becomes particularly interesting, and here we see a fast-moving succession of gardens which indicates just how quickly taste was changing. Although very busy developing the gardens at Woburn, by 1673 the earl and his gardener Gilbank had also altered the Bedford House gardens. Comparing the layout on Lacy's plan with that shown by Hollar, we see that they have simplified the left-hand parterre into four grass squares, each with a central statue, and replaced the original wilderness of dense trees on the right-hand side with a form of maze currently fashionable. This consisted of a geometrical pattern of closely trimmed hedges, in this case of thorns, cut through with diagonal paths leading back and forth to a central space and passing a series of 'rooms', quite possibly each with a seat, on the way. It may be just this kind of maze that Celia Fiennes described in 1712 as being one 'in which are slaunt cut ways'.[57] Although the two banqueting houses on the raised terrace are still clearly shown, it is not known if the grotto beneath the terrace remains functional during this time. In addition, the orchard seems to have been removed and the site is now annotated as belonging to Mr Bingley, the earl's steward throughout this period, who also had rooms of his own in Bedford House.

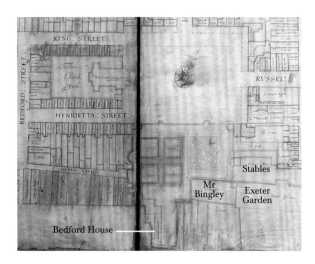

ABOVE Mr Lacy, *Gardens at Bedford House*, 1673.

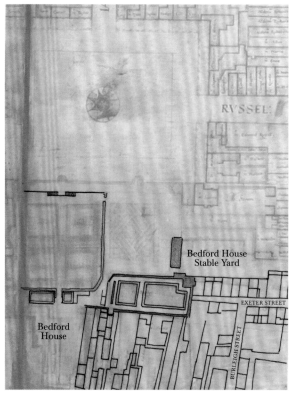

ABOVE Alterations and additions to the gardens shown by Lacy, from a plan by Thomas Smith, *Gardens at Bedford House, c.*1690.

By the 1690s, the whole context of these gardens had changed, as the market developed at Covent Garden and the gardens of Exeter House next door were swept away by the development of streets and houses, but it is clear that, even after Covent Garden Piazza became the location of an increasingly busy market, the 1st Duke continued to use Bedford House on a regular basis. We can imagine that, espcially after he was widowed in 1684, he looked forward to, and was cheered up by, regular visits by his son Lord William's widow, Lady Rachel, and his grandchildren, from nearby Southampton House, Bloomsbury; and it is entirely possible that some of the changes we see in the gardens at Bedford House during these years were in response to the changing needs and enthusiasms of the children. Although we can reasonably assume that any number of new ideas and plans for both Woburn Abbey and Bedford House were left unrealized when he died in London in 1700, it is also possible that he may have had the satisfaction of knowing that he had successfully passed on his knowledge, experience and enthusiasm for such projects to his 20-year-old grandson and heir, Wriothesley, 2nd Duke of Bedford.

CHAPTER TWO

*'. . . the upper hills of the park command good prospects,
and are beautifully cloth'd with wood; so as to form a
grand amphitheatre around the house'*

(Hon. John Byng, 1789)

WRIOTHESLEY RUSSELL, 2ND DUKE, AND JOHN RUSSELL, 4TH DUKE

Sir Godfrey Kneller,
*Wriothesley Russell, 2nd Duke
of Bedford* (1680–1711) *and
Elizabeth Howland, Duchess
of Bedford* (d.1724), 1695.
Kneller painted this lovely
image of the young couple
the year they got married.
Despite their youth, it
was to prove a happy and
productive marriage, but
one cut tragically short by
their early deaths.

On their wedding day in 1695, Wriothesley Russell, heir to the 1st Duke of Bedford, was 15 and Elizabeth Howland, his bride, was barely 12, so immediately afterwards the two returned to their respective mothers until he, at least, reached his majority. Of Elizabeth's substantial inheritance, the manor at Streatham was granted to her mother for life, while the manors of Tooting Bec in Surrey and Dry Drayton in Cambridgeshire, along with the valuable London docklands at Rotherhithe, came into the Russell estates. After his marriage, Wriothesley went up to Oxford in 1696, and set out on his Grand Tour the next year. Travelling with his tutor, Mr Hicks, he first visited Holland, where he was presented to King William III at The Hague.[1] Although William was busy with both political and military matters, he was also completing his gardens at Het Loo, and we can imagine that he encouraged Wriothesley to visit some of the outstanding gardens in and around The Hague. Following this visit, the pair travelled on through Germany, finally arriving in Rome in 1698. Here Wriothesley was following in the footsteps of a number of his predecessors, in particular his uncles Edward and Robert, but few of them had embraced the experience in quite the same way; he thrived, and visiting Rome seems to have marked a seminal moment in his life. Gladys Scott Thomson sums up vividly the impact that Rome had on him:

An imposing, a painted, a gilded Rome; such was the city about which Wriothesley drove, as he told his mother, in a barouche – an early use of the word – drawn by two horses and attended by a couple of running footmen . . . [and] the spell of an Italian summer took hold of him . . . But it was especially the charm of the Italian summer night . . . that intoxicated the young Englishman. To his mother he drew a picture . . . of himself driving about town on a night of moonshine . . . listening to music . . .

[talking] to acquaintances . . . with all the best company in town taking the air until long after midnight.[2]

He was clearly both excited and enchanted, soaking up his surroundings – the atmosphere, art, literature, theatre and music – and we get the feeling that, after the sombre surroundings of Southampton House following his father's death and the quiet company of his elderly grandfather at Bedford House, an entire new and exciting world was opened up, infecting him with a sense of enthusiasm for art and culture that remained undiminished when he arrived back in England in 1699.

Scott Thomson has no doubt about the importance of this trip and its influence on his life. She writes that, at this time, 'Society . . . was making great strides in its appreciation of art in all its forms. In his short life, Wriothesley, Duke of Bedford, stands out as the man who introduced into Southampton House and into Woburn Abbey fashions in the library, among the pictures and in the way of entertainments which were so new as to be almost revolutionary.'[3] The interesting question, for our purposes, is: could the same have been said about the changes he started to make in the park at Woburn had they not been cut short by his premature death so soon after they were begun?

It is clear that both Wriothesley and Elizabeth had grown up amongst a considerable amount of activity in garden design and new ideas about landscaping on a large scale, with works being carried out by his grandfather at Bedford House and Woburn Abbey, by his parents at Southampton House in Bloomsbury and Stratton Park in Hampshire, and by her maternal grandfather, Sir Josiah Child, and her uncle Sir Richard Child at Wanstead House. Their interest in these things is reflected in a visit the young couple made in 1701, when, returning home from Bath, they stopped off at Badminton House, the home of Elizabeth's aunt Rebecca Child. Henry Somerset, 1st Duke of Beaufort, had died the year before, but he was survived at Badminton by his redoubtable duchess, Mary Somerset, and their daughter-in-law Rebecca, wife of their recently deceased son Charles and mother of Henry, who had inherited as 2nd Duke of Beaufort.

Together, the 1st Duke of Beaufort and Duchess Mary had rebuilt the house at Badminton in the 1660s, with new gardens being laid out by George London between 1682 and 1711, but in addition to all this activity, Mary, who died aged 84 in 1714, was also one of the leading plant collectors of her generation. Seeds came to her from all over the world, and she was helped in collecting, propagating and developing these by nurserymen such as George London and Dr William Sherard, the latter having risen to prominence in the field of botany assisting the leading botanist John Ray in his research for the *Historia Plantarum Generalis* (1704).[4] At this time Sherard was resident at Badminton, where he acted as tutor to the Beaufort children, and one of the highlights of their visit will have been the chance to tour the duchess's greenhouses where thousands of plants were looked after by Sherard and his staff.

The Bedfords had both grown up amongst the work of George London and his partners – who included the Woburn gardener John Field – at the Brompton Park Nursery, and this visit to Badminton would seem to confirm Wriothesley's growing interest in horticulture and plant collections, an interest that perhaps they both shared. Jeremiah Wiffen, librarian to the 6th Duke and the first chronicler of the Russell family, was to write later in his inimitable style: 'To floriculture, as well as landscape-gardening and agriculture [Wriothesley] appears to have been much devoted.'[5] In the event, William Sherard left England for Turkey in 1702, but not before he had introduced his brother Dr James Sherard to the duke and duchess. James, who had worked with William on their nursery at Eltham, London, was hired by the Bedfords as a horticultural advisor, and went on to become an important and trusted member of the household, sharing an interest not just in garden design and horticulture, but also in the duke's other great passion, music.

But it will have been his parents' new gardens at Southampton House and the extensive landscapes at Stratton Park – both of which had been built by his maternal grandfather and came into the family on Rachel Wriotheseley's marriage to Lord William – that will have most caught his attention. At Southampton House, which his parents had occupied since their marriage in 1669, they had created gardens that echoed the structure of those at Bedford House. John Evelyn, visiting four years before they moved in, had noted that there was only 'a naked garden to the North' but praised the area for its 'good aire';[6] by turn of the century, the naked garden had been replaced by new gardens laid out by Lord William and Lady Rachel, which incorporated the bastions of a section of the Parliamentary fortifications dating from the Civil War. The substantial W-shaped embankment provided the site for an unusual raised terrace with views to the fields beyond to the north, and back

Anon., *Two Batteries at Southampton House.* A view from the north of Southampton House in the late seventeenth century. The house itself is seen over the walls of the gun batteries, a remnant of London's Civil War-era defences, which were used to create the raised terrace that ran across the end of the first gardens to be laid out. This layout survived until the gardens were extended north in the eighteenth century. The lane that became Southampton Row can be seen running south down the left-hand side of the garden.

towards the house over the large parterre gardens: an up-to-date version of the gardens overlooking Covent Garden. It is quite possible that this work at Southampton House was carried out at much the same time as, or even before, Lady Rachel's half-sister and her husband Ralph, 1st Duke of Montagu, built their Montagu House next door in 1675 and created new gardens in the fields beyond.

Of equal interest to young Wriothesley, perhaps, were the park and gardens at Stratton Park, Hampshire, a property his mother, Lady Rachel, retained until her death in 1723. Here, apart from all the landscaping that had been done by his parents, we have the fascinating possibility that Wriothesley will have known a young man, of much the same age, who grew up in the village and may also have worked there in the gardens as a 14- and 15-year old during the mid-1690s. The son of one of the large tenant farmers at Stratton, Stephen Switsur (or 'Switzer' as he later called himself) had been born at East Stratton in 1682,[7] and he wrote later that as a young man he had known 'the meanest labours of scythe, spade and wheelbarrow'.[8] These 'labours' may well have been at Stratton Park, and certainly by the time he was 16 he had gained sufficient knowledge and experience somewhere – and a sufficiently influential patron to propose him – to be offered an apprenticeship with London and Wise at Brompton Park Nursery, from where, alongside that of his fellow apprentice Charles Bridgeman, his professional career was developed.

It is tantalizing to imagine those times when the young heir to the Duke of Bedford might have met Stephen as he laboured with his scythe, spade or wheelbarrow on the grounds at Stratton, and perhaps discussed the work or exchanged views on the garden and how it might develop in the future. Although there is no recorded contact between the 2nd Duke and Switzer, the latter's evident awareness of the content and quality of the park and gardens that William and Rachel created at Stratton Park and Southampton House, his description of them as 'some of the best that were made at that time', and his noticeably personal description of Lord William as both 'Master', 'Gardener' and 'Friend' would certainly indicate a much stronger connection to Stratton Park than simply being born in the neighbourhood.[9]

Reading the opening of volume 3 of Switzer's *Ichnographia Rustica* (1718 and 1742) and his emphasis on the 'Decoration and Embellishment of a whole Estate, or at least, that Part of it that lies most contiguous to the Mansion House', it is possible that he was drawing on his experiences at Stratton, and that Lord William and Lady Rachel's landscaping may in fact have been part of a new departure in consciousness and style. Switzer urges his readers to look beyond the garden area itself and consider the 'Estate . . . that lies most contiguous' which is usually neglected, and argues that instead of installing large and expensive walled gardens, it is better to make a modest garden round the house and, through judicious improvements of the park beyond, include the whole into a pleasurable experience, incorporating as much of the 'natural' as possible. This idea was later to become recognizable in the *ferme ornée*, and also in the work of Lancelot 'Capability' Brown, and it is discernible in the developments at Woburn we saw in the last chapter. It may also enable us to reimagine more of what lay behind William and Rachel's 'orchards, and avenues, planted groves, wildernesses and other ornaments' at Stratton, and it is noticeable that the summary of Thomas Browne's 1729–30 survey of Stratton Park makes no mention of large parterre or formal gardens.[10]

One thing is for sure, when we look at the surviving elements of the gardens that Wriothesley was to go on to build at Woburn as 2nd Duke, as they are shown on the Browne's 1738 map, we notice that the emphasis is very much on linking the house to the wider parkland beyond, with a minimum of separation. Parts of de Caus's 1630s garden layout remain recognizable but much has been removed, the overall design simplified rather than enlarged; and with the walls, entrance court, gatehouse and wilderness gone from the west front of the house, the views beyond are now powerfully focused out down the Great Avenue, past the new axially positioned formal pond and on to the far horizon of hills and woodland. These elements contain strong echoes of his father's layout at Stratton Park, where woodland plantations spread out across the rising ground behind the house, while in front, the house, courtyard garden and bowling green look out over open parkland featuring an axially located pond. Certainly, it was during the 2nd Duke's lifetime that the parkland beyond the garden walls at Woburn started to become an integral part of the setting of the old abbey and of the family's use of the landscape that surrounded it, with new features, such as the Serpentine Terrace and the Great Circle, appearing in more distant parts of the park.

After Lord William's death, Lady Rachel and her children, Wriothesley and his sisters, had lived for while at Woburn, but once they began their married life Wriothesley and Elizabeth returned with his mother to Southampton House. They also paid numerous visits to Elizabeth's mother at Streatham, but after he achieved his majority and took over running the Bedford estates, they spent increasing amounts of time at Woburn Abbey, opening the windows, sweeping out the cobwebs, reanimating the rambling house with the busyness of family life, something it had not known since his father and uncles and aunts were children fifty or sixty years before. All of this meant that Wriothesley had to decide what to do with the old family home at Bedford House in Covent Garden. His solution was quick in coming and proved to be pragmatic and unsentimental, and to make

Browne's 1738 Woburn estate map, annotated detail of Bason Pond, Great Avenue and Serpentine Terrace.

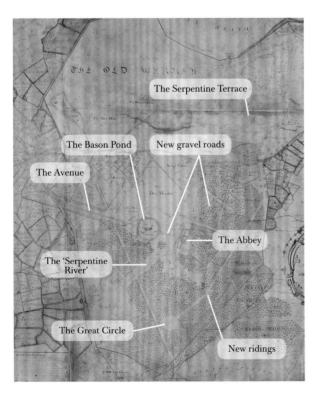

The Serpentine Terrace

The Bason Pond

New gravel roads

The Avenue

The Abbey

The 'Serpentine River'

The Great Circle

New ridings

STRATTON PARK, EAST STRATTON, HAMPSHIRE

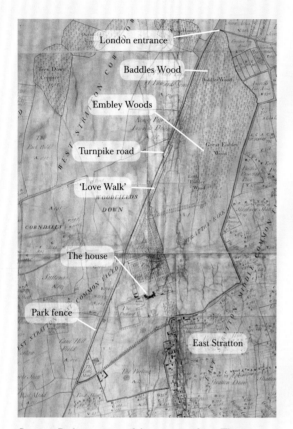

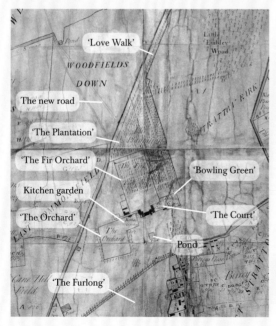

Stratton Park, overview of the property from Thomas Browne's 1729–30 survey.

Thomas Browne's survey of Stratton from 1729–30 describes the estate as situated 'in a clean "Champaign Country" with excellent sporting facilities and good land for sheep and corn'.[11] It notes that after his father-in-law's death *c*.1667 Lord William Russell added the two wings visible on the plan at either end of the original house, built a series of service buildings, and laid out a landscape with 'orchards, and avenues, planted groves, wildernesses and other ornaments to adorn and accommodate this beautiful and pleasant seat; he also pulled down part of the village of Stratton and laid it into his deer park.'

As shown on the survey, the park, enclosed by its paling fence and running north and south of Lord William's house alongside the main road from Winchester to Basingstoke, represents the largest landscaping project undertaken by any of the Russell family to date. Much of what was created is still visible today at least in outline, including the park boundaries, some of the trees round the orchard and the open parkland to the south, the woodlands of the plantations immediately north of the house, the locations of Embley and Baddles Woods, and the entrance from the road at the northern tip of the park, now known as the London entrance. The village of East Stratton lies to the south, and we can see that the north-eastern section of the village had to be cleared to create the park with its pond and 'Furlong' enclosure south of the house.

To the north of the house, the back of which was built into the hillside, steps led to an enormous walled garden area running up the gentle slope. A walk ran up the centre of this garden through a wide terrace with two grassed plots to 'The Fir Orchard', between what may have been two rectangular pools along the north boundary, and out into 'The Plantation' beyond. Along the eastern side of this garden a further walled plantation, the 'wildernesses', ran north from the 'Bowling Green' and 'Court' up into 'The Plantation' above, where all these paths converge on the long tree-lined avenue which ran up beside the Basingstoke road to the London entrance. Known as 'Love Walk', this provided access to the acres of woodland beside it.[12] Laying out and planting these gardens was a considerable and ambitious undertaking, which the 2nd Duke will have witnessed and learnt from as a child. The landscape at Stratton, particularly the walks through the woodland plantations, were also to have an influence on Lord John, who had bought the property from his brother the 3rd Duke and planned to make Stratton Park his principal residence. In the event, due to his brother's early death, John succeeded as 4th Duke, but the influence of Stratton can be seen in the substantial and complex plantations John went on to create at Woburn.

Central London properties of the Russell family, 1706–1800.

❸ Covent Garden
❹ Southampton House, renamed Bedford House 1734, demolished 1800
❺ Bloomsbury Square
❻ Montagu House, built 1675
❼ Bedford Square, laid out *c.*1775

excellent business sense: demolish the old house, now well over 100 years old, and use the resulting space to create a lucrative housing development beside the thriving Covent Garden market. Thus, in 1705, work started on the demolition of the house and gardens, and, by 1707, the site was being developed into the streets and terraces of houses that we see today between Henrietta Street and the Strand, and Bedford Street and Wellington Street, a project completed by the Trustees, pre-eminently his mother, during the 3rd Duke of Bedford's minority between 1711 and 1729. It was at this moment that de Caus's grotto was recorded for posterity before it and everything else, including gardener Gilbank's prized topiary maze, were demolished. In fact, an inventory of the contents of the house, taken on the death of the 1st Duke in 1700, indicates that things were already in decline. The list of contents for the garden – '3 stone rollers, 5 Seates, A Leaden Cistern and a Stone Table' – would seem to suggest that just about everything that was not too heavy to move had already been transferred to other properties.[13]

Further inspiration and new ideas were provided for the Bedfords in 1706 – when Elizabeth's uncle Sir Richard Child started a major programme of works in the grounds at Wanstead House outside London, working with George London to lay out huge formal gardens of avenues and ponds east and west of the house – and in 1709, when they paid a visit to his sister Rachel, Duchess of Devonshire, her husband, William, the 2nd Duke, and their five children at Chatsworth in Derbyshire. By 1707, the year he died, the 1st Duke of Devonshire had just completed a stylistically groundbreaking new house and the new 'baroque' gardens designed, again by George London working with the architect Thomas Archer. Here, as at Wanstead, London

Leonard Knyff and Johannes Kip, 'Bird's-Eye View of Wanstead House to the West', from *Nouveau Théatre de la Grande Bretagne*, 1728.

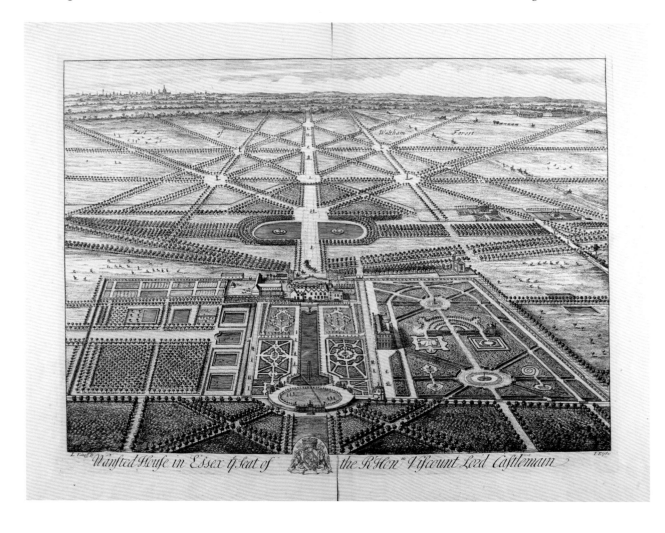

created a large formal layout, including the 'Great Parterre' cut into the hillsides above the house, fountains, garden buildings, temples and classical sculptures. This work was then further enhanced by a new enlarged version of the grand Cascade in 1701, and the Cascade House at the top added by Thomas Archer in 1703.

By the end of 1707, stimulated by his experiences on the Continent and by all the activity of their extended families, Wriothesley and Elizabeth were ready to start work on the wider landscape at Woburn – to finally move beyond the boundaries of the 4th Earl's walled gardens and the 1st Duke's orchards, and beyond the traditional layout of parkland. Following his parents' example at Stratton, he sought to include the wider setting of the Abbey, a landscape now seen as a place full of potential to expand the horizons and pleasures of their family life, to enrich their cultural and artistic interests, and to satisfy their new curiosity about the worlds of nature, botany and horticulture. Given what he knew of Stratton Park and what they had seen at Badminton, Wanstead and Chatsworth, who knows what they might have gone on to create at Woburn had not Wriothesley's early death in 1711 brought the whole project to an end? Although incomplete, what Wriothesley and Elizabeth set out to do marks the moment when the park at Woburn moved from being simply an economic and sporting asset to one which also enriched their cultural and aesthetic lives.

A witness to the start of the work was Wriothesley's uncle, Admiral Edward Russell, who visited Woburn in 1707. The admiral had been very busy himself with similar work at his home Chippenham Park, where he moved part of the village to extend the park and developed his gardens with new ponds, parterres and a great fountain.[14] After leaving Woburn he wrote approvingly to the Dowager Duchess Rachel:

> I am newly come from Woburn, where I stayed a week; and upon my word, I never was better pleased than to see the Duke and Duchess of Bedford both so extremely easy in their house . . . Your son busies himself with improving his park and grounds, and has got the reputation of a great husbandman. I have told him, the fear I am under is, his growing too careful; which is, I think, a mistake . . . I endeavoured to persuade him . . . to allow himself more, that he may complete his house for his dwelling, to his mind.[15]

The admiral was clearly looking forward to major developments at Woburn, and his letter seems to confirm that plans were under way.

From 1705 to 1710 the accounts record consistent building work within the Abbey itself, largely it would seem repairs to the structure, chimneys, door and window frames, plaster and paintwork, and 'a new door case for the Grotto', but also including the relaying of floors, steps and stairs and a considerable amount of brickwork. Large quantities of Portland and other cut stone were salvaged from the demolition of Bedford House and brought to Woburn for this work, and this may well indicate that some alteration of the fabric or layout was under way, but no details exist. Mention here of the grotto is interesting, because we can imagine that with the arrival of Wriothesley there was perhaps a resurgence of interest in it. Here, for the first time since the days of Francis and Katherine, was someone for whom this was not simply an exotic novelty, but who had experienced these things first hand in Italy. He had, no doubt, spent many enchanted candle-lit hours in just such settings during those long, magical summer nights in Rome, and will have passed on to his family his views on their joys and value. It is also entirely possible that, although himself too young to have shared such experiences with his father before he died, the 4th Duke too was fully aware of the unique nature of the grotto, and that this knowledge lay behind his insistence on retaining it intact when the Abbey was rebuilt in the 1750s.

Outside the Abbey we can build up at least a partial picture of what was under way. James Sherard may well have been the duke's close advisor, and perhaps directed things on the ground, but a number of bills from Brompton Park seem to indicate that the nursery was not simply supplying trees and new plant material, but that the duke was also paying for the services of George London, and possibly also Henry Wise.[16] London may well have been responsible for laying out the Great Avenue, the Serpentine Terrace, and constructing the Bason Pond. Closer to the house, while it seems that the old gardens round the Abbey were still intact by 1708, since in that year Joseph Stringer bills for '1 day for Wilderness pruning' in April, '4 days that week pruning Wilderness', and '3 days that week pruning in the wilderness and pruning the tubs in the Privy Garden' in May,[17] by the next year radical changes were under way. As Gladys Scott Thomson points out, from 1709 there are 'constant allusions to the building of peers [piers] in the park or adjacent to the house',[18] and although the nature and purpose of these are never specified, we can perhaps assume that foundations were being created for new walls, walks and possibly new terraces, cut into the rising ground to the north, south and east of the Abbey. Perhaps the basis for extensive new pleasure grounds like those at Wanstead and Chatsworth was being prepared, but, frustratingly for us, just as all this was getting under way, the 2nd Duke contracted smallpox at his mother's house in Streatham and died at Chenies in May 1711, aged just 30, at the start of what might have been a major transformation of the house, park and gardens at Woburn.

Amongst all the influences on the work that was done at Woburn by her husband and later by her second son, Lord John Russell, 4th Duke, it is worth noting the two houses that came from Elizabeth's family. One of these was Dry Drayton Manor, Cambridgeshire,[19] which, although never an important family home, remained in the family for 100 years and seems always to have been kept in good repair until sold in 1795 by the 5th Duke.

Browne's 1738 map, detail
of gardens, Bason Pond
and Great Avenue.
Most notable perhaps
of the changes recorded
in Browne's map of
1738 is that in the areas
immediately in front the
Abbey all the small field
boundaries and the formal
walled gardens have been
removed, and what was
previously agricultural
land or gardens has now
become parkland. This
has provided the space
for a layout similar to
that at Wanstead to be
created, a new gravel road
running straight down to
the circular Bason Pond,
complete with posts and
chains, and continuing
out across the park, over
the road and up the hill
opposite. In turn, new
ridings and 'circles' have
been laid out through the
woodland of the park, and
a new serpentine access
road laid out to the Abbey,
winding through the woods
from Froxfield Lane. What
we are looking at suggests
the establishment of the
basic design with much
more to follow, a process
cut short by the duke's
death in 1711 and never to
be completed.

The other was Streatham House, where Lord John grew up, and it clearly remained important to him. Following her husband's death in 1711, Elizabeth left Southampton House and took her young children – Rachel, Elizabeth, Wriothesley and John – back to her childhood home at Streatham. It must latterly have seemed a somewhat sad and lonely place following the marriages of their sisters and their mother's death there in 1724, but appears nevertheless to have remained of some importance to both boys. It was one of the few family properties that was used on a regular basis by Wriothesley after he became 3rd Duke of Bedford in 1729, and when Lord John, as the 4th Duke of Bedford, rented out the house and estate in 1739, he made two very interesting exclusions from the lease: 'the rooms which were occupied by his gardener and curiously, the lauristinus, cedar and yew trees planted in the grounds'.[20] In short, for different reasons, both brothers seem to have held close attachments to the house, and judging from what he excluded from the lease, the 4th Duke's attachment would suggest that the gardener had been an important adult figure in his life, someone with whom he spent time and who encouraged the interest in plants and plantings which was to become such a feature of his development of Woburn. Certainly, some

William Ellis, *Streatham House*, 1780s, engraving.

STREATHAM HOUSE, Surrey.

magnificent trees can be seen in the garden in a surviving image from the late eighteenth century, and the tree species excluded all went on to become a major component of the 'Evergreen' collection he developed after 1742.

While John, as 4th Duke, went on to create the house and grounds that still largely shape what we see at Woburn today, his elder brother, the 3rd Duke, left a somewhat darker legacy. In his short and unsettled life he seems to have struggled to assume a sense of responsibility for the family estates in which he had little interest or emotional attachment; indeed, although he periodically spent time at Woburn, he did no work on it, and left to his own devices he would have cut and sold the timber at Woburn; he also considered selling Southampton House. Apart from Streatham, the only other properties in which he showed any interest were Thornhaugh and Thorney. At the former he may have built the new house at the New Farm site, closer than the original manor house to the hunting park of the Bedford Purlieus, while at the latter he seems to have had plans to make the house built by his great-grandfather his principal home. At Thorney from 1728, 'Furniture was put into the house, the gardens were planted with fruit trees, and he gave lavish entertainments for his tenants'; he seems also to have actually enjoyed the landscapes around, taking trips along the rivers and canals in his specially ordered 'Pleasure Boat'.[21] The 3rd Duke, however, was to die just four years later on a trip to Portugal designed to improve his failing health, and, following his death, interest in Thorney as a residence came to an end.

Lord John, on the other hand, seems to have eagerly embraced the family legacy, and was happy to take on both the responsibilities and the way of life that came with it. As early as 1724, when she died, 'his mother had left him lands in several counties . . . and made him a residual legatee',[22] with the result that by 1729 he was in a position to buy the family estate at Stratton Park from his indifferent brother the duke and, not expecting to inherit the dukedom, planned to make it his principal country residence. In 1730 an additional property came to him when the combined manors of East and West Cheam were gifted to him in the will of its late owner, the Reverend Robert Lloyd. An eminent churchman and archaeologist, Lloyd felt himself 'indebted to Russell for preferment in the church',[23] specifically, his appointment as Rector of St Paul's, Covent Garden. It was thus as a considerable landowner that the young Lord John set off in 1731 with his tutor Mr Hetherington for his tour of the Continent, taking in France and Italy. While abroad he kept his eyes peeled for interesting furnishings for the grand house he planned at Stratton Park – perhaps the most significant of which was his inspired decision to commission a series of paintings from the artist Canaletto. By the time these started to arrive c.1732, however, Lord John had become 4th Duke of Bedford, and instead of going down to Hampshire, the paintings were initially installed in Southampton House before moving to Woburn in 1800, when the former was demolished, and where they can still be seen today.

In 1731, on his return from abroad, Lord John married Diana Spencer, the daughter of Charles Spencer, 3rd Earl of Sunderland, and granddaughter of Sarah, Duchess of Marlborough. Diana was the firm favourite of her redoubtable grandmother, who took a keen interest in the young couple, expecting great things for them when Lord John became duke in 1732, and she liked nothing better than to give the couple advice on how their various homes might be improved. After touring the Abbey in 1732 once the couple had moved in, she was full of ideas and commented, 'I'm sure if it was my house, I would not pull it down, but I would alter several things in it by degrees and make it a better house than any architect can build now.'[24]

Immediately following their marriage, however, the young couple were more interested in the house at Cheam, to which they appear to have become very attached. Along with the house, the Reverend Lloyd had also willed Lord John the contents, including his extensive library, his collections of flowers and exotic plants, and some furniture. We catch a glimpse of the newly-weds at the house together in Diana's letters to her grandmother, to whom she describes spending their time 'sorting out books and riding on the Downs', while the furniture 'included some of the "best Japan" she had ever seen'.[25] In addition to sorting out the contents, they were also making plans to improve the house, and by the spring of 1732 work was under way. Clearly, for the next few years until Diana's death in 1735, the house at Cheam and perhaps everything it stood for – the Reverend's tidy collections, his well-organized library, his interests in botany and horticulture, and the domesticity of the relatively small house and its flower gardens – appealed

After Gainsborough, *John Russell, 4th Duke of Bedford* (1710–1771).
This picture shows qualities of authority and comfort in Lord John's role as Duke of Bedford that we have not seen since the days of his great-grandfather William, and consciously or unconsciously he has adopted the same gesture we saw in William's portrait (see page 50). Certainly, he was to go on to develop the grand family home depicted in the prominently displayed plan and the lifestyle that went with it.

strongly to the young couple. They seem to have found here a quiet private world where they could enjoy each other's company and their shared interests, away from the concerns of the world and the worries about his late brother's stewardship of the Russell inheritance.

Yet it was the property at Stratton Park that the couple determined to turn into their principal home, and, as Marie Draper puts it, 'By 1732 a much grander architectural scheme than Cheam . . . was occupying Lord John's mind.'[26] We get an indication of the architectural style they were interested in when, early that summer, they set off on a tour to Bath, stopping first at Stratton, before going on to visit Wilton. The house there was a renowned

Thomas Howland, *Lady Diana Spencer, Duchess of Bedford* (1710–1735). Sharing interests and tastes, the couple were full of plans for their homes that were to be tragically cut short by her death four years after their marriage. Although he remarried, the development of the houses they planned together at Cheam and Stratton Park was not to happen, and both were later sold.

example of the Palladian style. It had been built by Inigo Jones, with gardens laid out by Isaac de Caus,[27] in the early 1630s, when they were also working for Francis, 4th Earl of Bedford, and great changes to the gardens at Wilton and the surrounding landscape were being planned by the 9th Earl of Pembroke, 'the Architect Earl', and Roger Morris.

By this time Diana was also about four months pregnant with their first child, and it must have been a time of much happiness, optimism and planning for the future. By late summer they had determined to fulfil his grandfather's plans for the house at Stratton, to pull down the remains of the original house and to build a new range of living rooms between the two end wings Lord William had added, and they had decided that the new buildings should be in the Palladian style, designed by John Sanderson. In one of her letters at this time, Sarah, Duchess of Marlborough shared their enthusiasm for the new house: 'My taste is exactly yours as to the country and I am glad you have everything at Stratton you can desire,' and she went on to point up one aspect of the property's appeal: 'For fine walks and trees would be my first wish, yet 'tis agreeable to have fine downs near one's house.'[28] This was certainly the case at Stratton and echoes what they enjoyed about Cheam's proximity to Banstead Downs.

By the end of 1732, however, their carefree summer tour must have seemed a distant memory, because two events occurred which put these activities on hold. First, in October, the 3rd Duke died on board ship en route to Portugal, and so, instead of immersing himself in their plans for Stratton and Cheam, Lord John suddenly found himself head of the family as the 4th Duke. Second, a month later Diana gave birth to their son John, Marquis of Tavistock, only for the infant to die within a few weeks. Everything had suddenly changed, not least because Diana's fragile health never really recovered. She was to die just three years later, aged 25. The house at Stratton remained unfinished at Diana's death, and although the duke and his second wife, Gertrude Leveson-Gower, whom he married in 1737, saw the work through, it was never to become the family home they had intended.

Once again, we will never know quite what was planned for Stratton apart from the new house, but Browne's 1729–30 survey does suggest that changes were also planned for the grounds, as evidenced by the new road pencilled in across 'Woodfields Down' (see page 70). This section of road survives today, enclosed by its rows of mature trees, and would seem to have been designed to provide easy access from the main avenue of the gardens, across the turnpike and up past the pond on to the wide open spaces of the 'West Stratton Cow Down' beyond. Seeing this we are reminded of John and Diana's love for riding on the downs, and clearly they were looking to include these in their everyday enjoyment of Stratton.

In the end, once the duke and Gertrude had completed the house, the Stratton estate was settled on their eldest son, Francis, Marquis of Tavistock, but following his sudden death in 1767, 'the house was surveyed by William Chambers in 1768 and over the next two years the interior was dismantled, the fixtures sold off . . . and one of the wings taken down'.[29] Their grandson Francis, the 5th Duke, may never have known the finished house, since it was stripped out just three years after he was born, and when he sold the property in 1801 to Francis Baring, the house passed out of the family, never quite having fulfilled its potential as a major home for the Russells. Fortunately for us, however, Baring commissioned a Red Book from Humphry Repton in 1801, and in its pages we have a unique record of the site as the Russells left it and before a new house and gardens were built.

Thomas Hudson, *Gertrude Leveson-Gower, Duchess of Bedford* (1715–1794). Less sensitive and artistic than her predecessor Diana, the duke's second wife's strengths lay in her confidence and forcefulness, attributes she needed to help steer the 4th Duke through a turbulent political career and to run the Bedford estates as Dowager Duchess during the minority of her grandson Francis, 5th Duke. During this period she oversaw the consolidation of the family finances and the development of the Bloomsbury estate along Gower Street.

ABOVE Humphry Repton,
Red Book for Stratton
Park, Plate Vb, 1801.
Repton's view of the downs,
seen from the house.

OPPOSITE ABOVE Red Book
for Stratton Park, Plate
VIIa, 1801.
The existing house in 1801.

OPPOSITE BELOW Red Book
for Stratton Park, Plate IIa,
1801.
Repton's view of the park
fence beside the turnpike,
with 'Love Walk' running off
to the right. Repton felt that
the road ran too close to the
walks in the plantations, but
his suggestion to reroute it
was not carried out.

The Red Book shows us the house in its setting of park and woodlands. Although the east wing, the 'Court', the walled 'Fir Orchard' and perhaps the 'Bowling Green' have been removed, we can still get an impression of the wider landscape, with the downs rising beyond the house, which would have been recognizable to Lord William and Lady Rachel, Wriothesley, the 2nd Duke, and Stephen Switzer, and which was still fresh in Lord John's mind as he started work at Woburn.

Meanwhile in Bloomsbury, Southampton House, which had remained largely empty during the 3rd Duke's time, needed refurbishing and enlarging. Sarah, Duchess of Marlborough writes approvingly in 1734 of the new additions, commenting that the house 'is so much mended by the new wing . . . and the two courts that are placed on each side of the house for the stables and offices are better placed than any I ever saw in the town or in the country,'[30] adding that the name should be changed to Bedford House: 'the name I think it should now go by'.[31] Between 1764 and 1766 the interiors were completely refurbished, and new gardens were laid out. Twenty years earlier, in 1747, the new gardener David Brown had reported: 'I have viewed your Grace's garden, and find it in very bad condition, quite over-run with weeds . . . It will require three or four men for some time to put it in order; and the gravel in the Pleasure Garden is so full of weeds as that unless the whole is turned over it cannot be made clean.'[32] In the process of 'turning it over' the gardens were simplified, and by 1768, 'the

wilderness has disappeared . . . no flower beds are indicated. The Pleasure Garden remained a place of grass plots with shady trees.' Although Scott Thomson goes on to say, 'The trees and the open view from the terrace . . . must have been a pleasant spot,'[33] that view too was rapidly changing with the inexorable development of the fields beyond into streets and housing.

While work at Stratton and Bedford House went on, however, circumstances meant that Woburn had now become the duke and duchess's principal home, and from 1732 onwards the 4th Duke was to concentrate on an extraordinary programme of improvements to the Abbey. Unlike his brother the 3rd Duke but like his father, grandfather and great-grandfather, the 4th Duke embraced his role as landowner and immediately started work on improving the estate, and he did so with what was clearly a deeply felt interest in the land. It would seem that someone during his childhood – and it could well have been the gardener at Streatham whose rooms he excluded from the agreement when the house was leased in 1739 – awakened in him an enduring interest in plants, botany and the natural world. Looking at his life as a whole and the way in which he interacted with Woburn, it is clear that he was in fact closer to the landscape of the park and gardens than many of his predecessors and successors. With a memo book and a pencil in his back pocket, he took a genuine and abiding pleasure in his regular, solitary, often early morning walks round the park. Walking up to five or six miles, he would take in the remotest corners and out of the way places, and he noticed and observed everything, from a tenant's untidy hedges to

Pieter Andreas Rysbrack, *Bedford House, Bloomsbury, c.1730.*
A view of the house around the time that its name was changed from Southampton House to Bedford House at the urging of Diana's grandmother Sarah. On either side we see the 'two courts' which Sarah was so pleased with, and atop the gate posts are two statues which reappear at Woburn following the demolition of the house in 1800. In front of the house lies Bloomsbury Square laid out in a style very similar to the original garden at the centre of Covent Garden Piazza, a design of pathways that was replaced by grass in the 1780s. In the distance to the right of the house, far off in the countryside, lies Highgate Hill.

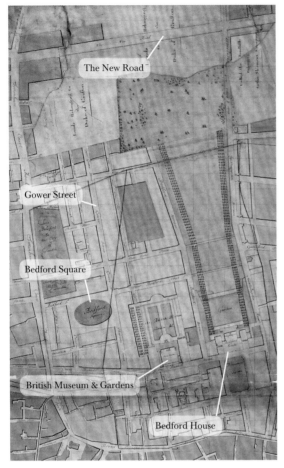

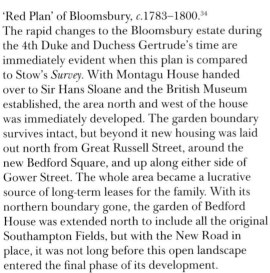

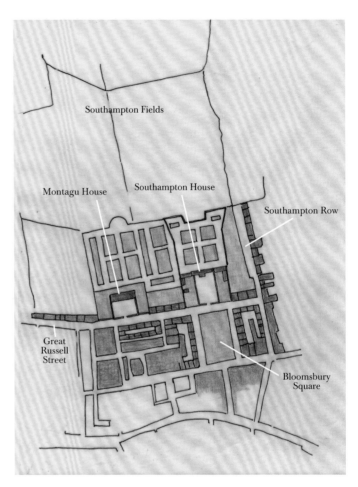

'Red Plan' of Bloomsbury, c.1783–1800.[34]
The rapid changes to the Bloomsbury estate during the 4th Duke and Duchess Gertrude's time are immediately evident when this plan is compared to Stow's *Survey*. With Montagu House handed over to Sir Hans Sloane and the British Museum established, the area north and west of the house was immediately developed. The garden boundary survives intact, but beyond it new housing was laid out north from Great Russell Street, around the new Bedford Square, and up along either side of Gower Street. The whole area became a lucrative source of long-term leases for the family. With its northern boundary gone, the garden of Bedford House was extended north to include all the original Southampton Fields, but with the New Road in place, it was not long before this open landscape entered the final phase of its development.

Southampton House, c.1720, after Strype's edition of Stow's *Survey of London*, 1720.
This drawing shows the houses and gardens at Southampton House and Montagu House before the removal of the old fortifications. At Montagu House the wall has been altered to include a semicircular viewing platform. From both gardens there were extensive views over the fields beyond towards Highgate. This was all to change as the fields were developed and the 'New' road (now Euston Road) was built.

weed on the ponds, a stile or gate in need of repair, a 'greasy' path or a broken fence. On his walks, he watched the seasons turn and the activity of the wildlife, noted the health of trees, and marked trees for cutting, jotting it all down in his little notebooks, and from the very start these tell us of his concerns and priorities.[35]

As he explored the estate, he discovered a park that had undergone considerable transformation as his father's landscaping projects had got under way – not least the extensive removal of hedgerows – and the area west of the Abbey moved from tenanted agricultural land, as seen in the 1661 estate map, towards the much more open landscape seen in the 1738 map. The 'Large Circular Piece of Water' (the Bason Pond) and the tree-lined 'Great Avenue' were now in place, but much of this work had, of course, been left unfinished on his father's sudden death, and the 4th Duke's first priority was to clean up everything around these new features. Thus, we see from 1736 onwards notes directing his staff 'to level in all the Hedge Rows that are cut down . . . particularly that at the Streights . . . and what other Hedge Rows are not now levelled in the new Park . . . To scour up Ditches, and to lay even the little ridings between the long riding and the Bason.' The fact that these activities truly mark the moment when the surroundings of the old abbey moved from their traditional medieval appearance to that of modern parkland is clearly illustrated by another entry of this time: 'That part of the Terrace which lies from the Turn before you come to the Pond, quite up to the top of the hill, which lies in Ridge and Thorou [furrow], to have its turf paired off, and to be laid level.'[36] The grassed-over lumps and bumps of the ridge and furrow terraces and the hedge lines of the old field systems that stretched out across the slopes of 'Windmill Hill' around the 'Terrace', and the network of the old hedgerows that were removed to create the Great Avenue, were replaced by the new park: the smooth, sweeping parkland we know today. It is not clear exactly when the 'Serpentine Terrace' was laid out along the top of the ridge: it could have been the 1st Duke or, perhaps more likely, it was part of the 2nd Duke's grand schemes of *c.*1710.

The fact that the duke was also starting to think of changes and additions of his own is clear from an album of designs from John Sanderson, the architect then at work completing the new house at Stratton Park. The album contains drawings dated 1733 for a grand stone gateway

Moore's 1661 map, detail of fields and woodlands removed by 1738. All the field boundaries and lengths of park fences within the red lines had been cut down and dug up. The belt of woodland running down the west side of the park between the fence and the Long Pond had been felled and, on the other side of the park, the fence line excluding the woodlands of Dutton's Copse and Somerley Spring had been removed.

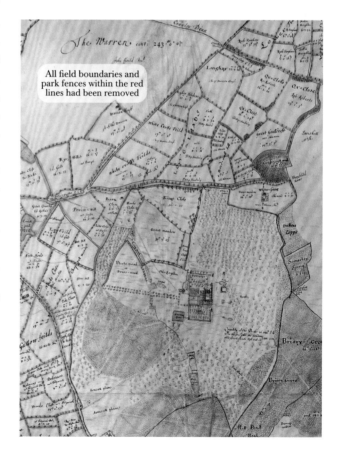

All field boundaries and park fences within the red lines had been removed

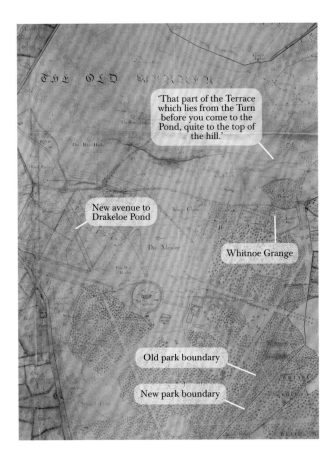

LEFT Browne's 1738 map, detail of Bason Pond area.

'That part of the Terrace which lies from the Turn before you come to the Pond, quite to the top of the hill.'

New avenue to Drakeloe Pond

Whitnoe Grange

Old park boundary

New park boundary

Apart from the removal of hedges and fences, the park itself had been enlarged down the east side, and both Dutton's Copse (renamed Parson's Wood) and Somerley Spring (renamed Somerley Grove) have been included within the park. Elsewhere, to the west of the Abbey the area has now been combined into the large open spaces of the Deer Meadow, while north of Froxfield Lane the old fields have become a grand sweep of open grassland dotted with trees, an area almost as large as the old Warren opposite. The old farm of Whitnoe Grange, leased for several generations by the Gregory family (the Masters of Horse to the Russell family), retains its old boundaries and was later to become the site of the 5th Duke's kennels and kitchen gardens.

RIGHT John Sanderson, drawing for gate and lodges, 1733.
Perhaps the grandest of Sanderson's designs was for this gateway arch with flanking pedestrian gates and lodges. Very much of its time, the grand gateway may have been designed to sit at the point where the 2nd Duke's Great Avenue met the London road before running up Wayn Close, but there is no record that it was ever built there or anywhere else.

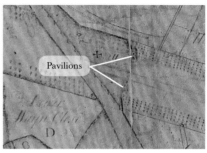

LEFT John Sanderson, drawing for two-storeyed pavilion, 1733.

ABOVE Browne's 1738 map, detail of the Great Avenue beside the Woburn road. It is not entirely clear whether Sanderson's drawing is concerned with a single pavilion or a pair, nor is it clear where the possible location was. Intriguingly, however, this close look at Browne's 1738 map seems to indicate that a pair of very similar pavilions were in fact built facing each other across the Great Avenue just before it meets the road. These would have been significant elements in the view west from the Abbey, and it is difficult to imagine why, if they were built, they would have vanished without trace by the end of the century.

with flanking lodges, a stone-built two-storeyed pavilion, or banqueting house, and two versions of a stone bridge with decorative mouldings; while it appears none of these were built at this time or in these forms, ambitious plans were obviously afoot.[37]

By 1736, the duke was turning his attention to finishing aspects of the park that his father had started, noting: 'The Stairs down to the Bason, and the Drawbridge into the Bowling Green, to be settled with Sanderson.' Also during this period, the duke was consulting with Charles Bridgeman, and gives orders 'about pulling down the Garden Walls, and putting the Pheasant Garden in order according to Mr Bridgeman's directions' as well as the trees 'Mr Bridgeman marked to be cut down, [and] to order the road between the Abbey and Gregory's House'.[38] It would seem that Charles Bridgeman was asked for his opinion on aspects of the landscaping around the Abbey that the duke's father had not got around to, including what additional parts of the old 1630s formal layout should be removed, and to choose a new route through the woods for a more direct road to the Abbey to and from the Serpentine Terrace and 'Froxfield Lane' at Stump's Cross Corner. This new road is now the exit road from the visitor's car park at the Abbey.

Throughout this period, as the duke continued his daily walks to distant parts of the estate, we soon get hints of a new project. John Sanderson's album had also contained 'Three Different Designs for a Temple on Warren Hill above Drakely Pond', and in 1737 the duke notes that the 'island on

RIGHT John Sanderson, two drawings for stone bridge, 1733.

Another interesting drawing from Sanderson's album, this time two slightly different designs for a bridge. Once again, there is no indication where the proposed site for this may have been, although another close look at Browne's map (see page 105) offers a possibility. Clearly visible on the map are inked-in alterations proposed for the Bason Pond. We will be discussing these proposals in some detail later on, but for now it is worth noting that it appears as though it was planned to bridge the extension of the pond to enable the road to run to the west front of the Abbey rather than retaining the old route to the stables at the back. Sanderson's bridge design would seem to be suitably grand for such a location, and anticipates the bridge built at much the same spot some forty years later, this one designed by William Chambers.

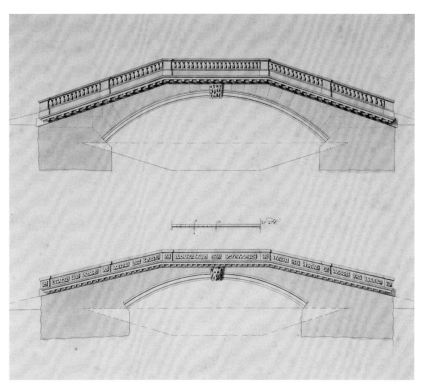

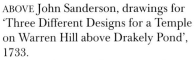

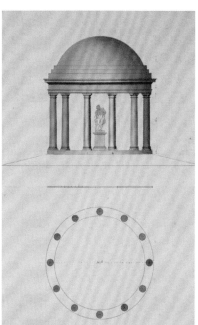

ABOVE John Sanderson, drawings for 'Three Different Designs for a Temple on Warren Hill above Drakely Pond', 1733.

Marking the start of interest in the slopes running down from the old Warren to Drakeloe Pond, these designs for a temple suggest the 4th Duke was looking to create an eye-catching structure which could provide excellent views of the pond below and landscape beyond as well as a destination for the family when they took rides or walks out in the park.

Dracklow should be planted'; clearly, Drakeloe Pond and the venerable old Warren were being drawn into the new vision for the park as these plans for the development of the slopes down to Drakeloe Pond got under way.

There is no record of this temple ever having been built in any form, or where it would have stood, possibly because by 1738 the duke had even more ambitious plans for the area. This is the year that he commissioned the new estate map from Thomas Browne, who a few years earlier had produced a very similar map for Stratton Park, and it contains evidence that the duke's new vision for the park landscape at Woburn was expanding to areas not covered by his great-grandfather's map of 1661. Looking closely at Browne's map, which hangs today in the Abbey vaults, it is clear that it was used extensively, not just by the 4th Duke, but also by the 5th Duke and his advisors, to assess what was there and to pencil in the changes they were proposing to make, inking them up when a decision had been made. In 1738 those decisions were to do with the duke's new venture – an extensive plantation of pines and conifer trees on the slopes of Warren Hill above

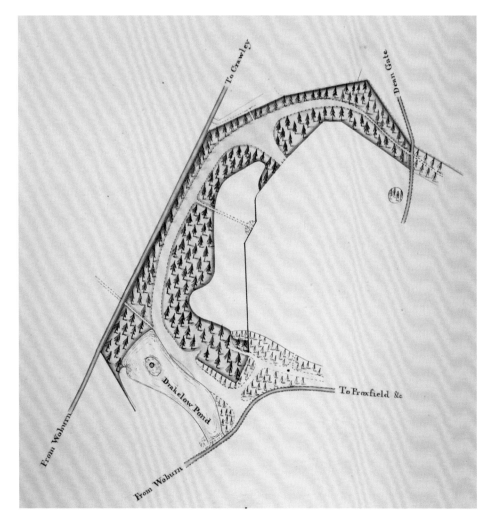

Robert Salmon, plan of the 'Old Evergreens', surveyed 1802.
The first phase of 'The Evergreens', an extensive plantation of evergreen trees curving round as it followed the contours of the ridge, soon came to dominate the duke's plans for this entire area; it is recorded here by Robert Salmon for the 5th Duke. The plan shows the rapid development of this area with the new road from Woburn to Froxfield in place: a crucial change which placed this relatively remote corner of the park into the heart of people's experience of Woburn.

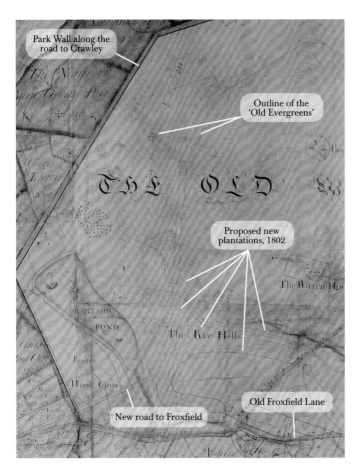

Park Wall along the road to Crawley

Outline of the 'Old Evergreens'

Proposed new plantations, 1802

Old Froxfield Lane

New road to Froxfield

Browne's 1738 map, detail of Drakeloe Pond and the proposals for 'Evergreen' plantation.
The first major enlargement of the Evergreens was undertaken by the 5th Duke, when trees were added on either side of the new road from Woburn. Today some of these trees are still visible as the visitor drives in from Woburn over the causeway between the two ponds.

Drakeloe Pond, known as 'The Evergreens'. This project was still expanding in the 1830s under the 6th Duke and remains a major feature of the park today.

We have already noted the duke's long interest in horticulture and trees, and by this time he was in contact with Phillip Miller, director of the Chelsea Physic Gardens, about supplies of seeds for a range of evergreen tree species and was turning areas of the park over to create nurseries for their propagation and growing on the trees. Surveying these plantations for the 5th Duke in 1802, Robert Salmon studied the surviving trees carefully and produced a plan of the area, which he considered 'by the specimens of Timber appears to have been planted in 1746',[39] and which he called the 'Old Evergreens'. Taking a closer look at the area on Browne's 1738 map, we see that the rough outline of this plantation has been pencilled in, curving round the hillside above Drakeloe Pond and north alongside the road.

The wider recreational purpose of the Evergreens is immediately clear from Salmon's plan, with the emphasis on the wide grass walk running along through the middle of the plantation, a place to be enjoyed on foot, on horse or in a carriage, to which the duke could take family and friends to admire the tree collection and spend a pleasant afternoon, which also included boat trips out to the island in Drakeloe Pond. Here, in 1740, Sanderson 'directed the temple on Drakeloe Pond', to which the duke adds a 'table for 10' in 1741.[40] Whether this 'temple' resembled any of those in his drawings is unclear, since no drawings or accounts of it survive, but it would seem to have been a kind of summer house, making it a place the family could visit and spend time, even have a meal; within a decade, as we will see, this structure was replaced by a summer house in the 'Chinese style', and a kitchen was added nearby to prepare meals for eating on the island.

In addition, at some point during the 1740s, what is later referred to as the 'Temple in the Evergreens' was built. Again, there is no image of this structure or any indication of its location, nor is it mentioned in the accounts until 1756, at which point it is in need of repair and repainting. It would not appear that this 'temple' was the one 'directed' by Sanderson in 1740 'on Drakeloe Pond', and it could well be the square structure of brick, dressed stone and flint surviving in a ruinous state in the Evergreens today.

Quite apart from the importance of the Evergreen plantation to the recreational potential of the park for the family and their guests, the scope and ambition of the duke's collections made it a very special project. Not only was he consulting Phillip Miller at Chelsea, but he was also, through friends such as fellow members of the Dilettanti Society,[41] in touch with plant collectors in America and the Far East. Most importantly, he was in contact with the American seed collector John Bartram, who, through his London agent Peter Collinson, was sending back the famous 'Bartram Boxes' of seeds to be distributed amongst his select group of clients. Something of the complexity and the contemporary importance of the growing Evergreen plantation at Woburn is caught in the following letter to the duke from Collinson written in 1759 after a visit:

April 1759:
I cannot forget the Duke of Bedford's Extensive Plantations of Evergreens when it is in my power to Add to it, which I now hope to Do, by this present of Siberia White Firr seed and Russian Larex.

It gives me real pleasure to hear of its prosperity, because with your Grace's leave I think myself in Some Small Degree interested in it, by

Square temple in the Evergreens, 2014, derelict from at least 1773.
An enigmatic ruin, this building stands today in the Evergreens, but its original form, date of construction and subsequent history remain a mystery. It is impossible to confirm at this time whether it is the 'Temple in the Evergreens' referred to by the 4th Duke in the 1750s, but graffiti on the remaining interior plaster indicates that it was a ruin as early as 1773. Most mysteriously of all, it was not painted by either Burgess in the 1830s or Bourne in the 1840s when they recorded the other features to be found in the Evergreens, both trees and structures.

procuring the Variety of North American Pines, Firrs and Cedars etc of which it is composed.

For Mr Miller knowing I had correspondence abroad in our Colonies desired Mee to send for a Collection of Seeds from thence for your Grace. Accordingly I brought Over in the years 1742, 1743, 1744, each year a Large Chest of Seeds of Trees and Shrubs from Pennsylvania. From these I hear'd Sprang up the principal Materials for raiseing this Noble Plantation which I am informed excells all other in this Kingdom.

[Collinson goes on to add:]

The trouble and pains in getting these Seeds Over is amply Compensated by the Success that has attended them besides the Pleasure it gives Mee that I can oblige my Curious Friends as well as Improve (or at least Embellish) my Country. I am with Due Respects and acknowledgements for the favourable Reception you gave Mee and my Friend Allen last Tuesday.

Your Grace's Friend, Yours etc, Peter Collinson[42]

Beyond the tree specimens themselves, the Evergreens are also interesting because their location in an area of the park both distant and out of sight of the Abbey itself catches the mood of the times as the wider landscape beyond carefully manicured gardens came to be valued as a setting for social and recreational occasions. Picking up on the creation of the Serpentine Terrace, there was a sense now of family life moving out beyond the confines of the gardens and creating interesting destinations, places for the family to set off to, to spend time enjoying themselves together and to entertain guests. It is interesting, too, that at this time social events such as cricket matches became a regular feature of park life, with annual matches at Woburn being held on the 'wide and cricket place' in the 1740s between the Woburn 11 and Lord Halifax's 11, Lord Sandwich's 11 and Lord Gower's 11, with the duke wagering 5 guineas on the last.[43] The landscape of the park, properly adorned with suitable buildings and specially prepared venues, was now seen as a place for the family's cultural, artistic and recreational life; the removal of the garden walls had finally opened up the potential of the park beyond, and created a space that is still recognizable today to thousands of visitors.

But change was under way not only in the grounds, because it was right at this time that – along with the remnants of the ridge and furrow fields, the old monastic fishponds and winding approach roads – many of the surviving medieval monastic buildings were replaced. As early as 1733, John Sanderson had drawn a series of images which recorded the ground plan and the west and north elevations of the Abbey, but work did not start until 1749. Resigning from office in 1751 after being accused, amongst other things, of neglecting his duties by spending so much time at Woburn, the duke settled down for the next six years and concentrated on creating the new Abbey.

REBUILDING THE ABBEY 1747–88

The years between 1747 and 1788 saw two main phases of work on the Abbey.[44] After more than a hundred years of fitting family life into what was still largely the remains of a medieval abbey, the 4th Duke and his son Francis, 5th Duke sought to create an imposing new house that celebrated the Russells and their place in the world. As the building itself was rationalized and enlarged, it also became the focal point for a series of symmetrically aligned service buildings, framing the Abbey for the first time within an architectural landscape which in turn was extended by formal gardens.

PHASE 1, 1747–68: 4TH DUKE, HENRY FLITCROFT AND SIR WILLIAM CHAMBERS

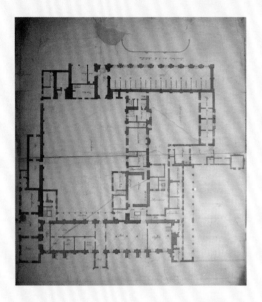

LEFT Woburn Abbey: Sanderson's record ground plan, 1747. This second plan of the Abbey by Sanderson shows the buildings just before work began on the 4th Duke's renovations. Comparing it with the 1733 version (see page 38) indicates that very little had changed by this time, although we know from the letters and accounts that parts of the old structure, particularly the south-west corner, were in a very bad condition.

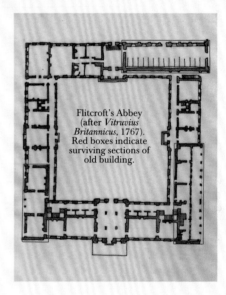

Flitcroft's Abbey (after *Vitruvius Britannicus*, 1767). Red boxes indicate surviving sections of old building.

Between 1747 and 1749 the 4th Duke consulted with the architect Henry Flitcroft,[45] and a letter from Flitcroft confirms that they agreed to 'rebuild the body of the House between the library and Grotto apartments, make good the North and South Wings. New build the Kitchen and Offices proposed at the last end of the Court . . . But that your Grace was determined to keep up the Library and Grotto Apartments, and to build the West Front agreeable to the present disposition of the ground before the House . . . all the slopes, and the approach from the Bason, would be the same as present . . . Mr Moore [would be] Clerk of Works.'[46]

Demolition work was carried out between 1750 and 1751, at which point new building started on the west and south wings. Following this, to the east of the Abbey, construction began in 1757 on two new service buildings designed by Flitcroft: the north court, mainly stables, and the south court for the carriage house and offices.

Finally, some ten years later, in 1768, Sir William Chambers was called in to modify the south wing, replacing the rustic stonework on the surviving twelve-bay portico on the south front with Portland stone and creating new rooms within.

ABOVE What got built is recorded on the 1767 ground plan from *Vitruvius Britannicus*. The 4th Duke insisted that the original grotto range and the south-west corner of the Abbey containing the Library above the arcade be retained. Between these two the west range was largely rebuilt, although the anomalies of the different floor levels along the length of it were retained and are evident to this day. At this time the surviving footprint of the chapter house and vestry was changed, although the stables remained pretty much intact, albeit one bay shorter. The south range beyond the arcade was then rebuilt entirely to continue the line of the building, extending through the old 'Still Room Court', and the north range was extended to complete the quadrangle. All the interior buildings were demolished and a new corridor was run round the inside walls of the four wings, with windows looking out into a new, symmetrical court.

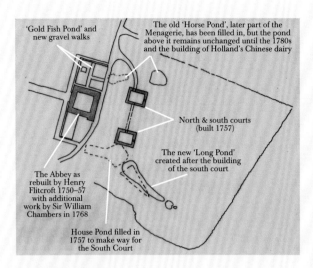

'Gold Fish Pond' and new gravel walks

The old 'Horse Pond', later part of the Menagerie, has been filled in, but the pond above it remains unchanged until the 1780s and the building of Holland's Chinese dairy

North & south courts (built 1757)

The new 'Long Pond' created after the building of the south court

The Abbey as rebuilt by Henry Flitcroft 1750–57 with additional work by Sir William Chambers in 1768

House Pond filled in 1757 to make way for the South Court

ABOVE Plan of Woburn Abbey showing Flitcroft's Abbey and the new stable blocks.

RIGHT J. C. Bourne, *Woburn Abbey from the South-West*, 1842. Bourne's image shows the Abbey as rebuilt and landscaped by Henry Holland working with the 5th and 6th Dukes. This is the phase of development that we still see, basically unchanged today.

BELOW Jeffry Wyatville, *A Sketch of the West Front of Woburn Abbey 1816*, showing 'A: Portico to drive under on the Basement floor level' and 'B: North Portico to drive under on the Principal floor level', 1816.[48]
Wyatville's plans for an even grander version of the Abbey with a new 'drive under' portico giving protected access to what was now the basement level of the north range, and another providing access to the 'Principal' floor level. It is not entirely clear what the impact of this enormous development would have been on the grotto and its garden.

PHASE 2, 1788–9: 5TH DUKE AND HENRY HOLLAND

In 1788 Henry Holland was commissioned by the 5th Duke to rebuild the state rooms on the principal floor (the *piano nobile*) of the south and east ranges, adding new kitchens and offices to the latter, and to complete the scheme he raised the ground level along the south and east fronts to permit direct access to the new rooms from outside. It was at this point that the old stables on the ground floor of the east wing and the twelve-arch arcade on the south become, as Duggan puts it, 'subsumed in the basement',[47] a radical alteration of the Abbey's relationship with the landscape around it.

THE ABBEY'S SUBSEQUENT HISTORY

At least one other major alteration to the Abbey was proposed by Jeffry Wyatville in 1816 but was never followed through, leaving the structure essentially unchanged from the 1790s to the 1950s, at which point the east wing (and the parts of both the north and south wings attached to it) were all demolished, removing the last surviving remnants of the monastic foundations of the east wing. This work left the three ranges of the Abbey we see today.

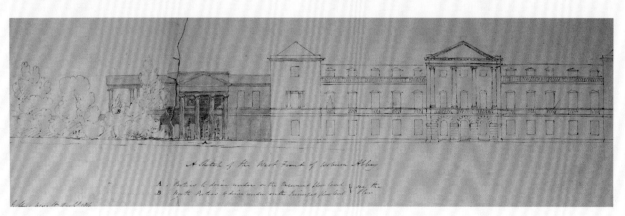

Outside the Abbey, although the duke had insisted that alterations to the west front should be 'agreeable to the present disposition of the ground before the House . . . all the slopes, and the approach from the Bason, would be the same as present,'[49] all this activity had a considerable effect on the grounds and gardens, particularly to the south and east where there were new buildings and raised ground levels. Although there does not appear to have been any kind of master plan, between 1740 and 1770 the layouts immediately around the Abbey on these sides developed piecemeal as work on the building continued, one idea succeeding another, one garden replacing another, as the layout was extended and the family's interest in new outdoor spaces grew.

In the gardens, the first indication of renewed activity is the recording of a new greenhouse being built in 1742, followed in 1746 by a 'new' garden being laid out, complete with orangerie, both designed by Philip Miller.[50] The location of any of these is not clear, but accumulating hints in the records suggest it was on the rising slopes east of the Abbey, the general area of the service buildings around the 1661 map's 'Horse Pond' and the woodlands of the 'Rookery'. The duke orders Miller's garden to be set out, a paling fence erected, and a 'Reed Hedge' created to divide the new garden from the Old Pheasantry. He then orders plants from Miller to be set around the orangerie. Given that this garden was close to the Old Pheasantry and that the greenhouse and orangerie were both demolished in 1757, once the duke had 'settled absolutely about the plans for the Stables', it seems likely that it was located close to, or on part of, the site of Flitcroft's new north stable block.

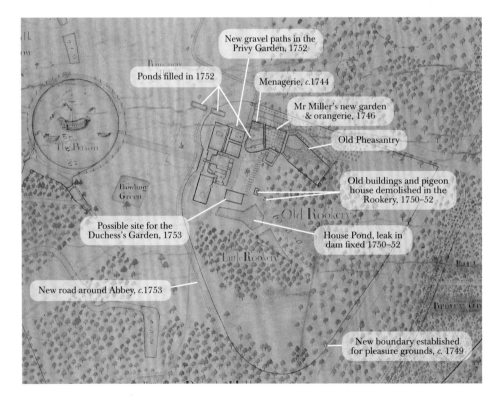

New gravel paths in the Privy Garden, 1752

Ponds filled in 1752

Menagerie, c.1744

Mr Miller's new garden & orangerie, 1746

Old Pheasantry

The Bason

Bowling Green

Possible site for the Duchess's Garden, 1753

Old buildings and pigeon house demolished in the Rookery, 1750–52

Old Rookery

House Pond, leak in dam fixed 1750–52

Little Rookery

New road around Abbey, c.1753

New boundary established for pleasure grounds, c. 1749

Browne's 1738 map showing suggested locations of gardens, buildings and other features mentioned in the accounts, 1742–57. Although there are no plans or other surviving evidence of the locations of the various features created in the gardens, or of the various alterations that were made to the ponds, roads and buildings, it is possible, using the very detailed representation of the area in Browne's 1738 map, to make some educated guesses as to where things were before the new stable blocks, built in 1757, imposed a sense of order and symmetry on the landscape. Those areas that can be identified with some confidence are shown on this plan.

Records then show that between 1748 and 1750 up to seventy labourers were busy working on ground works associated with the new building – 'digging and levelling the Court', 'digging and carting earth from the New Road', and carting earth and sand to the New Pheasantry and the Rookery.[51] This in turn suggests that materials from the road and Abbey site development were being used to alter large areas east of the house, removing the Pheasantry to the site that was soon to become the new Menagerie, and converting at least part of the Rookery from undeveloped woodland to the site of new 'pleasure grounds'. Not only does this development of the Rookery alter its traditional uses, it also marks the moment at Woburn when garden spaces started to be complemented by the newer idea of pleasure grounds. Pleasure gardens – or, increasingly, pleasure grounds – introduced the idea of alternative garden spaces to the older privy, or private, gardens: complementary places which were laid out and ornamented for communal activities and amusements, for exercise and games for family and guests, and increasingly open to the 'public',[52] leaving the private gardens for the family. These distinctions remain largely intact today.

The first mention of the pleasure gardens at Woburn comes when the duke reminds himself in 1749 'to speak to Mr Carter to have always those flowers that are in season in the pleasure Gardens to come up the one after the other',[53] and the same year the accounts tell us that a 'Chinese Temple for the Pleasure Grounds' was commissioned.[54] This is particularly interesting because it is the first reference we have to the duke and duchess's interest in Chinese design since Lord John and his first wife inherited some of the 'best Japan' furniture they had ever seen at Cheam, and the building of this temple coincides exactly with the introduction of Chinese wallpaper to the Abbey interior. Indeed, many of the same craftsmen, joiners and painters who were working on the Abbey interiors were also used to create the Chinese detailing on a succession of features in the grounds. It is quite possible that the Bedfords' interest in Chinese design was stimulated by the duke's colleague at the Admiralty, Lord Anson, who, on his return from his circumnavigation of the world, which included a stay in Canton, had helped his brother Thomas Anson develop their Chinese-themed park at Shugborough between 1747 and 1748.

Work on the Woburn temple got under way in 1749, with the joiners Philips & Co. 'driving piles. Building scaffolding to put up Chinese leaves' and 'putting up Mr Linnell's ornaments', embellishments that included 'Chinese and Gothic Balustrades . . . [and] Arches', a 'Circular Chinese pedestal' and 'Chinese and Gothic mouldings'. Meanwhile, 'paving for the Chinese Temple' was installed, and the next year the painters Spinnage & Co. billed for 'Painting the Chinese Temple in the new Pleasure Ground', specifying 'various colours, the roof striped in imitation of linen, ceiling flat white, and painting the floors'. Both William Linnell, the cabinet-maker, and John Spinnage and his painters were also involved at the same time in the

Chinese-style fittings and decorations for the duke's bedroom. Unfortunately, we have no idea where this temple was built, what it looked like, or how long it survived. There is a possibility that it is the same structure which the duke later refers to as the 'Chinese Seat in the garden' that he decides to demolish in 1764, but other than this no further mention of the temple is made.

Development of the pleasure grounds, however, goes on apace, and the specifics of the accounts confirm their location in part of the original Rookery immediately east of the house. Between 1750 and 1752, the accounts of George Stephenson, the duke's foreman organizing the seasonal labourers, detail work on improvement of the area, including 'levelling ground before Stables', which at this time were still in the basement of the old east wing of the Abbey. In addition, they are 'clearing away Stuff from Old Buildings by the Rookery', and then 'pulling down old Buildings by Rookery', 'pulling down the old Pigeon House . . . levelling ground at Rookery'. They then 'Take up the palings around the old Pheasant Ground' and 'level ground and cart earth to the New Pheasantry'. In addition to this reorganization of the area for the pleasure grounds and the New Pheasantry, workers were also 'stopping the leak of the House Pond' and 'making good gravel walks at end of Privy Garden', probably a reference to one of the walled gardens at the north and south ends of the Abbey.[55]

With all this preparation of the areas around the Abbey in place, work starts on the demolition of those parts to be changed, digging foundations for Flitcroft's new west wing and repairs to the structurally unsound south-west corner tower. Materials generated by all this activity – earth and turf from the west front and south Privy Garden – were then reused in the pleasure grounds, and the duke enquires if 'there is sward enough left to turf the new Garden, and the hill by the house pond behind the Abbey'.[56] While the area between the west front of the Abbey and the Bason Pond is to remain untouched, the duke is also interested in making use of this material to start his redevelopment of the slopes to the north-west of the Abbey.

Here, in 1752, soon after building work begins, the duke instructs Stephenson to 'Carry earth which is to come out of the foundations to fill up to the ponds, and fixing the level of the hill from the slope above the ponds down to the Gravel Walk', and Stephenson bills 'for digging and loading carts with earth, and unloading and levelling the Stews [fishponds], wheeling mould and turfing parts of the Stews'.[57] With the filling in of the 'Stews' on the hillside, we see another major part of the 4th Earl's terraced gardens of the 1630s replaced, and the different levels of these terraces finally smoothed into the grassed slopes we see on that side today. Importantly, having filled the ponds to 'fix the level of the hill', the duke finally had the space to bring an access road round from the north to the west front of the Abbey.

Having made best use of all the materials produced by demolition work, as the new building work got under way the duke turned his attention to the pleasure grounds again, and in 1753 we have the first mention of the

'Duchess's Garden', when the duke is ordering that 'some sweet Bryars, roses, and honeysuckles' be added 'to fill up some of the clumps in the Duchess's Garden'.[58] Two years later, Philip Miller had this garden in mind when he sent the duke 'two plants of the Broad leaved Andromeda which are just arrived from America. It is one of the most beautiful flowering shrubs of that Country, and is very rare in Europe . . . I think they should be planted in the Duchess of Bedford's Garden.'[59]

Once again, quite where this garden was located at this time is not clear, but if the present location of the Duchess's Garden is anything to go by – and this dates back certainly to the time of Georgina, second wife of the 6th Duke, in the first decade of the nineteenth century – it was just to the east of the south Privy Garden. A further indication that this was the general location comes in 1757, when its proximity to the new stable courts built by Flitcroft that year requires the duke to 'show the Gardener how he is to hide the new wall of the Stable next to the Duchess's Garden'.[60] If so, it occupied at least part of the ground 'before the Stables' – the old stables, that is – that Stephenson's men had levelled when they fixed the leak in the House Pond in 1752, and will have incorporated some of the trees associated with the old Rookery.

Along with work on the Duchess's Garden, the facilities and features of the pleasure grounds were also being developed. In addition to the Chinese temple that had been built in 1749, and was still presumably a major feature of the garden, in 1753 accounts appear for work on building 'an Alcove round the Great oak', painting '4 seats fixed round trees', making '3 new seats fixed round trees', and making '2 long rail seats';[61] we can imagine, too, the gravel paths laid through the trees leading round the grounds to these various stopping places. This work was followed in 1756 with the construction of a second 'temple', this time in a section of the pleasure grounds called 'the Lady's Folly'.[62] Nothing more is specified at this time about this intriguing sounding area, or where it was, but 'the Temple in the Lady's Folly' appears to have featured a spring head adapted to form a decorative fountain. The accounts for its construction include work by the stonemason John Devall, who provided 'backing ashlars for the Temple in the Lady's Folly', along with carpenters 'making a centre for the Spring Well', and 'covering the Fountain head with rough boarding', 'battening joists, and hanging curtains at the Temple in the Folly'.[63] The site of this temple is lost today, as is the site of the very essential 'Privy' added to the pleasure grounds at the same time.

Two years after the temple in the Lady's Folly was built, another innovative structure appeared in the pleasure grounds, one which marks an important change of both fashion and the look of the park to the west of the Abbey. For some 120 years the Bowling Green had sat just beyond the Abbey, enclosed at one time or another by a ditch and fence complete with entrance drawbridge, and furnished with benches and the Great Stand. The Stand and the Bowling Green had been a central focus of the experience of the park from the family's initial adoption of the Abbey as their principal country residence, and then, suddenly, they were both gone. Although the accounts tell us that the Bowling Green at least was occasionally maintained from the 1740s onwards, the old style of bowling was abandoned in favour of the fashionable new game of nine-pin bowling,[64] and a new bowling alley, rather than a 'Green', complete with seats of its own and Purbeck stone from the Abbey court, was laid out in the Lady's Folly in 1759. In the park any traces of the old Bowling Green were levelled and turfed, and some fifty years later the site was buried altogether under the hill that Humphry Repton created to hide his 'Viaduct' from the Abbey.

While development of the pleasure grounds continued, the duke's final decision in 1757 to go ahead with the two new stable blocks east of the Abbey had immediate implications for the gardens that had been laid out over the previous decade, since the new stables were the first service buildings associated with the Abbey to be laid out in a formal, symmetrical relationship to it. Unlike the randomly positioned buildings that had just been pulled down, these two stable courts, rather than fitting amongst the existing features, were to be sited in a specific relationship to the footprint of the Abbey, even if that was at the expense of those other features. In a sense, the 4th Duke was completing the process that his father, the 2nd Duke, had initiated when he removed the old field enclosures and fishponds to create the Bason Pond and Great Avenue in a symmetrical relationship to the Abbey's west front. Now, the same was to be done on the east side, and for the first time, instead of being incidental to the layout of the park, field systems and woodland which surrounded it, the Abbey and its buildings became the focal point of the park and grounds that lay on the main axis

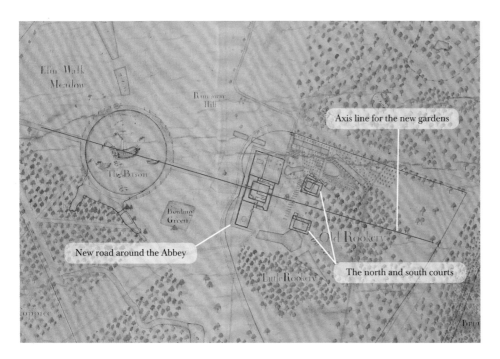

Browne's 1738 map overlaid with new symmetrical layout around the Abbey in 1757.
The symmetry of Flitcroft's new layout of roads around, and buildings behind, the Abbey meant that a number of the original gardens, structures and ponds had to be removed. From this time on, all the gardens built east of the Abbey were laid out in relation to the new axial centre line which ran down the Great Avenue, through the new building and out to the back of what became the pleasure grounds.

Sanderson's record ground plan, 1747.
One aspect of Sanderson's plan is particularly interesting: the annotation added to the short range of rooms along the south side of the 'Still Room Court'. During monastic times this had been the monks' reredorter (toilet block), while on the 1733 plan (see page 38) its use is unspecified. By 1747, however, the note tells us that the ground-floor rooms in it were 'Offices under the new Greenhouse', suggesting that the greenhouse was built along the upper floor. Accounts tell us that the new greenhouse was built, but just what it looked like is something of a mystery. No other examples of such a structure have come to light.

of the house. The implications of this development were immediate. As the decision on the stable blocks is made, George Stephenson's teams of labourers start 'Altering the House Pond and making the foundations for the new Stables', a major project which was still being completed in 1760.

Looking at the plan of this area with the two new buildings superimposed on what existed (see page 95), it is clear that most of the old House Pond had to be filled in to allow the ground levels to be adjusted sufficiently to provide the space for the south stable block, while the pond above it was reshaped to become the 'Long Pond', now known as the Camellia Pond. At the same time, the accounts show that the 'old' greenhouse (built 1742) and the orangerie (built 1746), both associated with Philip Miller's 'new' garden, were demolished, suggesting that they were on or near the site of the new north stable block. Although nothing like the orangerie was built again, at least until Henry Holland added the Camellia House in the 1790s, the greenhouse was replaced in 1758 when the 'new Greenhouse' was built over the offices in the south range of the Abbey. It is hard to imagine exactly what this structure looked like, but it was a major new addition to the surviving assembly of buildings round the old 'Still Room Court' of the monastery, and will have had a good view out over the south Privy Garden.

It then appears that little more was done in the gardens until the Abbey, with new roads round the north and south ends, and the stable blocks, with their new access roads, were all completed. Following this, in 1763–4, we see a new garden being laid out between the south Privy Garden and the south stable block, where space had been created when the House Pond was filled in, and an 'Arch' is built to permit access to it from the Privy Garden and on

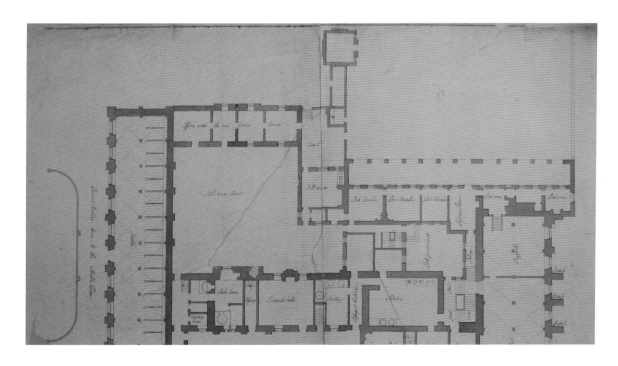

to the pleasure grounds. Although no contemporary plan of this new garden exists, it seems to have been primarily an ornamental flower garden, since orders are given for 'Trenching plats of the ground in the new Garden for Roses and Sweet Flowers',[65] and added to the sense of the Abbey being set amongst decorative gardens. In addition to this garden, a few years later the Duchess's Garden is enlarged, and, on the north side of the Abbey, the duke orders a 'small building' to be added to the 'Grotto Garden' which already featured the 'Gold Fish Pond'.[66] Some hint of what this small building might have been comes in a letter from Robert Butcher, the duke's agent in London, to Flitcroft: 'His Grace . . . asks that you will order Mr White to plant immediately as many yews, as will be necessary behind the Necessary lately built in the Grotto Garden.'[67] Clearly, family comforts while out in the garden and pleasure gardens were being addressed.

Thus, in the space of some ten years, the ground to the east of the Abbey was transformed from the old woodland of the Rookery, interspersed with equally old deer barns, service buildings, pigeon house and pheasantry, into formal gardens laid out around the stable blocks; it also included the new gravel paths of the pleasure grounds leading away through the trees to the Chinese temple, to the Lady's Folly complete with a temple of its own, past a series of seats built round the tree trunks, before leading back past the new Long Pond, all the while providing glimpses of the deer park stretching away beyond the palings. And out in the park the duke had been equally busy during this period, not least in the continued development of the Evergreens.

Here, as the planting programme continued, in 1747 the area was fenced off and the 'Temple in the Evergreens' was joined by a decorative feature the duke refers to as 'The Arch' set amongst the trees in one of the small valleys that ran down the slope. These points of interest were then added to few years later by a Chinese-style 'Summer House' or temple on the island in Drakeloe Pond. Clearly, this had become a popular spot for the family to visit, and at the same time that the Chinese temple was being built in the pleasure grounds, a wooden structure was put up on the island, using some of the same craftsmen. In 1754 new wharfing is completed, no doubt making access to the island easier, and the next year Whittle and Norman, the carvers also working on Chinese designs in the Abbey, bill respectively for 'carving 8 columns in the Chinese taste, done in oak, for Drakley Pond Summer House', and for 'gilding the Chinese Temple',[68] while the mason, John Devall, submits a bill in 1756 for 'Preparing paving for island, at Drakley Temple'.[69] This is the structure referred to on the Anon. 1738 map as 'Drakly Pond with a Chinese Building on ye Island', and although there is no contemporary image or plan of this structure, it seems we might be able to catch a glimpse of it some fifty years later when Humphry Repton produced an image of just such a building on Drakeloe Pond in his Red Book for Woburn of 1805 (see illustration on page 104).

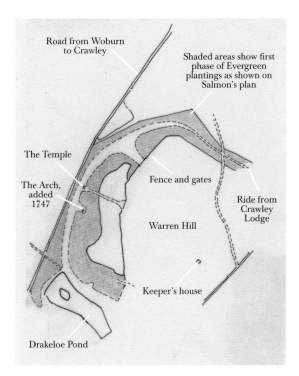

LEFT The Evergreens, 'Square Temple' and 'Arch' location plan. This shows the first phase of Evergreen plantings as drawn by Robert Salmon (see page 90). Although the building of the temple is not recorded, the 'temple in the Evergreens' is mentioned by the 4th Duke in 1756 as needing repair, suggesting that it had been built some time before. More certain is the addition of the Arch, which the duke orders to be built in 1747. These appear to be the first two structures built in the Evergreens, but more were to follow.

BELOW H. W. Burgess, *View in the Evergreens* (showing the 'Arch' and 'Colonnade'), 1837.
The 4th Duke's Arch can be seen on the left, standing at the head of its own little valley. The sweeping cedar on the right still stands today, while the Arch and the Colonnade below it are only visible as piles of stones. The Colonnade was added to the scene by the 6th Duke in the 1830s. Part of this still stood in the 1970s but was knocked down by a falling tree and, like the stones of the Arch, became lost in the encroaching rhododendrons.

Elsewhere in the park, the duke had been busy completing another major project, the creation of a wide, elegant grass ride from Parson's Wood up past Froxfield Gate and out round the entire north-east quadrant to the Red Lodges at Crawley Gate and back across the park, past Long Lands Barn to the Abbey. Accessed from the northern end of the 'New Long Riding', this ride was regularly rolled and was lined on either side with paired blocks of elm trees, of which some forty-eight pairs are visible on Browne's 1738 map, and called 'The Platoons'.[70]

No mention is made of when this great undertaking was begun, but we do know that planting was being completed in 1742, arguing that this was one of the first projects the 4th Duke undertook, and it will no doubt have been part of the route for his regular walks around the park. In addition to these plantings, the duke turned his attention to the Bason Pond. Throughout this period, as we see from Browne's 1738 map, he had kept a yacht on this pond, large enough to use as an office for conducting his Admiralty business, and we catch sight of both the boat and the pond in a description of them by Daniel Defoe, who visited Woburn as part of his 'Tour through Great Britain' in the early eighteenth century: 'before the house is a large bason of water, surrounded with a fine broad gravel walk, which is bounded with posts and iron chains. On the water is a most beautiful yacht . . . completely rigged, and mounts 10 guns, which are fired on occasion of entertainments . . . given on board by his Grace.'[71]

With the Platoons completed, the 4th Duke began a series of alterations to his father's grand but very simple circular pond. First, the Great Avenue from the Abbey to the turnpike road was re-gravelled, and then, from 1755, once the fish had been relocated, the pond was drained and work started on alterations to its shape, which continued for the next six years. While the duke's Memorandum Book for 1755

Humphry Repton, Drakeloe Pond and the Evergreens, Red Book for Woburn, detail of unnumbered image on p. 41, 1805.
Repton's view of the Evergreens, seen across Drakeloe Pond, shows the new plantations added by the 5th Duke in the late 1790s. In the background to the left, we catch a glimpse of the older trees of the 4th Duke's original plantations of the 1740s. Equally interesting is Repton's representation of the 'temple' on the island. Close inspection of his image shows a simple structure with a conical roof supported by eight columns. This is the number specified by Whittle and Norman when they invoice for 'carving 8 columns in the Chinese taste, done in oak', and since the original columns were of oak, it is quite possible that the structure was still standing when Repton painted it. Certainly, there is no record of another building replacing it during the intervening years. This suggests that Repton's image shows us the original structure from 1747.

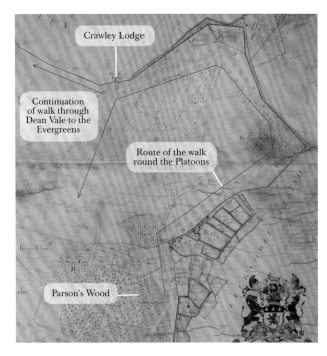

Browne's 1738 map, route of walk round the Platoons. The Platoons consisted of paired blocks of elm trees down either side of a wide grass ride. Striding along this route through the gentle mists of early summer mornings, memo book and pencil in his pocket, was one the 4th Duke's favourite pastimes at Woburn. To keep it in prime condition the grass was regularly rolled, but not before the duke's walk, since the staff had strict instructions not to leave footprints in the dew-soaked grass before he had passed.

gives specifics of the work – removing the gravel, turf, posts and wharfing from around the pond, altering and re-claying the banks – nothing is said of the shape of the new design, but it is noticeable that at the same time work was also being done on a 'New River'. All this strongly suggests that at this moment the alterations inked on to Browne's 1738 map, showing the Bason Pond altered to include what looks like a pre-existing decoy beside it, were carried out. A new, informally shaped pond was created, the basis of the Bason Pond we see today, and it was linked to the water source above it, the Hop Garden Pond, by a new, more direct route into a new 'Lower Hop Garden Pond' and a 'Long Pool' below it, creating the 'New River' and eliminating the older 'Serpentine River' which meandered off along the contours to the south but never joined up with the Bason.[72]

Looking closely at the alterations shown on the map, it would appear that part of the plan was that this new river should be bridged, providing the opportunity to eliminate the road from Bowler's Gate to the south and east side of the Abbey, where there were now to be gardens, and replace it with a far more interesting route round to the spectacular new west front. Although a permanent new bridge and the new road were not put in place until 1770, when William Chambers provided the design, an additional decorative feature was added to the Long Pool when an 'Arch' designed by the Marquis of Tavistock was created in 1756.[73]

There was also one other significant addition to the park landscape at this time: the building of another summer house, this one known as the 'Temple in Parson's Wood', in 1756.

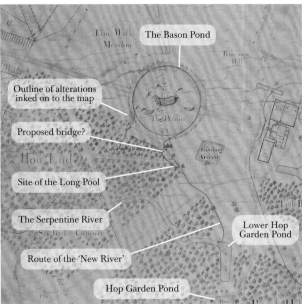

ABOVE Browne's 1738 map, the Bason Pond alterations.

LEFT Browne's 1738 map, route of new road to west front of the Abbey.

Rerouting the road from Bowler's Gate to the Abbey served two purposes. First, it ran the road past the new setting around the expanded Bason Pond and gave visitors the best view of the Abbey as they came over the decorative bridge. Second, it meant that the old road round the south-east corner of the Abbey could be eliminated, providing new space for the development of the gardens in this area. As mentioned before, it is possible that Sanderson's bridge design of 1733 was an early version of this idea. Perhaps it took the 4th Duke's visit to Stourhead, where Henry Hoare had added the Palladian bridge in the 1740s, for the duke to decide to build his own.

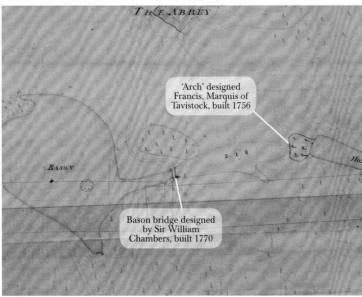

ABOVE Detail of estate map showing the bridge by William Chambers (1770) and the 'Arch' designed by Francis, Marquis of Tavistock (1756).

As well as indicating the possible location of the Arch, it also gives us a good view of the plan of the bridge designed by Sir William Chambers, in which we can clearly see the four pedestals at each corner on which the tall obelisks stood.

ABOVE The Arch at the New Pond, 2015.

Due to the fact that Repton raised the water level of the Long Pool by as much as two metres when he replaced Chambers's bridge with his 'Viaduct' in 1806–7, what we see today tells us little about the original look of the structure. It is likely that in the original design the water fell from the Arch down some form of cascade to the pool below, making a spectacular show when seen from the bridge. Any such feature is today below water level. Today, part of the Arch still survives, but the trees on top and later additions of piping have taken their toll on the structure.

RIGHT Pompeo Batoni, *Francis Russell, Marquis of Tavistock* (1739–1767), 1762. The portrait captures the young Marquis of Tavistock amongst the ruins of Rome and commemorates his Grand Tour of Italy between 1761 and 1763. The trip was clearly an inspirational time for Francis, and he records that while there he felt 'an awakening interest in art and architecture'. Other portraits show him pursuing his other passion – fox hunting – but this one seems to suggest his underlying interests and perhaps tells us something about what he might have done at Woburn had he not died young following a hunting accident.

BELOW Barratt, *Chambers's Bridge and West Front of Abbey, c.*1770–1805. This is the best image we have of the Abbey towards the end of the 4th Duke's life. The alterations have all been made to the Bason Pond, Chambers's bridge is built, and the new road is visible running up to the grand west front, a scene still recognizable today. '. . . and so down to the bridge, whose pyramids I shou'd instantly level' was Lord Torrington's verdict when he visited in 1789, and others, perhaps the 5th Duke, seem to have agreed, since the 'pyramids' were gone by the time Repton drew this scene in 1805 (see page 136). Although we cannot see the south side of the Abbey, it does show us the low garden wall running up the slope to the north, and provides a glimpse of the plantings of small trees and shrubs in the Grotto Garden and Privy Garden beyond. The painting also suggests that the pleasure gardens behind the Abbey were still surrounded by very dense woodland to the north and east.

Looking at Browne's beautifully delineated map of the park outside the immediate gardens round the Abbey, we notice that certain areas of woodland are drawn in more detail; not only are these areas more densely planted with a variety of tree sizes, they also have finer patterns of small walks running through them, and are enclosed by paling fences. Distinct from the parkland around them, they have been given names – 'Parson's Wood', 'Somerley Grove', 'Part of Briary Grove', 'Hockley Wood' and so on – indicating that these were individually maintained pieces of decorative woodland, fenced off to keep out the deer, and places of special interest to the family. A hint of how they looked comes from the duke's orders in 1753 that Mr Shackleton should 'plant sweet bryars and honeysuckles by the side of the serpentine path in Somerley Grove',[74] providing an intimate woodland of flowering trees and shrubs, festooned with honeysuckle and briars, for the family to walk or ride in. Parson's Wood and Somerley Grove, features of the kind that later became known as 'shrubberies', would seem to be particularly important in this context since they are close to the new pleasure grounds behind the Abbey and are on the way to the start of the Platoons. Thus, in Parson's Wood, although its exact location is lost, a new, equally decorative and elaborately furnished summer house was built as a destination for the family.

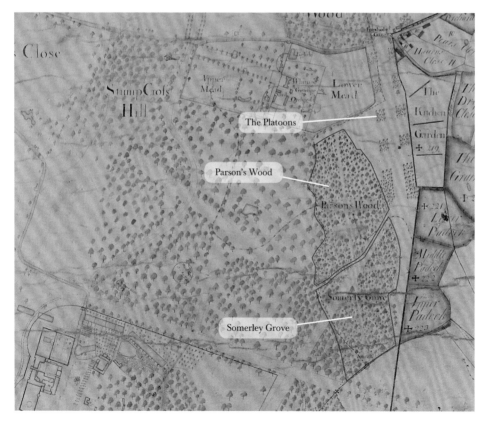

Browne's 1738 map, detail of Parson's Wood and Somerley Grove. The fenced-off, decorative woodlands of Parson's Wood and Somerley Grove, where the parkland trees were heavily interplanted with smaller flowering trees and shrubs to form an intricate network of paths, represented a significant extension of the 'pleasure grounds' out into the park. Once the 'Temple in Parson's Wood' had been added in 1756, these woodlands will have represented an important element in the family's experience of the landscape around the Abbey during the childhood of the young brothers Francis and John, who went on to become 5th and 6th Dukes.

In 1756 the duke's surveyor Thomas Moore 'measures' for the temple in Parson's Wood, and the materials he specifies include Tottenhoe stone, Portland stone and a black marble floor. John Devall bills for 'mouldings and stone work done at the New Temple in Parson's Wood', before Lloyd and Johnson (plasterers) bill for 'whitewashing the cornice and ceiling of the Temple'. In 1757 the roof is slated and the windows glazed, before the building is furnished with '2 large couches for the Temple in Parson's Wood' and '4 beds, 4 mattresses, bolsters, chinzes and fringe'.[75] This was clearly an elaborate and highly finished 'Temple', the most elaborate of all in fact, and a place where the family not only stopped off but spent some time, possibly even staying overnight.

Looking back over the development of the park and gardens during the 4th Duke's time, we see not just an agenda of the duke pursuing his interests in plants and horticulture generally, but also a consistent effort both to provide entertainment for the family in the gardens around the house and to extend that experience out into the park. Although at various times professional designers such as Philip Miller and Charles Bridgeman were called in, and there can be little doubt that the duke also knew and hosted Capability Brown at Woburn,[76] the overall impression is of the family coming up with their own ideas and designs. The duke, the duchess and their son Francis, the Marquis of Tavistock, all seem to have contributed ideas, and to have had an ongoing interest in and engagement with the landscape around the Abbey. In this context it is interesting to note that although both Tavistock and his sister Caroline had married and left home (she to the Duke of Marlborough) by 1764, a whole new family soon emerged to keep the duke and duchess company. Initially, they were joined by three of Gertrude's nieces, by then young women,[77] and subsequently – following the death of the Marquis of Tavistock after a fall while hunting in 1767 and that of his heartbroken wife, Elizabeth, the next year – Tavistock's three young sons, Francis (aged 3), John (aged 2) and William (aged 1), joined the household. We can imagine that at least some of the developments in the gardens at this time were designed to entertain the children.

Although by now the duke was suffering increasingly from gout and was operated on for cataracts in both eyes in 1768, the duchess seems to have relished her role as grandmother, and Georgiana Blakiston paints a vivid picture of the children's life at Woburn. She quotes the duchess, who tells the duke in a letter 'that in hot weather [she and the children] breakfasted upon the pavement', and felt cheated when it was cold, 'which is a very great misfortune to my little companions and me, for we have lived out of doors and not found the hay too long'.[78] This provides a fascinating glimpse of the 5th and 6th Dukes' upbringing, and we can just imagine them setting out for the temple in Parson's Wood to spend a day, playing amongst the honeysuckles and sweet briars of the ornamental woodland, riding in the carriage with their grandmother through the long grass of summer, along the open spaces of the ridge-top Serpentine Terrace or down the grass ride of the Platoons, and on round through the dark woodland of the Evergreens, to pause in the open glades where they found the 'Arch', the 'Temple in the Evergreens', taking a boat trip out to the island in Drakeloe to sit in the Chinese summer house, before returning to the Abbey along the new road through the park. Steadily, the park had been remodelled to sharpen the focus on the Abbey, to make the experience of arriving more impressive, while also providing a new internal infrastructure of roads and rides from the Abbey out into the park itself, enabling the family to reach all the new places of interest.

Perhaps the full extent of what the duke and duchess had achieved since the 1740s is best summed up by the following account of his visit to Woburn written by Arthur Young, a leading writer on agricultural matters, in 1770, the year before the duke died:

Sir Joshua Reynolds, *Gertrude Leveson-Gower, Duchess of Bedford.* By reputation a proud and overbearing woman, this portrait nevertheless conveys something a little warmer, the loving grandmother whose letters to the duke tell of her adventures in the grounds with her young grandchildren, who came to live at the Abbey following the deaths of their parents.

Woburn park is 10 miles around, and contains variety of hill and dale, with woods of noble oaks; we drove from the house through them towards the south, and looked up the great glade which is cut through the park for several miles, and catches at the end of it a Chinese temple; then winding through the woods we came to the Duchess's shrubbery, containing 16 acres of land beautifully laid out in the modern taste, with many most glorious oaks in it. From thence we advanced to the hill at the north end, from which is a vast prospect into Buckinghamshire, Hertfordshire, and Bedfordshire; turning down the hill to the left, the riding leads to the evergreen plantation of above 200 acres of land, which thirty years ago was a barren rabbit warren, but now a close winter's ride, on a dry soil, with all sorts of evergreens of a growth. About the middle on the left hand, is an handsome temple, retired and pleasing. At the end of this plantation, we came to the lower water, which is about ten acres, and in the center, an island with a very elegant and light *Chinese* temple, large enough for thirty people to dine in; and in the adjoining wood is a kitchen, etc. for making ready the repasts his Grace takes in the temple. In front of the house is a large bason of water with several handsome boats; formerly a large yacht swam in it, but rotting, it has not been rebuilt.

This park, which is one of the largest in the kingdom, contains 3,500 acres of a great variety of soils, from a light sand to a rich loam, which

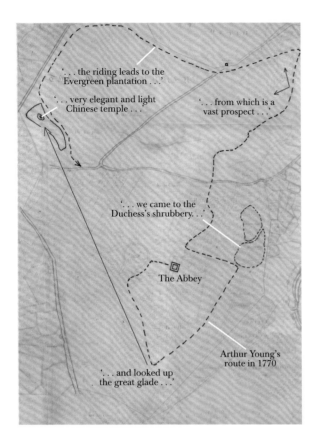

'. . . the riding leads to the Evergreen plantation . . .'

'. . . very elegant and light Chinese temple . . .'

'. . . from which is a vast prospect . . .'

'. . . we came to the Duchess's shrubbery. . .'

The Abbey

Arthur Young's route in 1770

'. . . and looked up the great glade . . .'

Plan of park showing Arthur Young's probable route around the park, 1770. Young left a fascinating account of his visit to Woburn which tells us not just about the things that caught his eye, but also about the route that visitors would take around the park. Whether they were accompanied by a guide, or perhaps a family member, is not clear, but no doubt they were directed towards what were considered to be the interesting views. Sadly, the two-mile view right across the park to Drakeloe Pond is no longer open, but it must have been as impressive as the 'vast prospect' from the Serpentine Terrace, which also is no longer visible. Gertrude's shrubberies do not seem to have survived her, and are not shown on later maps.

yields grass good enough to fat large beasts: It is all walled in; was there a greater variety of water, it would be much more beautiful, but the nature of the soil in the low parts makes that acquisition very difficult; but what might be much easier gained, are buildings scattered about it, which would give a pleasing variety to the ridings, and for want of which, most of them are very melancholy.[79]

While written very much in the language of the agriculturalist, we nevertheless get a vivid idea of the park as still being a place of long views to distant places of interest, specifically the view of some two and a half miles down the 'great glade' to the Chinese temple on Drakeloe Pond, and the 'vast prospect' of three counties from the Serpentine Terrace along the ridge line. We also catch a glimpse of the duchess's decorative woodlands, her 'shrubberies', of Parson's Wood and Somerley Grove, and of the 'retired and pleasing' experience of the Evergreens, where the hundreds of trees planted from 1742 were rapidly growing to block a number of those long views. It would appear, however, that Young did not have access to the pleasure grounds or the shrubberies, since he seems not to have seen the temple in Parson's Wood, or that in the Lady's Folly, or the Chinese temple in the pleasure grounds, the Menagerie, the aviaries, or the seats and benches under the trees which the family so clearly enjoyed. Instead, Young picks up on a pervading sense of melancholy, a sense perhaps of the end of an era. By 1770 Woburn park had gone quiet: the huntsmen, like the sadly missed Marquis of Tavistock, were long gone, the rides were empty, and the increasingly frail duke no longer strode forth through the morning mists, notebook in hand. The kitchen in the woods no longer provided meals for thirty people on Drakeloe island, and even the guns on the once beautiful yacht had fallen silent as it rotted away in a corner of the Bason Pond. The great sweep of landscape that surrounded the house and its pleasure grounds needed a sustained injection of energy, ideas and commitment to bring it back to life, and the duke's grandsons – the two brothers, Francis and John, who had spent their childhoods there – were to provide just that.

CHAPTER THREE

*'Much has been done here, but much remains to be done,
and something I think to* undo'

(John, 6th Duke, 1805)

FRANCIS RUSSELL, 5TH DUKE, AND JOHN RUSSELL, 6TH DUKE

John Hoppner, *Francis
Russell, 5th Duke of Bedford*
(1765–1802).
When he reached 21 in
1786 Francis took his place
in the House of Lords
and turned his attention
to developing the estate
at Woburn. This portrait
catches him at this moment,
a serious young man setting
out to put in place his 'plans
for national improvement'
and surrounded by the
necessary boxes, papers
and books.

If Woburn had appeared as a quiet and melancholy place towards the end of the 4th Duke's life, this was soon to change as, over the next fifty years or so, Lord Francis and Lord John, the 5th and 6th Dukes, turned it into one of the most vibrant, complex and innovative estates of its time. Picking up on the horticultural, scientific, artistic and cultural interests of their father and grandfather, and full of ideas of their own, they worked with a succession of the country's leading figures – from William Smith, the geologist, to Humphry Repton, the landscape designer – as they went on to create many of the features of the Abbey and park that we see today. It was a period of sustained development and expenditure at Woburn – one for which the wider Bedford estates paid a price – but it provided the setting for the extraordinary lifestyle of the Victorian and Edwardian Russells, and survived until the Second World War, when other forces came into play that changed the Abbey and its park forever.

We can follow the known facts of Francis Russell's life and what he was interested in, and add other people's comments, but the lack of any personal diaries, letters or notebooks (all of which he had destroyed before he died) makes it impossible to hear his own voice or understand what he was really thinking. What is clear is that he inherited the dukedom in 1771 as a 6-year-old, and from this period until he reached his majority in 1786 the estates were run by his grandmother, the Dowager Duchess Gertrude. She lived on until 1794, and, as we have seen, she appears to have brought up the boys, Francis, John and William, in 'remarkable freedom',[1] while at the same time overseeing the estates and the development of Bedford Square and Gower Street in Bloomsbury, central London.

After attending Cambridge, Francis left for Europe, where he travelled, particularly in France, between 1784 and 1786. Whatever his initial plans may have been, his time seems to have been spent largely in Paris, where he had met and formed a lasting relationship (the exact nature of which is unclear) with Nancy Parsons and her husband, Lord Maynard. Abandoning any other plans he may have had, he travelled to the south of France with the Maynards, before eventually returning to England with them in late 1786. Their close friendship continued – Lord Maynard even went on to have his own room at Woburn Abbey[2] – but, living in London on his return, Francis also became a part of the group close to George, Prince of Wales, sharing their interests in London life, going to the theatre, gambling enormous sums on cards and extravagant wagers at Brooks's club, and attending the horse racing at places like Newmarket and Epsom.

By 1787, however, on achieving his majority, he had taken his place in the House of Lords, participating as a strong adherent of Charles James Fox's Whigs, and after what may have been a somewhat tense period of negotiation with the Dowager Duchess, he took control of the estates and Woburn itself. Surveying his inheritance, and perhaps because, unlike any of his predecessors, he had no strong personal connections with any of the other properties or houses, he seems to have instinctively prioritized Woburn; and realizing that his plans for it would require a substantial injection of money, he prepared to raise the funds required by a radical rationalization of the sprawling Bedford estates. To this end, in April 1787, he agreed the first major sale, which included land and the 'the Honor and Manors or Lordships' of estates in Middlesex, Surrey, Hampshire, Buckinghamshire, Hertfordshire, Northamptonshire, Huntingdonshire, Bedfordshire, Cambridgeshire, Devon and Cornwall.[3]

With the estate coffers refilled, Francis set out to realize his vision of a thoroughly modern agricultural and sporting estate built around an enlarged and updated Abbey and the Park Farm, the latter to be a model of its kind and the first 'home' farm on the estate. This was to be a ducal seat and a setting for it that reflected what his brother John would later describe as Francis's 'plans for national improvement'[4] – whereby estates such as Woburn would set new national standards of efficiency and productivity, securing their position and status at the centre of an invigorated rural economy, increasing and stabilizing food production, and steadying the country at a time of great social unrest and radicalization.

Many of these plans took time to develop as Francis put together the finances and the team of people who were to help him realize them, but by 1787 he had met Henry Holland, the architect who would realize his ambitions for a modern Woburn Abbey.[5] Holland was already working for the duke's relatives and London acquaintances when he started work for Francis, first remodelling the dining room at Bedford House and then acting as his surveyor, 'surveying and valuing' houses for leasing on the London estate and Covent Garden. As this work continued, Holland submitted new designs for the south and east wings of the Abbey which, when complete, would link up with the old north and west ranges to close in the inner court with new

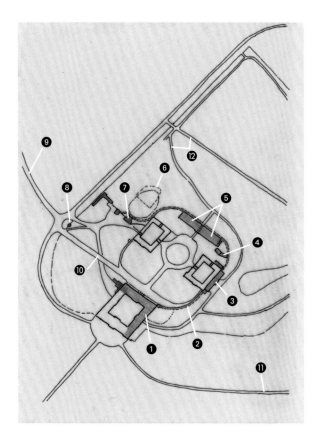

buildings: plans which placed the quadrangular structure of Berwick Manor once again at the heart of the family home, this time in the grandest form yet. In Holland's scheme, the new south wing would include a suite of rooms – dining room, library and study – on the first floor above the old twelve-arched arcade, with new bedroom apartments above them, while in the new east wing, the old basement stable block and coach house would be converted into a kitchen and range of offices, with a first-floor series of reception rooms and attics above them. In both cases the old basement level – the arcade and the entrance to the stables – were buried on the outside as the ground level was brought up to the principal floor.

Work on the Abbey continued until 1792, at which point the new approach road to the west front was created from Holland's design for the London entrance, running across the park past the south front, while on the other side, the road from Woburn was brought in from Stump's Cross Corner, past the porter's lodge and over a bridge to arrive at the new front entrance facing the east court.

ABOVE Plan of Henry Holland's new south and east ranges of the Abbey, with the bridge to the east entrance and new buildings around the north and south courts. This figure indicates the amount of work that was done on the Abbey and its relationship to the landscape around it by the 5th Duke working with the architect Henry Holland between 1787 and 1792. It established the basic layout that we still see today.

❶ East and south ranges of the Abbey.
❷ Covered walkway from the south range round to the Chinese dairy.
❸ Conservatory.
❹ Greenhouses.
❺ Tennis court and riding house.
❻ Existing pond enlarged to create the fishpond in front of the Chinese dairy.
❼ Chinese dairy.
❽ Porter's lodge.
❾ Road from Stump's Cross Corner.
❿ Road over bridge to the new east entrance of the Abbey.
⓫ Holland's new approach from the London entrance.
⓬ New gravel paths.

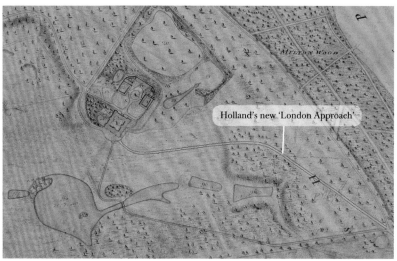

ABOVE Plan of Holland's new approach road from the London entrance, highlighted detail of anonymous estate map, c.1810. Holland's choice of a new route for the London approach to the Abbey, leaving the old road from the London entrance via Chambers's bridge to run east of the ponds, meant that visitors' first sight of the Abbey was of his new south front. Repton did not approve.

While building work got under way, the duke was also looking to improve the amenities at the Abbey and the attractions in the pleasure grounds. It is unclear whose idea it was to create a Chinese-style 'Dairy' – whether it was Holland, inspired by his work on the 'Chinese Drawing Room' at Carlton House, or the duke reviving the theme used by his grandparents both inside the Abbey and in the gardens – but the highly decorative structure was built 1787–9 behind the north stable block on the edge

of the fishpond. Such buildings were very much in vogue at the time as places where the ladies of the family could entertain themselves acting as dairymaids, making cream and soft cheeses, but exactly who the bachelor 5th Duke had in mind to use it is not clear. Nevertheless, it remained popular with the family throughout the nineteenth century, and survives intact as a building of great interest. Repton, too, was very taken with this building in 1805 when preparing his Red Book for the 6th Duke, producing a wonderful image of it and proposing the development of the Chinese theme around the pond.

Other developments by Holland at this time were also concentrated around the two stable courts: a new conservatory attached to the south stable block facing the south gardens and then, immediately east of the two courts, an entirely new double-height structure housing an indoor tennis court and a riding house. One gets a vivid picture of this building from a contemporary account in the *Sporting Magazine*, which tells us that the duke had built 'the Tennis Court and Riding House (with apartments between the two to dress in) . . . there are flues run along the walls and under the pavement of the Tennis Court to keep off the damps . . . the walls of the Riding House are painted in panels, with high pilaster, and the ceiling is painted to represent a clear sky.'[6]

These new structures were then linked to the Abbey by a covered walkway which curved round the east court from the Abbey to the conservatory, past the riding house and tennis court and all the way round through a Chinese-style 'Moon Gate' to the Chinese dairy. For the first time, the pleasure grounds and the recreational facilities were fully integrated with the Abbey itself, and they took on a new artistic aspect in 1801, when the duke converted the conservatory into a sculpture gallery. This development was perhaps precipitated by the ongoing development of the Bloomsbury estate, which in 1800 had seen the demolition of Bedford House and the arrival at Woburn of a number of artworks, from the 4th Duke's Canalettos to an array of sculpture collected over the years by a succession of family members on their Grand Tours. Francis now created a home for all this art,

Humphry Repton, 'The Chinese Dairy', Red Book for Woburn, Plate XXIX, 1805.
Repton's image of the Chinese dairy tells us two things. First, it emphasizes the time and effort that Repton took in preparing the Red Book for Woburn: a beautifully finished painting, full of light and shadow, crystal clear reflections in the still water of Holland's pond, indications of tree species in the foliage, while the pair of ducks amongst the water lilies and plump peony blossoms all add life and animation. Second, it tells us just how much Repton enjoyed the style and atmosphere of the scene, adding his pavilion on the right, and emphasizing the pleasure he felt this setting added to the experience of the garden as a whole.

THE DUKE OF BEDFORDS STABLES WITH THE NEW TENNIS COURT & RIDING-HOUSE AT WOBURN ABBEY.

'The Duke of Bedford's Stables, with the new Tennis Court and Riding House at Woburn Abbey' (seen from the east court), *Sporting Magazine*, February 1795.

Henry Holland's new building, depicted soon after it was constructed, ran between Flitcroft's north and south courts. The tennis court (on the left) and the riding house (on the right) stood behind the courtyard wall and were illuminated by rows of large windows. The dressing rooms occupied the middle section beneath the cupola, and a central open passage ran through to the east gardens beyond. It is noticeable that the building had a flat roof, a design choice which may explain the fact that it appears to have leaked, needed repairing a few years later, and was stripped off and completely rebuilt in the 1830s.

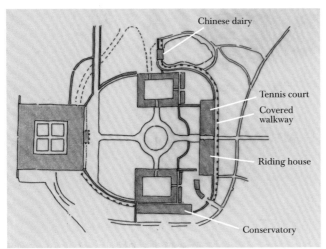

Chinese dairy

Tennis court

Covered walkway

Riding house

Conservatory

Plan showing new buildings in the pleasure grounds and the covered walkway.

This plan indicates the full complexity of the architectural landscape east of the Abbey once Holland's buildings (the conservatory, riding house, tennis court and Chinese dairy) had been integrated into the layout of Flitcroft's north and south courts. The plan also illustrates the central role of the covered walkway as it provides the crucial link between these new buildings and the garden paths beyond to the family rooms in Holland's new south range. This arrangement appealed strongly to Repton, who went on to propose an extension of the walkway to provide an all-weather link to the buildings he designed for the central terrace of the pleasure grounds.

part of which was his 'Temple of Liberty' on the eastern end containing busts of Charles James Fox and other current and historical political heroes.

At the same time as this building work got under way, on coming to Woburn the duke was eager to enter fully into country life, pursuing two of his favourite interests – hunting and horse racing – and building facilities for both in the park. In 1787 he co-founded the Oakley Hunt with his fellow horse-racing enthusiasts William Lee Anthonie of Colworth, Bedfordshire, and his near neighbour Samuel Whitbread, who had bought Elstrow. The hunt had the run of an enormous area, and kennels for the hounds were built spaced out to facilitate hunting across its range, at Oakley House, Wroxton and Woburn. Of the kennels at Wroxton, Lord Torrington in 1794 considered them so well built that 'The truth is, they would make the best cottage in the village,'[7] while the elaborate kennels at Woburn were described in the *Sporting Magazine* in 1795 as the 'completest in England [with] 11 apartments for bitches and puppies, with yards ... plus apartments for the Keepers, and two very long lodging rooms for the hunting hounds ... in front is a large pond and between 60–70 couple of working hounds are kept in the Kennels.'[8] The complex also included a house for the huntsman.

Woburn kennels (LEFT) and stud and groom facilities (ABOVE), details of *Woburn Park & Abbey*, 'plan made 1810', 'copied by T. Evans 1817'.
The detail LEFT indicates the location of the 5th Duke's new kennels, in the top left-hand corner, just south of the Froxfield road on ground that had previously been part of Whitnoe Grange farm. Within about twenty years the site was taken over by the 6th Duke's new kitchen gardens and gardener's house. Lord Torrington considered the site far too close to the Abbey, creating 'a nuisance to the house by the noise', and would have chosen a more distant site.

The magazine goes on to say that one wing of the Woburn stables was large enough to 'contain stalls for 36 hunters, with 11 hospital apartments for sick and lame horses'.

All this makes abundantly clear the elaborate scale on which Francis was building, although, in terms of the hunt, his interest does not seem to have matched his father's, who had been 'mad for it', and while he continued to pay a subscription and allowed the hounds to be kept at the three kennels, he steadily withdrew from participation. The pack was kept going by Anthonie and Whitbread until 1809, at which point the new Marquis of Tavistock, also Francis (and later 7th Duke), took over as Master, serving three times in this position, and retaining a lifelong interest in the hunt. In 1834, new permanent premises for the pack were established at Milton Ernest, and the Russell family interest was maintained by the 9th and 10th Dukes, only ending when the 11th Duke finally conveyed the family's share in the premises to the trustees of the hunt in 1903.

The 5th Duke's other great passion, horse racing, proved more enduring, and besides attending races he also became a successful breeder. Soon after he became duke, new facilities – no doubt as elaborate as the kennels – were built at Woburn for housing the racehorses and four grooms. Located at the west end of what became Park Farm, the facilities had access to paddocks on one side and the wide open spaces of the park beyond.

The stud was clearly a success, producing three Derby winners, Skyscraper (1789), Eager (1791) and 'Colt by Fidget' (1797), and three winners of the Epsom Oaks, Hippolyta (1790), Portia (1791) and Caelia

(1793), all trained by the duke's personal trainer Matthew Stephenson, who also rode Eager to victory in 1791. His racing colours, described on the race card for Bedford Races in 1794 as 'Purple and Buff', continued to be used by the 7th Duke, as purple and white stripes, and were re-registered by Lord and Lady Tavistock when the Bloomsbury Stud was established in part of the buildings at Park Farm in 1966. As Henrietta, Dowager Duchess of Bedford, says, 'We were told [recently] that the colours are the third oldest in the world still being carried by their original owners. Only the Queen's and the Duke of Devonshire's are older.'[9] It is more than likely that in the 5th Duke's time the long rides running through the park were alive with thundering hooves as Skyscraper and the other horses were prepared for their Derby runs, but as Henrietta says, circumstances have changed too much for the park ever to be used again for training runs. Today, the facilities at Park Farm are leased out and new generations of horses can still be glimpsed as they are turned out in the paddocks behind the old buildings.

Other than the building work at the Abbey and the pleasure grounds, by far the most direct impact on the appearance and uses of the park and estate beyond at this time came with the 5th Duke's wider improvements: new roads and lodges, the brand new and carefully planned 'model' Park Farm, the efforts to create productive water meadows from the marginal boggy areas by drainage and irrigation, and the development of woodland plantations in the park, including the expansion of the Evergreens. From 1787 onwards, Francis steadily put together the team of people who would help him realize his 'plans for national improvement', a team which was to include such figures as John Farey, mathematician and civil engineer,[10] Robert Salmon, administrator,[11] Dr Edmund Cartwright, inventor of the 'Spinning Jenny', who oversaw the experimental programmes at Park Farm,[12] and William Smith, geologist and drainage expert.[13]

Browne's 1738 survey, annotated detail showing the new road from Woburn to the 'Star of Roads' junction and ❶ The new road across to Froxfield, ❷ The new road to the Abbey, and ❸ The road down to Park Farm.

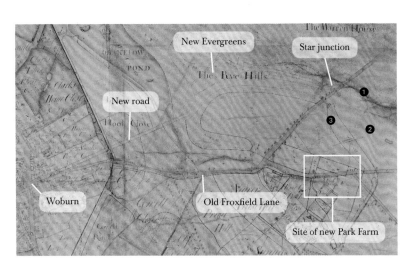

Apart from creating the new road to the Abbey's west front from Holland's London entrance, and upgrading the approach to the Abbey across Stump's Cross Hill, Robert Salmon also oversaw the creation of a new road from Woburn, running beside Drakeloe Pond and across the park to Froxfield Gate. The first hints of this road can be seen pencilled in on Browne's 1738 survey, which, despite being some fifty years old, was evidently still the most accurate rendering of the park.

It would seem that this was designed to run the new approach road from Woburn through the new Evergreen plantations and, at the same time, to clear the site where the new Park Farm was being built. With the exception of the road shown running across the park to the Abbey (which seems never to have been laid), it is the layout we see today. New lodges were added at the end of Park Street (*c.*1800) and at the 'Star of Roads' junction in 1810; both are still there, along with the gated entrance to the Evergreens. The tree-lined road that ran up to the 'Red Lodges' now serves as the exit road for the Safari Park.

At the end of its road from the Star of Roads junction, Park Farm was built by Robert Salmon between 1795 and 1801, replacing the random collection of old barns and rickyards with an entirely new complex of farm buildings, yards, workshops and a timber yard, some of which can still be seen. More than simply the estate farm, it was soon to become famous nationally as the location for an annual agricultural show, known as 'The Sheepshearing', for exhibiting new and improved breeds of cattle, oxen, sheep and pigs. Visitors came to watch competitions and award ceremonies, inspect the state of the art buildings, meet people, exchange ideas, and participate in the livestock sales and auctions. Begun in 1797, the show was hosted by the duke at the Abbey, where up to 200 guests were fed lavish meals over the course of the week, and continued by the 6th Duke until the 1820s when, largely due to its enormous cost, it was discontinued.

In 1802, William Smith, the geologist and 'drainer' (as he was described on his business card), after draining the 'infamous Prisley Bog', wrote a monograph in 1806 on how the work was carried out called *Observations on the Utility, Form and Management of Water Meadows, and the draining and*

RIGHT George Garrard, *The Sheepshearing, c.*1804, engraving. This wonderful image by George Garrard gives us a glimpse of Park Farm as it was finally built in the late 1790s. The buildings, from the left, include the 'Exhibition' shed with its display of fleeces, the sheepshearing shed (erected 1801), the stable block and piggery along the back, and the conical roofed poultry shed behind the 'Great Barn' on the right. In the crowded large yard in front of these we see the 'Sheepshearing' show in full swing. At the centre of it all, the 6th Duke sits on his horse, while on the right, Sir Joseph Banks sits watching the shearing surrounded by the scientific community, including Sir Humphry Davy standing behind his left shoulder.

LEFT Robert Salmon, *Design for Farm Yard*, 1794. Dated 1794, this plan by Robert Salmon appears to be his first version of the new Park Farm. The image shows the new model farm to be built immediately south of the old Woburn to Froxfield road and of relatively modest size. It consisted of stables, cart shed, barn, threshing barn and stack yard, poultry yard, piggery, and a small abattoir, all spaced around a further series of yards. Beside this were the bailiff's house and garden, extensive workshops, a large timber yard and a weigh bridge at the common entrance to the timber yards, threshing yard, stack yard and kitchen garden beyond. With the creation of the new road from Woburn, however, and a larger site available, Salmon soon produced an expanded version of these plans and a much bigger complex was created.

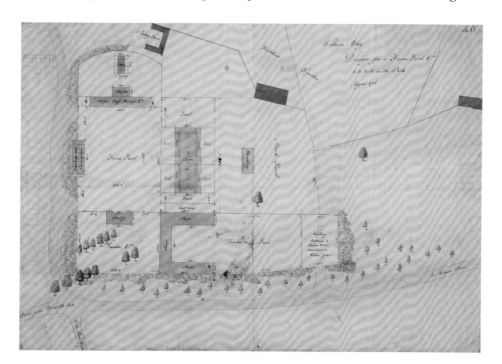

WOBOURN SHEEPSHEARING.

Dedicated by Permission to
His Grace the Duke of Bedford,
By his Grace's most obedient and very humble Servant
GEORGE GARRARD.

RIGHT Park Farm 2015. In this photograph, taken from much the same viewpoint as Garrard's image, the main yard at Park Farm is still largely recognizable today. The stable block with clock and cupola still runs along the back, and although the exhibition room, which stood on the left-hand side, and the 'Great Barn', which stood on the right, have been replaced, the space in the centre is little changed. Most noticeably, the yard is now much more open since the trees shown by Garrard have been removed.

irrigation of peat bogs; with an account of Prisley Bog . . .;[14] in this title Smith alerts us to one of the central concerns of the 5th and 6th Dukes' plans: the creation and management of water meadows by draining boggy ground and installing controlled irrigation, enabling them to bring otherwise marginal land into production. To gain control of this land, the duke obtained a series of enclosure orders between 1795 and 1797 effective in the parishes of Crawley, Ridgemont and Maulden, and he 'procured the insertion of a clause in the Acts of Enclosure . . . by which a liberty was given to make use of the various brooks for the purpose of irrigation, by turning their courses . . . and making due satisfaction to the parties injured'.[15]

Drakeloe Pond was also used as part of this land improvement programme, when the 'Deadlands', which lay between Birchmoor Farm and the Crawley road from Woburn, were transformed by John Farey under the guidance of Smith. Between 1795 and 1801 they converted the pond into the 'Temple Reservoir' with the addition of sluice gates, after 'throwing down the hedges, filling ditches and swamps, levelling inequalities . . . The ridge and furrow parts of the meadow are irrigated by conducting water by the carriers on the crowns of the ridges, and the furrows act as drains to carry it away.' T. Batchelor goes on to tell us that the meadow is 'floated and kept dry alternately', and that since this ground was 'close to the Park . . . it was an object to carry out in the neatest manner'. This last comment suggests that the process by which parts of the park and the estate around it were being transformed was calculated to ensure that the practical made allowances for the aesthetic, and this seems to be confirmed by the locations chosen for further enclosures, this time of heath land for a programme of tree planting.

Heaths such as Wavenden in 1789 and Crawley and Ridgemont in 1795 were converted into extensive plantations of trees, and with much the same dual practical and aesthetic purpose. At Wavenden, the enclosure of Old Wavenden Heath for planting, and the duke's purchase of 300 acres of New Wavenden Heath for the same purpose, created a heavily planted decorative belt of woodland across the rising slopes from Aspley Guise to Bow Brickhall Heath, designed as much as anything to create the perfect backdrop to views across the valley from the Evergreens; much the same was achieved with Crawley Heath where the new woodlands of the Dean Hills and Vale added significantly to the views from the old Serpentine Terrace.

Inevitably, these improvements to the land came at a price. Many local people's lives were changed by the loss of their traditional rights to exploit the resources of what had been common land. Often the compensation offered was perceived as wholly inadequate, and the injured parties were far from satisfied. At Maulden, for example, feelings ran so high about the loss of the common in 1796 that the local militia had to be stationed at Ampthill to control the crowds attempting to prevent the enclosure survey being carried out.[16] Similarly, given the task of encouraging the sometimes reluctant tenant farmers to adopt new methods in 1800, John Farey issued detailed lists of new

Plan of park showing the new water meadows, Wavenden plantations, park outline and perimeter belts.

As the development of the park spread north beyond the Froxfield road, we see the incremental inclusion of the landscape beyond as part of the park experience. Started by the 4th Duke with the creation of the Platoons and the Evergreens, the landscape now comprises three main areas: the original park around the Abbey, the area including the old Warren and Crawley Heath, and the ridge of hills round from Aspley Guise beyond the Crawley road to the north-west. Rather than the Abbey, the Evergreen plantations are now the central focal point of the landscape, and both the water meadows and the Wavendon plantations are created to improve the views from the rides and viewing points of the Evergreens. While the views from the Evergreens become more expansive, the park itself, enlarged by enclosures, actually becomes more insular, with a series of perimeter plantations created around the line of the new and old park walls between 1788 and 1808.

procedures and new schedules for crop rotations. The result, his notes tell us, was on occasion the exchange of 'rough words' between him and some of the farmers who were either resistant to, or simply disagreed with, the new regimes.[17] The traditional relationship between the family, their tenants and the villagers of Woburn was changed forever.

During this period the rural economy was transformed from being based on long-leased smallholdings where tenant farmers, sometimes for generations, made a living by supplementing small-scale production on their piece of land with associated rights to grazing, foraging and fuel gathering on heaths and commons and paid seasonal work for their landlords, to one in which landless labourers' families rented 'estate' cottages, sometimes with small gardens, as part of a wage-based economy. At Woburn Abbey, its park and the land around it had entered the modern era, and building new estate cottages became a particular priority for the 5th Duke's immediate successors.

In actions that seem symptomatic of this new reality, in 1792 Francis commissioned Holland to extend the park wall to include all the land within the Husborne Crawley Enclosure, and set about planting a series of dense screens around the perimeter of the park. Starting at Froxfield Gate in 1792, these ran down to the London entrance, up the west side of the park alongside the turnpike road to the Great Avenue and around the Cowhill Pond. Beyond the Evergreens, these plantations continued up to Crawley Gate, and round the newly enclosed Crawley Heath to Sandy Lane.

PLANTATIONS
1 1788 Kennel Screen Clumps
2 1792 Purrat's Belt
3   Cowhill Pond Belt
4 1793 Stocking Leys
5 1794 Turnpike Belts 1–2
6 1789 Wavendon Old Heath & Wavendon New Heath
7 1796 Grange Plantation
8 1798 Crawley Belt
9   Sand Lane and Sand Pit Belt
10   Crawley Dean Hill & Vale
11 1802 Crawley Ridgemont Belt
12 1806 Ridgmont Stone Pit
13 1808 Hay Wood Screen

Meanwhile, Francis had also turned his attention to the Evergreens, and in the winter of 1801–2 John Farey's men are 'forming rides' and 'Planting Scotch Firs' in the 'new Evergreens'. Plant lists for the 'Evergreens Nursery' indicate that at this time there were, amongst other things, stocks of some 14,000 Scotch firs and 14,400 spruce being grown on.[18] It is not clear exactly where all this work was located, but from the evidence of alterations pencilled on to Browne's 1738 map and Salmon's plans of the plantations, the rides and Scotch firs of the 'New Evergreens' were concentrated on either side of the newly completed road running up the hill to the Star of Roads junction;[19] it is these plantations that we see newly planted in Repton's view of 1805, and through which we drive today. Given the number of plants in the Evergreens nursery it is clear that further plantings were planned, but the duke's sudden death in 1802 meant that further development was left to his brother.

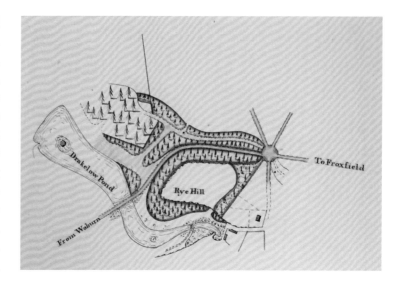

Robert Salmon, *Woburn Plantations in & about the Park in 1808*, no. 12: 'New Evergreens', 1802–5. With the new Woburn to Froxfield road completed, Salmon maps out the next major expansion of the Evergreens to include new plantations surrounding the end of the Old Evergreens and running along the slope above Drakeloe Pond to cross the road.

Also being built at this time was the 'Cold Bath', perhaps the most enigmatic of all Francis's additions to the park. No images of the completed building exist, there is no mention of it in contemporary diaries or memoirs, and what survives of it today tells us tantalizingly little about how it looked, who used it or what it was used for. What does survive is a single wall, an elaborate rustic construction of two arched niches and a central alcove, beside a crystal clear spring-fed pool and overlooking a small pool immediately in front of it, from which two grotesque heads were recovered during a clean out in the 1990s. Clearly, this was once an elaborate structure, and fortunately just enough remains on the ground, on maps of the estate, and in the account books for us to be able to piece together some account of it. There may well have been an earlier, unrecorded version of the bath – the site may have dated back to monastic times since it is mentioned in the 4th Duke's Memorandum Book in 1750 – but the structure we see today was definitely started by the 5th Duke, who died before it was finished, and it does not appear on any map before the early nineteenth century or in the accounts until 1803.

In January of that year they are 'making Cistern for Cold Bath in the Park' (perhaps this was the bath itself), and work continues, presumably on the walls and roof, until by August the 'Marble Floor at Bath' is laid and workmen are 'plastering', 'fitting doors', hanging 'Wind Shutters', and 'making iron rails for the Bath'. After 'fixing a temporary chimney piece, painting and plastering at the Bath' in October, they appear to finish work

Humphry Repton, 'The View near Woburn Gate', Red Book for Woburn, p. 41, 1805.
Arriving in 1804, soon after these New Evergreen plantations were laid out, Repton captures the view looking along the new road to Froxfield. In the foreground are the two Drakeloe ponds with the road running up between the young trees towards the Star of Roads junction. Today, of course, little of this view can been seen as the road runs into the deep woodland, but at least something of how it first looked can be glimpsed as the clearance of rhododendrons reveals once again the slopes of the hill and the rides woven amongst the trees.

in March 1804, when they are 'fixing the chimney in the Bath Dressing Room'.[20] These entries clearly do not account for all the building work, and it would seem that work on the foundations, walls and roof of the building, and on the landscaping outside, all falls into the eight-month gap in accounts which occurs between the duke's death in early March 1802 and the establishment, in late 1802, of a new regime of accounting by Robert Salmon for the 6th Duke. From what evidence there is, however, we can conclude that it was a substantial building with statuary in niches on the outside and at least two rooms inside, one possibly containing the bath itself decorated with statuary, and the other a cosy dressing room, complete with fireplace, where the duke and his guests could warm up after the rigours of immersion in the cold water of the bath.

Thus, by 1802 Francis had initiated a wide programme of improvements – agricultural, architectural and recreational – and amidst all this activity with the building projects at the Abbey and right across the park, he spent a good deal of time at Woburn. He evidently enjoyed both the relative solitude of life at Woburn and the bustle and business of building, and we can get a rare sense of how he saw the developing estate in the following exchange from 1787 with Sir Philip Francis, a close friend of both the 5th and 6th Dukes, who reported in his *Memoirs*:

> I was staying at Woburn without any party being there; and noticed that the park was full of strollers from the neighbourhood, and they even came close to the windows. I said to his Grace, 'I wonder that you, who love retirement, do not shut up your grounds . . . It is never private . . .' The Duke's answer was '. . . I consider myself a steward to do the best I can with the money placed in my hands . . . and [a rich man] should use it to promote as much general good as possible . . . If I were to shut up this place, many people who enjoy it as much as I do would be shut out of much innocent enjoyment and healthy amusement.[21]

This sentiment did not prevent the duke from extending the park wall by an additional three miles in 1797, but it seems to have been largely sincere, and this sense of the park being open to all is reflected in Lord Torrington's

THE COLD BATH

Surviving evidence allows us to build up at least a partial image of this structure.

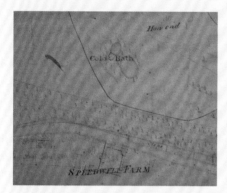

Cold Bath and its two pools, detail of untitled and undated estate map (after 1802).
Located in this tucked away corner of the park close to the London road, we see the otherwise unrecorded ground plan of the bath. The building stands on the edge of the lower, smaller pond, with what may be a cascade or perhaps the bath itself projecting out into the water, and perhaps the smaller room at the back was the dressing room with fireplace. At the bottom of the picture, just across the road, stands Speedwell Farm, built by Salmon at the same time as Park Farm, and the original house can still be seen beside the road.

Estate map of 1867, detail showing 'The Bath'.
Our last view of the Cold Bath. Although it may already have been largely ruinous, the bath was clearly still standing when this map was produced in 1867, but after this it vanishes from the record. There is some evidence that the surviving wall was retained as an interesting picturesque ruin in the nineteenth century, but after that it seems to have been forgotten and is remembered only in the name of the 'Cold Bath Pond' and a nearby plantation known as the Cold Bath Clump, marked 24 in this image.

The Cold Bath, 2015.
When the pond in front was cleaned out in the 1990s two 'grotesque' heads were recovered, but an accretion of soil and fallen masonry masks the original relationship between the bath and the pond. A lead pipe visible in the back wall of the central arch suggests that water once flowed out of – or out from under – the building down into the pond below, but how this was configured is now lost.

Washing the recovered 'grotesques'; and one of the two heads now displayed in the Shell Grotto in the Abbey Gardens.

Chambers's bridge by Barratt, detail of 'River God' decoration.
Covered in mud and lost perhaps for a hundred years, these two heads were recovered from the Cold Bath Pond. Cleaned off they are identifiable as 'River Gods' and would seem to bear a striking resemblance to the River God plaque just visible on the central arch of Chambers's bridge (and there was another on the other side), which was rebuilt by Repton in 1807–8. This may suggest that 'picturesque' details were added to the ruin at a later date, along with some decorative trees, to make it even more interesting.

comments following a visit in 1789. After walking across the park from the inn to see the new kennels – 'established in pompous stile – the huntsman has a charming house' – they walk to the front of the house, where 'We took our seat, on a bench on the hill . . . It is a grand place, with finely surrounding woods . . . there are more deer upon such a space as I ever saw before . . . who came around us in a most quiet manner . . . We were so pleased with our evening . . . that we stayed out till 9 o'clock; for the park, close to the town, was alive with walkers, mushroom pickers, and the quality of the place.'[22] Clearly, on a summer's evening, when the day's building was over and the workmen had all left, a peace descended on the park that no doubt reminded Francis of what had been important to him in his youth, of the time he had spent there with his brothers under the amused and watchful eye of their grandmother. He felt it only right to share this place of 'innocent enjoyment and healthy amusement' in a way that was, perhaps, not to be repeated for another 160 years, when the house and grounds were opened to modern visitors.

Sir Gilbert Eliot, however, suggests that, while the duke may 'love retirement', there was another person who may have enjoyed this 'grand place' on a summer's evening. In a letter to a friend about his visit to Woburn in 1789, he writes: 'The Duke is altering and enlarging it at great expense, although nobody ever inhabits it but Mrs Hill, an old Madame.' In addition to Lady Maynard, whom we have already met, the duke seems to have had relationships with a number of women: a Mrs Palmer of Curzon Street, the mother of his two children 'Francis and Georgiana', for whose care he left her 'a generous sum' in his will, in which he also 'disclosed responsibility for three other women living in Marylebone'.[23] Mrs Hill, however, seems to have been the only one who lived at Woburn, and it is possible that amusements such as the Chinese dairy were initially built for her entertainment.

Since his circumstances meant that he could not marry any of these 'Mrs', the duke had to look elsewhere for a wife, and in so doing attracted the attention of the notorious Jane Maxwell, Duchess of Gordon, who was looking for a suitable duke to marry her youngest daughter, Georgina. The Gordon 'tribe' was held in fascinated horror by polite London society, which recoiled from the wild stories of untamed children running amuck in the Highlands at Gordon Castle, and the equally scandalous tales of the free-spirited duchess, hostess of raucous Scottish-themed parties that featured dancing and Highland dress, the wearing of which was still officially proscribed by the government following the 1745 Jacobite rebellion. The degree of surprise and consternation the news of this possible marriage caused amongst his close friends is illustrated by the reaction of Georgiana, Duchess of Devonshire, who, in spite of thinking '*her* very pretty, very bewitching, and clever certainly', was still most alarmed since 'there have been stories enough to make one tremble . . . The very *amabilité* that some times arises from the grotesque originality of Scotch people is in a line very different from what one should have thought [suitable] for the Mistress of Woburn.' She concludes gloomily, 'We are all undone . . . No possible event could have so thoroughly overthrown our society as this.'[24]

But things progressed no further since, in February 1802, 'while playing tennis in the great court at Woburn he received an injury from a fast-flying ball,'[25] and after two unsuccessful operations Francis died a month later from a strangulated hernia. It remains unclear what his real intentions were to Georgina Gordon, or indeed whether they even became engaged, but, as we will see, his final gesture in requesting his brother John to ensure that a lock of his hair be sent to her had far-reaching consequences for both his brother and the story of Woburn in the succeeding years.

News of his brother's accident reached Lord John on a visit to Longleat following the death of his first wife, Georgiana Byng, in 1801, and he immediately returned to Woburn where he was able to spend the last few weeks with Francis. Finally, after giving John instructions 'relating to his servants and some of his private affairs . . . [he] ordered a simple burial and then expired in my arms.'[26] For a while after the funeral, the new Duke of Bedford seems to have concentrated on fulfilling his brother's last wishes, and no doubt this was the moment when instructions were given for all the personal papers to be destroyed, but he also took it on himself to travel down to London and deliver the lock of hair to Lady Georgina personally. Exactly what happened when they met is unrecorded, but it would seem that a shared grief brought the two together, with the result that they were married the next year. What is also unrecorded is the reaction of the Duchess of Devonshire and her circle to this news – although perhaps we can guess – but it is clear that this marriage introduced a considerable amount of 'amabilité' and 'the originality of Scotch people' to Woburn which led not only to rowdy house parties, but also to new sensibilities soon to be reflected in developments both there and on the wider estates.

Whatever the disapproval of London society, Georgina, who was 22 when she married the 36-year-old duke, had led both an unconventional and a very interesting life steeped in the culture and landscapes of the Scottish Highlands, a background suggested perhaps by the full-length portrait by John Hoppner hanging at the Abbey. This shows an immaculately dressed young woman out walking not along the terrace or neat gravel paths of the pleasure grounds as we might expect, but rather along a rough path through wild woodland, looking completely at home and unperturbed. Growing up at Gordon Castle, where her mother would host tremendous house parties with up to 200 people staying sometimes for three or four weeks, the children also spent many summers on long excursions with their mother ranging through the Gordon estates along the length of Strath Spey. In addition, from 1799 onwards she had spent the summers living with her mother in a small farmhouse at Kinrara, overlooking the Spey near Aviemore, where they were joined by a succession of guests who were expected to join in their

Sir William Beechey, *John Russell, 6th Duke of Bedford* (1766–1839), *c*.1786. John Russell shortly before he married his first wife, Georgiana Byng. As the second son, John Russell was not expecting to become duke and at this time was pursuing his interests at Oakley House and Stratton Park.

John Hoppner, *Georgina Gordon, Duchess of Bedford* (1781–1853), 1802.
A girl from the Scottish Highlands whose arrival at Woburn caused both alarm and consternation amongst those who knew the Russell family. Woburn Abbey, and in particular the Devon estate, were never to be the same again as the new duchess brought the influence of her eventful Scottish upbringing to bear on the previously sedate world of the Russells.

rustic lifestyle. Activities included excursions to nearby Glen Feshie and up into the Cairngorms beyond, before returning for traditional evenings of music and dancing. But for Jane Maxwell and her circle, which included such figures as Robert Burns and a young Walter Scott, this was not simply dressing up and playing at Highland life. For her, and subsequently for Georgina, this was a deeply felt rediscovery and celebration of who they were, of their Highland and Scottish identity, after the disasters of the Jacobite era and the proscriptions on Scottish culture that followed, and the picturesque landscapes of Strath Spey and Glen Feshie were central to this identity.

On her marriage, Georgina brought all of this to Woburn, where her high spirits and gregariousness, her sensitivity to landscape, tradition and the natural world seem to have both energized the duke and complemented his own interests and tastes. The couple went on to have ten children, once again filling the Abbey with the bustle of family life, and while her relationship with the duke's elder children by his first wife – Francis, now Marquis of Tavistock, and his brothers – steadily deteriorated and led to lasting animosity, her warmth and enthusiasm seem to have captivated most who met her. Typical of people's reaction is that of Dr Allen Thomson, who wrote in 1837, 'She . . . is a most astonishing woman, extremely clever, with information on all subjects, a great mimic and always ready for a joke. She is scrupulously attentive to the most minute arrangement of house affairs, kind and affable to everyone, but rigidly tenacious of dignity and rank.'[27]

In the short term, however, the new duke seems to have been closely focused on completing the programmes of improvement begun by his brother, and this is reflected in the letter he wrote to Arthur Young in March 1802. In it he says he is writing

on a subject, deeply interesting to me, because it occupied the last thoughts of my much lamented brother – his zeal for that first and most interesting pursuits, agriculture, did not forsake him even in the last moments of his Life, and on his death bed with an earnestness expressive of his character . . . he strongly urged me to follow up those plans for national improvement he had begun . . . He referred me to Mr Cartwright and to you for explanation and details . . . desirous as I am . . . to fulfil the best wishes of my brother [but] without the aid and advice of those most capable of assisting me I should utterly despair of attaining the objects so near to my heart.[28]

And so it was that in 1802 the Sheepshearing was held during the summer as usual, and – working with Young, Salmon, Cartwright and the other people his brother had assembled – the agricultural buildings and new cottages under way were completed and the new roads and lodges at the Woburn and London entrances were finished, as were the new greenhouse (Camellia House) and the Cold Bath out in the park. In the Evergreens, the new rides and plantings that became known as the 'New Evergreens' were finished and a complete survey of the plantations carried out by Salmon. Yet, while the new duke shared with his brother both an upbringing in the park and a vision for the future of Woburn, it soon became clear that different sensibilities were at work: new priorities and subtle differences in emphasis, reflecting the characters, tastes and outlook of John and Georgina.

In 1781, after leaving Westminster school at 15, Lord John had attended university in Göttingen, before travelling on to Brussels where he met Georgiana Byng, daughter of the British Minister to Brussels, George Byng, 4th Viscount Torrington. They married in 1786, and lived at Stratton Park, the last members of the family to do so, before moving to Oakley House, near Bedford, where their three boys were raised. It was while living at Oakley that John became acquainted with Dr Charles Abbot, the vicar of Oakley Raines, a man whose 'botanical enthusiasm used to afford me both instruction and amusement', and who sparked a lifelong passion which was to have a dramatic effect on the look and contents of the gardens at Woburn.[29]

As duke, John quickly emerged as a very different man from his brother; while clearly committed to completing his brother's plans, he was content to leave the practical work to the experts already in place, turning his own energies to pursue a growing interest in botany. He was more sensitive not only to natural history and the natural world, but also to history itself and, like Georgina, to 'dignity and rank', having what has been described by John Martin Robinson as a 'more romantically feudal view of his position than his brother'.[30] With the arrival of the 6th Duke and Duchess Georgina, the Abbey and its landscapes entered a more romantic, sentimental and family orientated phase. One senses that he had never forgotten those childhood adventures in the Parson's Wood temple and, alongside the botany, we see a more decorative and fanciful aesthetic at work. It is also noticeable that as early as 1803 the 6th Duke authorized his agent William Adam to reverse the 'ruinous condition' of the old family home at Berwick, the building having fallen into disrepair in the years since his grandfather visited the tenant farmers there in 1751.

In terms of architecture, Robinson sums up the differences between the brothers and their implications:

> The estate buildings at Woburn are of exceptional interest in that they demonstrate two phases in the design of rural buildings . . . [those of the 5th Duke] are austere Neo-classical structures which reflect the mania for new materials and techniques and are evocative

TOP RIGHT Francis Nicholson, *Another View of the Pantheon Cottage, Stourhead, c.*1813, watercolour. Nicholson's picture captures the effect that a new interest in the picturesque was to have on gardens that had been dominated by classical and rococo design. Combining the romance of Gothic historicism with an emphasis on the natural world, a sense of a simpler life as it is lived beyond the rarefied worlds of art and culture, the 'picturesque' developed from being a new way to look at and record the natural world to one which could provide a sense of participation in that world.

BOTTOM RIGHT 'Gothic Cottage', Stourhead, 2015. The restoration of the Stourhead cottage is indicative of the continuing relevance of this kind of building to modern visitors and their fondness for it, and of the value that is still placed on the picturesque aesthetic.

of the utilitarian philosophy of the late 18th century . . . while those of the 6th Duke by contrast reflect the full flood of picturesque enthusiasm and romantic historicism. His old-world cottages, with their tree trunk verandas and Jacobean gables . . . point the way to the designs of Loudon's *Encyclopedia* and associated visual values of the mid 19th century.

Representing a style and a sense of aesthetics shared by both the duke and Georgina, this 'picturesque enthusiasm' became central to the new look of the park and gardens at Woburn. We can understand its appeal to Georgina given her upbringing in the Highlands, but it was clearly also something the duke was drawn to. During his stay at Longleat in 1802, he may well have met Jeffry Wyatt (later Wyatville), who during that year 'had designed a country cottage adjoining the Pleasure Ground on the west side of the house at Longleat'.[31] In addition to this, while at Longleat one of the places he visited with Lord Bath was Stourhead, 'to see Mr Richard Colt Hoare's fine and valuable collection of Pictures',[32] but he also accompanied 'Mr Davis' on a tour of the water meadows, as he had done at all his previous stops. These were located in the valley below the pond dam, and so they must also have walked through the gardens round the pond to get there. Colt Hoare, like Lord John, was an avid plantsman who had 'naturalized the plantings round the house' after inheriting the estate in 1783, and by 1802 he had been altering the feel of the gardens by removing a number of his grandfather's more fanciful structures. The 'Turkish Tent', the 'Chinese Alcove', the 'Venetian Seat' and so on were all demolished as he turned instead to 'the picturesque quality of the Gothic Cottage, which became a feature', adding a seat and a Gothic porch and 'turning the walk to it' in 1806.[33] This last comment is interesting in that it tells us that Colt Hoare's intention was to include his little cottage in the main circuit of the gardens, adding the picturesque experience to the classical theme. And as part of this move to the picturesque, to create suitably secluded glades and shady, mysterious walks he had also introduced the dense and prolific *Rhododendron ponticum* to Stourhead, a plant which was to figure heavily in the 6th Duke's development of the Evergreens at Woburn in the years to come.

Given this background, it is perhaps not surprising that one of the first structures to emerge at Woburn after 1802 that was not directly associated with the farm and agriculture was the 'Round House', created *c.*1805 when the duke and duchess converted 'the former base of a mock windmill' into a picturesque cottage.[34] This strange little building still stands today beside the road just beyond Froxfield Gate, and although it is not clear why it was created, it nevertheless set the theme for much of what was to come. It

Central London: the site of Bedford House, Bloomsbury, after 1800.

❸ Covent Garden
❺ Bloomsbury Square
❼ Bedford Square
❽ Russell Square (formerly Bedford House and gardens), laid out 1801

Modern Street layout

Humphry Repton, frontispiece, Red Book for Woburn, 1805.
In Repton's frontispiece the chaos of an unkempt natural world is pushed back out of sight behind the grandeur of the carefully crafted 'structure' of the landscape setting that he is proposing to create. Although Repton always referred to his ideas as mere 'hints', deferring in this case to the taste and eye of the duke and duchess, he nevertheless places his business card prominently in the centre of the image and surrounds it with the tools of gardener, surveyor and artist, all the special skills he will bring to the project.

will certainly have been of interest to Humphry Repton when he arrived at much the same time to work on his Red Book of designs for Woburn. Repton had, in fact, already worked for the 5th Duke in 1801, when he was commissioned to design Russell Square as the centrepiece for the development of Bedford House, Bloomsbury, where the old house and gardens were demolished and replaced by new streets and houses. Had the duke not died, it is quite possible he would have moved on to work at Woburn. As it turned out, it was not until 1804 that the 6th Duke called on Repton to help complete the development of the wider landscape of park and gardens, now that Henry Holland's new buildings at Woburn had been completed. As reported by Repton in the Red Book, the duke's brief to him stated, 'Much has been done here, but much remains to be done, and something I think to *undo*. I am not partial to destroying works recently executed, but some cases will occur . . . Freely give me your opinion as to what alterations or improvements suggest themselves to your judgement, leaving the executing of them to my own discretion or leisure.'[35]

It seems clear from this that the duke was not entirely convinced by the landscaping carried out by Henry Holland and was looking for fresh ideas from Repton, but with the understanding that he was not necessarily going to use all the ideas or require Repton to implement them; these vague terms were partly responsible for a number of problems that arose as the work was carried out. From its very first page, however, Repton's ambitions in the Red Book for Woburn are clear, the frontispiece being a striking example of the extra time and effort he took with this commission. Working at home, in this case over the winter months of 1804–5, writing out pages in meticulous handwriting, explaining the proposals and the thinking behind them, adding theoretical digressions on taste, beauty and aesthetics, creating maps and plans, painting images of the landscape, cutting out the paper flaps (or 'slides' as he called them) to create the 'before' and 'after' views, and carefully designing each of the pages to create a beautiful book: as if all this was not enough work, Repton also took the time to create elaborate pages such as the frontispiece, not so much to explain ideas but to set the right tone for the book.

From the great success of his early years of practice between 1788 and 1793, when he was averaging about eighteen commissions per year, Repton's career had steadily declined to averaging four or five between 1794 and 1804,

PLAN OF THE MAIN PROPOSALS IN REPTON'S RED BOOK FOR WOBURN

Looking at Repton's proposals, what stand out initially are the red lines indicating his alterations to the approach roads. On the left, Park Street, which he thought should be enhanced either by terraces of new houses or by avenues of trees, runs out of Woburn village to a new lodge. At this point the road splits; to the left an existing road runs between Drakeloe Pond, renamed Lower Drakeloe, and Repton's new pond, which became known as Upper Drakeloe, and on to Froxfield, while to the right a new road cuts down below Upper Drakeloe to cross the pond before curving up to the Abbey. From the bottom of the plan, the road runs into the park through Holland's London entrance before leaving Holland's route (shown in dotted line) and curving left to cross Chambers's bridge and turn up to the Abbey. In front of the Abbey, these two roads form a graceful and symmetrical layout, emphasizing the position of the building. To the north Repton shows the existing route out to the Serpentine Terrace to exit the park at Ridgemont, and at the top end of the terrace Repton has shown a new side road running left to his design for 'The Thornery'.

Taking a closer look, we see that Repton has included a considerable amount of detail. On the south side of the Abbey he felt that Holland's raising of the ground level was a 'mistake' and had compromised the view from the 'summer apartments'. His sense was that by creating a 'level plane' Holland had 'presented space without grandeur and extent without beauty',[37] and his solution was to re-excavate some of the soil, breaking the level plane and allowing him to place a fence in the valley created. This in turn would allow the deer and cattle in the park to come much closer to the house, animating the scene.

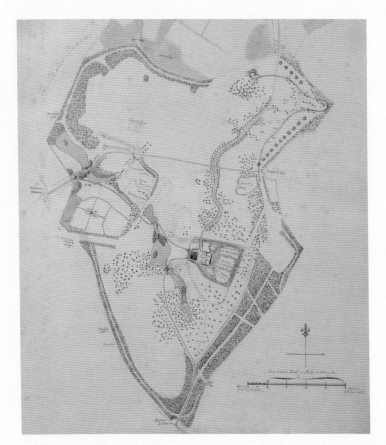

The soil excavated from this area could then be used for two further projects: first, to break up the banks of the Bason Pond with additional islands and promontories, and, second, to bulk up the slopes on either side of his curving approach roads, creating a more balanced landscape. All of these projects went ahead.

To carry his new approach roads over the ponds he proposed two 'Viaducts' (dams constructed to look like bridges), structures which would allow him to bridge the water, but also to raise the water level up stream. By doing this, he hoped to create a much more visible water course running down across the front of the Abbey through a series of ponds and streams. In the event, only the southern route was changed and Chambers's bridge, which was in need of repair, was replaced with the existing viaduct.

Humphry Repton, 'Plan of Proposals', Red Book for Woburn, Plate II, 1805.
Repton's carefully detailed plan of his proposals emphasizes once again the care he took with this book.

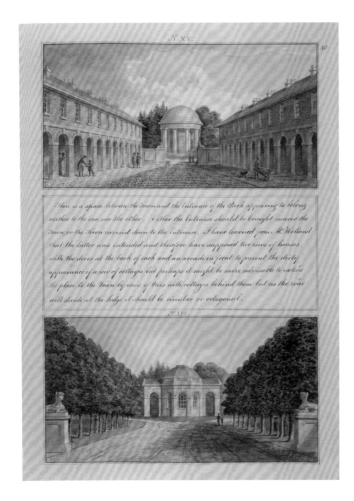

ABOVE Humphry Repton, 'Proposal for Park Street as
Entrance to the Park', Red Book for Woburn, Plate XV, 1805.
Another of the beautifully designed pages of the Red Book,
this time offering alternative suggestions for an enhanced
treatment of Park Street as it runs up to the park entrance.
He felt strongly that visitors should have a sense of arriving
somewhere important.

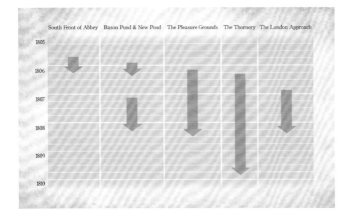

until he had just one in 1805: that at Woburn
Abbey.[36] Coming at this crucial time, Repton
threw all his energies into this commission,
and the book was designed to impress from
the start.

In Repton's eyes, and expressed implicitly
in the appearance of the frontispiece, the main
aim of all these proposals was to enhance the
'grandeur' of Woburn: to alert visitors at the
entrances, and by the approach roads to the
Abbey, to the importance of the place and
its inhabitants, to improve the setting of the
house when seen from both inside and outside
the building, to emphasize a sense of 'dignity
and rank', and to place the house and family
at the heart of the surrounding landscape. In
addition to this, Repton also caught the mood
of the times, seeking, as Paul Smith has put it,
to 'enhance the beauty of the house, make the
parkland and gardens attractive, amusing and
enlightening for the Duke, his family and his
visitors and to provide facilities which would
enable him to develop his interest in botany
and horticulture'.[38] All this meant that Repton
was trying to meet a lot of requirements with
these designs, some to meet specific briefs
from the duke and duchess, and some in the
form of 'hints' that he felt he should offer in his
role as a professional improver.

Work on Repton's proposals began in the
late summer of 1805, and reading through the
Abbey accounts for this time, we are able to see
exactly which of the ideas and hints the duke
decided to 'execute'. Looking at the timetable,
we see that the proposals adopted concerned
altering the ground at the south front by
digging out the shallow 'valley' into which

LEFT Timetable of work on Repton's Red Book proposals.
As Repton reports in his introduction, the duke
commissioned him on the understanding that the duke was
free to accept or reject the suggested changes. The result
was that only a small proportion of the 'alterations' were
adopted. This timetable outlines the main projects that
were undertaken.

TOP LEFT Humphry Repton, 'View to the West' (before), Red Book for Woburn, Plate VI, 1805.
Repton felt that this important view from the west front of the Abbey lacked interest, needing both more cohesion and variety. Of the Bason itself he wrote, 'A circular pool will always appear stagnant . . . but if the margin is enlivened by trees, and its line broken by creeks and bays and islands, the imagination will give motion to the flood and produce apparent intricacy.' He also felt the straight drive lacked interest, and he disapproved of the fact that the bridge was visible from the house.

BOTTOM LEFT Humphry Repton, 'View to the West' (after), Red Book for Woburn, Plate VIb, 1805.
Repton's solution was to break up the shorelines, raise the hill on the left to hide the bridge and produce a lovely symmetrical sweep of drives up to the front door. In his *Hortus Woburnensis* of 1833 James Forbes commented on Repton's work; in his view the form and size of the Bason Pond were 'much improved by Mr Repton in order to render it more picturesque'. Keenly aware of the potential influence Georgina had on whether or not the proposals were adopted, Repton also took care to introduce her into the image to engage her attention. The plan was only partially successful.

RIGHT J. C. Bourne, *The Thornery*, 1842.
This summer house was designed as a destination for the family. Here they could visit on summer afternoons and take tea while enjoying the views down from the ridge and beyond. We see the Thornery, which still stands amongst the trees above the lion enclosure of the Safari Park, some twenty-five years after it was built, time enough for the woodland and gardens to grow up and create a setting much as Repton must have imagined.

the fence could be dropped, carrying the earth dug out to build up the hills where the Bowling Green had been and reshaping the featureless bank of the Bason Pond, rebuilding Chambers's bridge as a viaduct and creating the 'New Pond' upstream.

As work on the south front was reaching a conclusion in early 1806, labourers were moved to the pleasure grounds to begin work on reshaping the ground for the great terrace, laying gravel paths and installing a new iron fence around the perimeter; work also began in the spring of 1806 on building on the highly ornamental summer house called the Thornery.[39] Once the cottage itself was completed, planting the collection of thorn trees around it began in 1808 and continued until the next year.

Although it was only a few years old, the duke clearly agreed with Repton that Holland's road past the south front needed 'undoing' and the new route was taken from the London entrance to the west front, over the new version of Chambers's bridge. The effect of this new crossing and the raising of the hills was reported by Stephen Dodd in his guide to Woburn of 1818: 'There was formerly a great deficiency of water but this has been recently remedied by the formation of several ponds, and the enlargement of more ancient ones. Over one of these, called the Bason . . . a bridge has been lately erected in place of another which has been taken down. A winding road leads over it by the side of a newly planted eminence, which conceals the view, till a sudden turn gratifies the eye with an immediate sight of the Abbey': exactly the effect Repton had been looking for.

With the exception of the Thornery, located out of sight of the Abbey, all these projects – the alteration of ground level at the south front, the new roads, the viaduct, and the Bason and New Ponds – were part of Repton's plan to enhance the grandeur of the Abbey and its parkland. As Repton states in the Red Book, the 'Object of Landscaping' was 'the art of displaying the beauties of a Place, and artfully concealing its defects without discovering the artificial means involved'. At Woburn these defects were largely to do with the low position of the Abbey in relation to the ground around it, and he saw his role as organizing the landscape to make the most of the house and its defective site, bringing, amongst other things, 'Symmetry, Order, Continuity and Grandeur' to it. Judging from his Park Street proposal, he clearly felt that the neoclassical aesthetic of the 5th Duke's era was still the most potent way of adding these qualities, but in other places he was also looking for 'Intricacy . . . Variety, Novelty . . . [and] Contrast', and for this he turned to the picturesque.

In the first case, grandeur was to result from an increased sense of continuity and order in the layout and land forms beside the main approaches to the Abbey from the London entrance and Woburn, the increased symmetry of the ground and roads below the west front alerting visitors to the special nature of the house. Largely approving of Holland's

The viaduct, 2015. Repton's viaduct today seen beside the hill he raised to screen it from the Abbey. One aspect of the new design stemmed from the fact that he wanted to lower the profile of the bridge itself: 'We often observe bridges raised so high as to make passage over them difficult, when there is no passage under them required, and this is the case with the present bridge at Woburn.' He also wanted to raise the water level upstream by means of a dam. Of the result he writes, 'There being at present no architectural form adapted to this purpose, I have ventured to suggest a hint for such structures as may support a road and raise the level of the water, rather calling it a Viaduct than a bridge.'

PROPOSALS FOR THE PLEASURE GROUNDS IN THE RED BOOK FOR WOBURN ABBEY

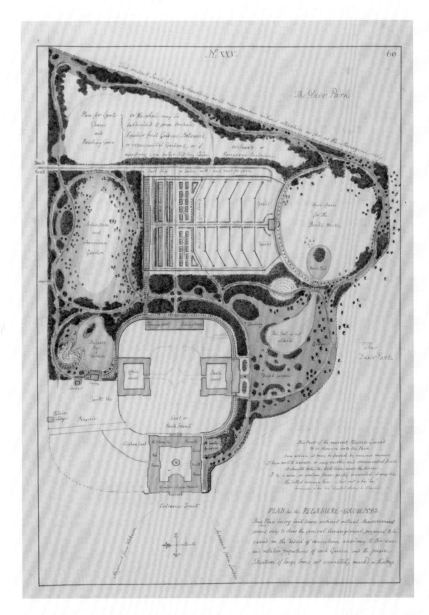

Humphry Repton, 'Plan of Proposals for the Pleasure Grounds', Red Book for Woburn, Plate XXV, 1805.
Plan showing Repton's 'hints' for developing the pleasure grounds. Designed to add an element of fantasy to the family's experience of their gardens, the plan expresses the decorative side of Repton's work, especially in the circular Menagerie on the right.

Towards the bottom of this plan we see the layout of the Abbey itself, its stable blocks and the building containing the tennis court and riding house as completed by Holland, while the pleasure grounds behind are dominated by Repton's central idea: a complex of buildings consisting of, from the left, heated greenhouses flanking a large conservatory, two hot houses (and hot walls in front) overlooking melon beds, a winter garden, and then a series of vegetable gardens laid out to the south. In addition, the new conservatory was to be linked by an extension to Holland's covered walkway, with further paths leading to the greenhouses and vegetable beds. This complex was thus designed to be used by the whole family, the covered walkway making the conservatory and hot houses accessible in all seasons and in all weathers, the former a place for the family to gather and for the display of the duke's rare and exotic plants, the latter both for the growing of these plants and for the duchess to select cut flowers for the Abbey.

Beyond this, gravel paths led to Repton's more fanciful and picturesque attractions, the decoration of the pond in front of the Chinese dairy, the creation of a 'Dressed Garden', and the development of the Menagerie. Beyond these, gravel paths would wind through an 'Arboretum and American Garden', a 'Place of Sports, and Bowling Green', and an area of orchards. Something, in fact, for all the family.

design for the new London entrance, Repton sought to create a similar effect at the Woburn end with his circular or octagonal designs for the lodge. Yet, while the duke saw the need to re-route Holland's approach, not being 'partial to destroying works recently executed' (Salmon's road was only about ten years old), he drew the line at creating an entirely new approach from Woburn, and so the grand scheme never happened. Today in front of the Abbey the road still runs straight down to the Bason Pond, unchanged since the 5th Earl's initial avenue of trees.

In the second case, picking up on suggestions from the duke and duchess, to whom he 'pays tribute to [her] good taste in her amendments to his initial schemes',[40] Repton turned to the picturesque to enhance not just the view west over the Bason Pond, but also the 'amusing' and entertaining qualities of the family's experience of the more private areas of the park and pleasure grounds. Although Repton's experience with the picturesque had not been entirely comfortable,[41] working at places like Blaise Castle from 1795 onwards, he had developed his vision of landscapes enhanced by the addition of small idealized rustic structures, such as cottages, dairies, root houses, water-mills, decorative gates, fences and gatehouses, embracing what he saw as the potential of a sense of romantic fantasy to enliven and animate a view and engage the viewer. As Nigel Temple tells us, this vision was recorded by one commentator who wrote of Repton's work at Blaise: 'The capricious taste of that sweeping improver, Mr Repton, has made this naturally beautiful place still more whimsically fantastical than it originally was.'[42] These elements of fantasy and whimsy make up one of the most detailed sections of the Red Book – Repton's proposals for the pleasure grounds – and represent, perhaps, his most original contribution to the look of the gardens at Woburn.

In the case of the Chinese dairy, Repton thought that the pond should enhance and develop the decorative Chinese theme, and because 'Most pictures of Chinese scenery consist of islands and bridges and small irregular inlets of water,' he suggested cutting an island on the far bank and 'raising the soil in a heap over a cave or boat-house; to the top of which may be removed the Chinese building from the Drakeloe Pond'. It would appear that the image illustrating this suggestion in Plate XXX actually shows a new, far more decorative Chinese-type structure rather than the existing one from Drakeloe Pond, since the building shown on the rockery bears no relation to that visible on the island in his panorama of the view of the Evergreens (see page 104), the latter being a different shape and apparently lacking any of the colour or decoration visible on the former. In addition, the structure shown here does not appear to have the eight columns described in the original accounts.

On the other side of the gardens, Repton wanted to develop the area in front of Holland's conservatory as a place for the duke to display his

TOP RIGHT Humphry Repton, 'Chinese Dairy Pond' (after), Red Book for Woburn, Plate XXX, 1805.
It would seem that the shape of the pond in front of the Chinese dairy was another aspect of Holland's landscaping work of which Repton did not approve. This proposal for improving the view across the pond from the Chinese dairy was not one of the hints that the duke took at this time. It would seem, however, that notice was taken of elements of the design, since the stone grotto, or 'cave' as Repton called it, is strikingly similar to the one Wyatville was to create further east in the gardens some twenty years later.

BOTTOM RIGHT Humphry Repton, 'The Dressed Garden', Red Book for Woburn, Plate XXVII, 1805.
For the formal garden that lay in front of Holland's conservatory, Repton returned to the style he had used successfully for the duke when they worked together on the garden at Oakley House a few years earlier. Here masses of flowers were formed in beds dotted across the area in front of the house and trimmed around with basketwork. In the 'Dressed Garden' Repton expanded this idea to include the pond beyond, at the end of which a Doric arch complemented the architecture of the conservatory. The garden never seems to have been developed in quite this way, although the great urn on its pedestal was still there in the late nineteenth century when Lady Ermyntrude Russell paused to lean against it long enough to have her photograph taken (see page 185).

collection of hardy rare plants, and use them to create a decorative garden which included the pond and the view up towards the Menagerie. On the plan, we see this area encircled by a looping gravel path and broken up with randomly sized and spaced flower beds, with a shrubbery spread across the grass and framing the pond itself, and two beds flanking the doorway from the building. It is only when we look at the accompanying plate, however, that we realize just how fanciful the 'dressing' was to be.

In this picture, the duke and duchess and one of the children are strolling down the path alongside the conservatory as the duke points out one of his plants, while other family or friends make their way along the gravel path above the pond towards the Menagerie, and Repton also includes two chairs to suggest this would be a garden to sit in, spend time and enjoy the views. In the background at the head of the pond, Repton is proposing to add a decorative bridge complete with an ornate Doric 'door' opening into the Menagerie behind, an area hidden from the garden by a screen of trees. His idea, as he explains, is to entertain the family by creating a little variety and surprise: 'The door in this design for the termination of the dressed ground may open into a covered seat of a very different character . . . this being formed of fir trees and cones of various kinds will make an unexpected contrast between the chaste style of the Athenian Doric and the fanciful decorations of the menagerie: and being placed at the back of each

Humphry Repton, 'The Menagerie', Red Book for Woburn, Plate XXXIII, 1805.
'The fanciful decorations of the Menagerie . . .': with the completion of work on the Menagerie in early 1810, we see perhaps Repton's key contribution to the pleasure gardens at Woburn. Although the structures do not seem to have survived into the 1880s, it was nevertheless a most imaginative piece of work, the creation of an 'unexpected' world. Note the 'rustic' fencing, the Pine Cone pavilion on the left, and the wire cages running round to the Aviary. With some of the buildings now restored, it is planned to reintroduce birds to the area.

J.C. Bourne, *The Aviary*,
1842.
The magical sunlit spaces
of Repton's Menagerie
were captured for us by
J.C. Bourne when he
painted this view of the
Aviary and the keepers'
cottages in 1842. Bourne's
caption confirms the
facts – 'The Aviary is from
a design by Repton, as
it appears in his plans,
which were prepared in
the year of 1804–5, and
completed in the year
1809' – but the picture
itself conveys something of
the atmosphere of Repton's
picturesque world.

other they can never be seen together.' This 'covered seat of a very different character' became known as the Pine Cone Pavilion.

There appears to have been a menagerie of some sort at the Abbey since at least 1744, and although there may have been interesting and different animals at Woburn for a long time, the first mention we have of an organized menagerie comes with the 1738 estate map, where it is shown to be located to one side of the stables (see page 96). At this time the collection most likely featured various bird species and, perhaps, some farm animals, and in 1744 we have specific reference to the 'pales across the pond in the menagerie',[43] suggesting, perhaps, that the pond shown on the maps was divided by a fence into different enclosures. The 4th Duke's son Francis, Marquis of Tavistock was born in 1739, and the menagerie may well have been organized as a place of interest for him; certainly, by 1752, when he was 13, he had his own canary aviary there. In 1750, as part of the 4th Duke's development of the pleasure gardens into what had been the old Rookery, a new menagerie was established in the location shown by Repton, but apart from some pheasant pens, just what this consisted of is unclear and unrecorded.

In the end it was to Repton that the job of creating a setting for the Menagerie fell, and his designs for it, as seen in Plate XXXIII, represent one of his best sustained essays in picturesque decoration. This was not simply an isolated cottage or lodge, but a complete world in itself, a collection of buildings set amongst trees and shrubs and enclosed by rustic fencing, which swept up those who stepped through his Doric doorway and transported them from the everyday order of the 'Dressed Garden' into an 'unexpected' fantastical and romantic world of exotic architecture, brought alive by the sounds and dazzling plumages of the birds within. The Menagerie was created in 1808–10, and the account books provide a vivid picture of the degree of detail that went into creating this special place. The 'Plan of the Pleasure Grounds' shows the basic layout, the semicircular Pine Cone Pavilion and the Duck Pond, with a gravel path leading round past the front of the wire pens to the Aviary and on round to a gate in the fence, which in turn carries on round to enclose the 'Open space for the Birds'. James Forbes's text in *Hortus Woburnensis* (1833) makes it clear that the Doric door on the bridge was the 'outer entrance' through which visitors were expected to enter the compound, and then follow the curving path past the wired compartments to the Aviary, all designed by Repton. In the Aviary, the 'lower part of the centre, or octagonal building, is devoted to the collection of canaries, and other small birds . . . [while] the upper half consists of a very complete Pigeon house.'[44] Dr Allen Thomson tells us in 1836 that the Menagerie 'with the exception of some peculiar deer and a tortoise, is exclusively an aviary',[45] and it appears to have subsequently remained that way.

As work went on building the Doric gateway and the Pine Cone Pavilion, inside the Menagerie – after 'levelling the ground' and building the long curving back wall of the wire pens – they built the 'dovecote, aviary and sheds', which they were thatching by 1809. The same year the gravel paths were laid out, and the rustic poles cut for the enclosure fence, while the Aviary and pens were being fitted out with 'wire-work nets', nesting boxes, and 'boughs and perches', and decorated with moss, bark and 'painted patterns'. The enclosure fence itself presented something of a challenge since, apart from the lovely image of the completed structure, no details of its construction were included. A note in John Farey's accounts suggests it fell to him to 'suppose' how he might make an 'Inclosure of Rough Firs and net or wire-work round the Menagerie Ground, the sort not exactly known (suppose)'. Resourceful as ever, Farey came up with a solution, and finally, in January 1810, they 'completed the walks', 'put up seats', 'painted the pheasant pens', and completed the 'nets' for the enclosure fence.[46]

Elsewhere in the gardens, round the outside of the complex of hot houses and vegetable gardens, were Repton's proposed series of plantings and open areas, all linked by gravel paths, leading round from the Chinese Dairy Pond to the Menagerie. Interestingly enough, the last of these, just east of the Aviary, is a space for 'Orchards or Kangaroo Enclosure', but whether this last option was in response to a suggestion from the family, or simply something Repton felt to be suitably picturesque that they might enjoy, is unclear. In the event, other than the Menagerie, only the basic framework of Repton's proposals for the pleasure grounds was adopted at this time: leveling the central terrace, laying the network of gravel pathways, and erecting the iron perimeter fence.

In the light of what happened next, it seems clear that the duke had his own ideas of where and what kind of botanical and experimental gardens and plant houses should be built, and what kind of trees he wished to collect and plant, and that both he and the duchess had other ideas as to how they wanted the rare plants displayed and how the flower gardens should look. And they seem to have felt that Wyatville understood those ideas better than Repton. The Menagerie, however, was too much to resist, and the way Repton designed it clearly fitted with their picturesque sympathies. Similarly, looking at the wider proposals, Repton's grand scheme for an enhanced approach from Woburn, and the resulting symmetry at the west front, was turned down, while the more decorative ideas such as the tree plantings along Park Street and the addition to the park of the picturesque *cottage orné* in the Thornery were adopted.

We can imagine too that at this time, with the Abbey filling with young children, the Chinese dairy really came into its own, and we catch a glimpse of it in 1826 when Prince Pückler-Muskau visited Woburn and described it as 'a sort of Chinese temple, decorated with a profusion of white marble and coloured glasses; in the centre is a fountain, and round the walls hundreds of Chinese and Japanese porcelain of every form and colour, filled with new milk and cream . . . The windows are of ground glass, with Chinese painting, which shows fantastically enough by the dim light.'[47] This extraordinary building retains this 'fantastical' atmosphere today, its intact painted windows still casting a quiet, shadowed light in the cool atmosphere of the room. We can perhaps still sense that feeling of the unexpected, of transformation from the everyday, provided by the picturesque that the duke and duchess seem to have found in buildings like the Thornery and experiences such as walking through the Doric doorway into the Menagerie, and that the family seem to have valued for so long in the 4th Earl's grotto.

This emphasis on the picturesque and, in particular, 'romantic historicism' was underlined in 1810 when Repton was called back to Woburn to design and build Aspley Lodge. During the course of a conversation, Repton reports that the duke commented on the lack of authenticity in 'the numerous cottages called Gothic, which everywhere present themselves near high roads', and went on to 'express his desire to have a cottage of the style and date of buildings prior to Henry VIII'.[48] In response to this and working with his son John Adey, Repton went on to design and build Aspley Lodge, which still stands beside the road outside Woburn Sands, a mixture of design references they put together after consulting antiquarian literature and images on the subject, and which evidently satisfied the duke's desire for authenticity.[49] A further picturesque building, a single-storey Gothic-style lodge, also to be seen from the road, was added in 1825 when Ivy Lodge was

Humphry Repton, 'Aspley Lodge and Gardens', *Fragments on the Theory and Practice of Landscape Gardening*, 1816.

J. C. Bourne, *Ivy Lodge*, 1842. Ivy Lodge, possibly designed by Repton, was built beside the Great Avenue at the point where it crosses the London road. It stands at the entrance to the footpath that runs down the side of the Avenue and into the park; this path may well have been used by visitors to the Cold Bath during the time of the 5th Duke. Ivy Lodge still stands today, although slightly altered.

built at the point where the Great Avenue crosses the road to run up Wayn Close. Both these buildings, along with the Round House and the Thornery, can still be seen today, a lasting legacy of the duke and duchess's interest in the picturesque.[50] However, there was more to come, and perhaps nothing better captures the true meaning of the picturesque than the duchess's project at Endsleigh in Devon.

No major house was built in Tavistock or on the Devon estates until Endsleigh in 1814. The family's official residence in the west had been in Exeter, and a moderate house on 'the monastic property outside town' seems to have sufficed in Tavistock itself, along with Crowndale Farmhouse just outside the town. Similarly, Longbrook House, a large, heavily modified farmhouse outside Milton Abbot, sufficed as a base for fishing trips on the upper Tamar river.

ENDSLEIGH HOUSE AND GARDENS

The site for the house at Endsleigh was chosen by Georgina in 1809, who was drawn by the 'picturesque' qualities of the view looking down to the Tamar river as it twisted its way through a steep-sided valley surrounded by dense woodland. An intimate world of its own, yet one which also provided long views out to the distant moors of Cornwall, it immediately reminded the duchess of the scenery of her childhood, particularly that of Strath Spey near Aviemore, and the decision was made to create a house that reminded them of the hunting lodges the family so enjoyed staying in during their yearly trips to Scotland. Although Repton was initially asked to design the house in 1809, his proposal was rejected and an alternative, designed by Jeffry Wyatville in 1810, was built instead. On completion of the house in 1814, Repton was invited back to work on the landscaping, before Wyatville went on to design a further series of structures around the valley in the 1820s and 1830s.

ABOVE Humphry Repton, 'House from across the River', Red Book for Endsleigh, Plate X, 1814. Endsleigh House as seen by Repton when he arrived back there to give his suggestions for the landscaping of the house. The river Tamar runs across the foreground, with the house above it and, to the left, the dairy built by Wyatville at the entrance to the dell site, Repton's original choice of site for the house. Of the proposals included in this view, the large terrace was created in front of the house, and small gardens were developed above it. Repton's grand scheme for terraces of fruit trees and vegetable gardens on the hillside above the house was not adopted.

BELOW Humphry Repton, 'View from the Library', Red Book for Endsleigh, Plate XI, 1814. It was this view, looking west from the house site out across the Tamar valley to the distant moors of Cornwall, that first drew Georgina to the site. It reminded her of views she had known growing up in Scotland and the places where she and the duke spent annual family holidays during the deer hunting season throughout their marriage, and epitomized those grand, wild qualities of the picturesque she so valued. Repton's reduction of the scene to this symmetrical, painterly composition, complete with a new mill cottage and cascade across the river and Doric temple in the woods to the left, suggests perhaps why so much of what he proposed beyond the immediate surrounds of the house was not adopted.

ABOVE H. Repton & Sons, 'Effect of the Cottage proposed for the Dell Site taken from the Oak on the same side of the Glen', 1809. In this picture we see the design proposed by Repton and his sons John Adey and George for the main house 'for the Dell site' at Endsleigh, Devon, in 1809. While his highly ornate, decorative interpretation of the picturesque may have suited their purposes at Woburn, Endsleigh was different and the proposal was turned down in favour of one by Jeffry Wyatville.

BELOW Jeffry Wyatville, *The Duke of Bedford's Cottage at Endsleigh in Devonshire*, 1814.
The house at Endsleigh as completed by Wyatville in 1814. In front we see the initial formalized landscaping as laid out by Wyatville, and which Repton was to radically change when he was called down later that year to help integrate the new house into its extraordinary setting.

F.C. Lewis, 'Endsleigh Cottage and Grounds: From a Seat under the Rock', *Views of the Tamar Valley* (album of engravings), 1823. This view by Lewis confirms that the rock seat was built and provided an interesting destination for family walks from the house. The seat was carefully positioned at the same height above the river as the house, and a level path, wide enough for donkey carts, was run all the way round the side of the valley from the house to it, eliminating the need to either descend or climb and making it a comfortable walk or ride. Quite what happened to this roofed site, or just how it was constructed, is not clear, but a seat still sits there today lost in the dense trees and undergrowth.

Jeffry Wyatville, untitled pencil drawing of the 'Seat under the Rock' and the Swiss Cottage seen from beside the Tamar, *Original Designs for Woburn Abbey and Endsleigh* (folder of drawings). Wyatville proved altogether more capable bringing the duchess's vision alive. In this lovely drawing he shows Georgina and one of her daughters down beside the river working on their sketchbooks. On the skyline above the woods opposite is his 'Swiss Cottage', and halfway down the slope we can make out the same rock cliffs that Repton included in his 'View from the Library'. Just below the craggy rocks Wyatville has drawn in the rock seat, a large horizontal slab supported on pillars, under which was a bench where the family could look out back towards the house. All traces of the slab and pillars are gone today.

Jeffry Wyatville, 'Rustic Seat for Warm Wood [Wareham Woods]', ink and wash drawing, *Original Designs for Woburn Abbey and Endsleigh* (folder of drawings).
Another of Wyatville's proposals that was adopted was this idea for a 'Rustic Seat', a structure to be sited at the top of Wareham Woods across the river opposite the house. The octagonal base of this seat was recently rediscovered by foresters working in the woods, and it was found to have spectacular views down precipitous slopes to the river far below and out towards Cornwall. In the late nineteenth or early twentieth century, one of the series of 'tea houses' built by the 11th Duke was located near the seat.

Photograph of the rustic seat, Wareham Woods, late nineteenth century.
The rustic seat was still standing in the late nineteenth century and clearly in use by the family. The identity of the two ladies is not known for certain, but it is likely that they are the 11th Duke's sisters, Ela and Ermyntrude. Like their mother, Elizabeth, wife of the 9th Duke, these two were extremely fond of Endsleigh, and through their shared interest in photography they captured a number of priceless family moments on their annual holiday. The absence of any photograph by them of the rock seat suggests that it may have already collapsed by this time.

Back at Woburn, with the completion of the Menagerie between January and February 1810, account entries for the park and gardens covering 'work on designs for Mr Repton' largely come to an end, and there is a lull in new activities as the duke and duchess take the family abroad for three years. Once the designs for Endsleigh had been settled, as work there got under way, the family travelled to Spain, Portugal and Italy between 1813 and 1815 (while in Rome, the duke commissioned the 'Three Graces' from Canova). By the time the family returned to Woburn, most of the work initiated by Repton's designs had been completed – the levelling of the central terrace, the network of gravel paths, the fencing and the Menagerie with the Doric doorway and Pine Cone Pavilion – and some of the new shrubberies were in place; not since the days of the 4th Duke had so much been added to the gardens, but much more was to come.

In 1810 and 1811, two interesting structures were added which continued the picturesque theme, a 'Cowhouse' and a garden seat, the former possibly, and the latter certainly, by Jeffry Wyatville. The Cowhouse was a decorative but functional structure, perhaps linked to the use of the Chinese dairy and may have looked much like the one built below the house at Endsleigh (see page 147). Its location is not known and no image

Jeffry Wyatville's garden seat. At Woburn, one of Wyatville's lasting legacies is this seat he designed for the pleasure gardens; it has recently been renovated.

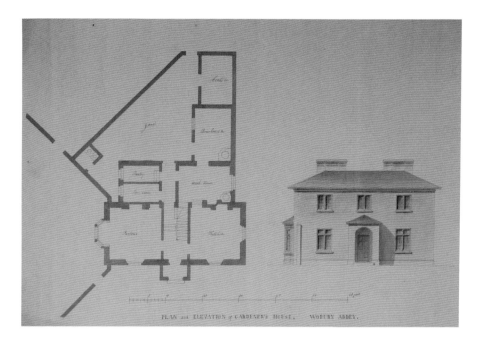

PLAN and ELEVATION of GARDENER'S HOUSE, WOBURN ABBEY.

LEFT Jeffry Wyatville, *Plan and Elevations of Gardener's House, Woburn Abbey*, 1830s.

LEFT BELOW James Forbes, 'General Plan of the Kitchen Garden', *Hortus Woburnensis*, Plate XIV, 1833.
The kitchen gardens as they were completed. Wyatville's gardener's house is visible set at an angle to the gardens in the top left-hand corner of this plan. Although the central garden layout and the greenhouses along the south wall are gone, the house is still ocupied and the row of offices, stores, potting sheds, bothy and workshops still stands awaiting renovation. Also still visible from the road is the elaborate gateway shown on the left of the plan which provided access for the family when they visited from the Abbey.

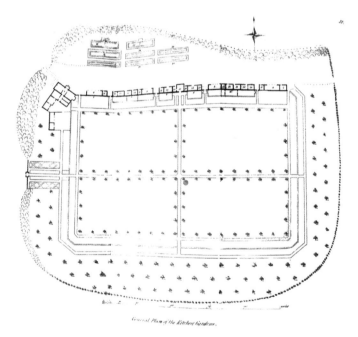

General Plan of the Kitchen Gardens.

exists, but it was a thatched building, with mangers and stalls, decorated by 'trellis and columns' to which were fixed 'hazels'.[51] The garden seat or 'Arbour', however, was definitely by Wyatville and can still be seen in the Abbey gardens today.

Also visible today beside the exit road from the visitor car park, and also by Wyatville, are the gardener's house and the elaborate 'doorway' into the duke's new kitchen gardens. Here, in 1826, the 5th Duke's kennels and huntsman's house were replaced by new designs, and in an interesting separation of styles Wyatville built a modern-looking villa for the practical world of the gardener's house, similar to his remodelling of Bedford Lodge, Campden Hill, the duke and duchess's London villa beside Holland Park, and very different from the picturesque designs of Repton's work.

One other structure created in the park at this time seems to sum up the picturesque sense of design, that combination of the romantic and the historic so favoured by John and Georgina: Purrett's Hill Lodge. This was

built in 1834 standing 'on an eminence in the north-east of the Park near the wall adjoining Froxfield'. J.C. Bourne's caption to his 1842 watercolour goes on to point out that it 'is a very good example of the architecture of the time of Queen Elizabeth'.

What is particularly interesting about this building is that 1834 entries in the account books concerning its construction – 'Work on cottage in the park', 'Cottage in the Park, fixing bargeboards and brick loggia' – are immediately preceded by an entry that says 'Taking temple down', but gives no further details and is not referred to again.[52] This would seem to raise the possibility that Purrett's Hill Lodge was built for much the same purpose as Repton's Thornery, a place for the family to visit and spend time out in the park, but what made it particularly special was that it may have replaced the dilapidated remains of the old Parson's Wood temple, reinvigorating for a new generation the site in or near Parson's Wood which had been so important to John and his brother Francis as children. It would further appear that the 'Swiss Cottage' shown on the 1881 Ordnance Survey map is the same building, and although the building itself was gone by 1900, this site is still discernible today.

J.C. Bourne, *Purrett's Hill Lodge*, 1842.
A great lost treasure from the heyday of the park at Woburn, Purrett's Hill Lodge (also known later as the Swiss Cottage) was one of the series of historically authentic cottages that had begun with Aspley Lodge. Although the building is long gone, traces of the site still exist. There is also some suggestion that it may have occupied the same site as the 'Temple in Parson's Wood', which had played such an important part in the 6th Duke's childhood experience of the park all those years before when he and his brothers were under the care of their grandmother, Gertrude.

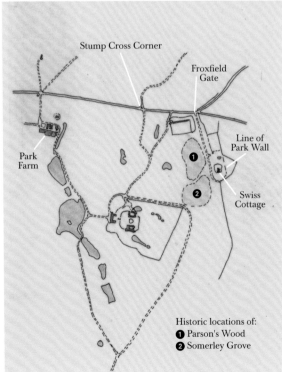

Stump Cross Corner

Froxfield
Gate

Line of
Park Wall

Park
Farm

Swiss
Cottage

Historic locations of:
❶ Parson's Wood
❷ Somerley Grove

ABOVE The site of Purrett's Hill Lodge today.
This is the corner of the park near Froxfield Gate that was once the site of Purrett's Hill Lodge (known by the late nineteenth century as the Swiss Cottage). It is not clear when this structure was demolished, but the house site is located in front of the trees in the background, just to the left of the large tree stump standing among the deer. It is possible that this stump is the large tree seen behind the house in Bourne's image. The park wall is still visible on the lower ground to the left, but has been replaced by fencing running up behind the site.

LEFT Location plan of Swiss Cottage, 1881.
The first indication of a building 'near the wall adjoining Froxfield' is the appearance of the 'Swiss Cottage' on the 1881 Ordnance Survey map. Its location would suggest very strongly that this is the same building that Bourne painted as Purrett's Hill Lodge, and its proximity to the eighteenth-century 'shrubberies' known as Parson's Wood and Somerley Grove might indicate that the 'temple' that was removed from the site before work began on the Lodge may well have been the remains of the old 'Temple in Parson's Wood'.

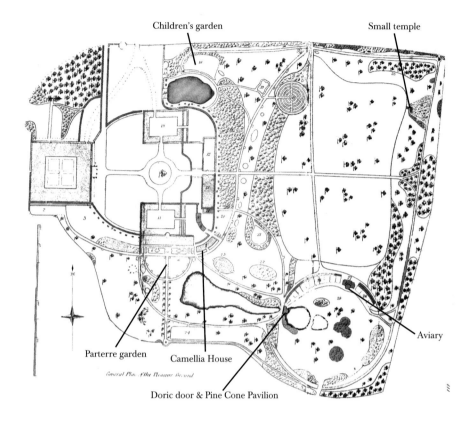

Children's garden

Small temple

Parterre garden

Camellia House

Doric door & Pine Cone Pavilion

Aviary

John Forbes, 'General Plan of the Pleasure Grounds', *Hortus Woburnensis*, Plate III, 1833.
This plan of 1833 indicates just how little of Repton's hints for the pleasure grounds were actually followed through. Clearly visible here are the Doric door backed by the Pine Cone Pavilion at the head of the Long Pond and the Menagerie, but a formal parterre garden has appeared on the site of his proposed 'Dressed Garden'. In fact, apart from the children's garden beside the Chinese Dairy Pond, only his wide central terrace was laid out. Forbes did, however, capture one feature of the garden in the Red Book: the little temple shown beside the path in the top right-hand corner of the plan. Looking closely at Repton's image of the Chinese Dairy Pond (see page 141), we catch a glimpse of a small open-fronted structure amongst the trees in the middle background.

Back in the pleasure grounds, in 1816 the 'Three Graces' arrived from Italy and an alcove was specially created for them within the sculpture gallery, known as the 'Temple of the Graces', and facing the 5th Duke's politically themed 'Temple of Liberty', a development which seems to encapsulate the differences between the brothers' personalities and wider interests. The alterations to the sculpture gallery inside were followed by a new design for the gardens outside, the first sign of a long sequence of additions the duke and duchess were to make to the pleasure grounds over the next twenty years, as each filled the spaces of Repton's basic layout with features which reflected their individual interests and their shared vision for Woburn. Just how much was done, and just how different it was to what Repton had proposed, are made clear by the 'General Plan of the Pleasure Grounds' which appeared in *Hortus Woburnensis*, an account of the gardens published by the duke's gardener James Forbes in 1833.

For the duke's part, we see developments that reflect his continuing interest in arboriculture, the use of scientific methods of chemistry and horticultural botany to raise improved varieties of plants and grasses and for controlling pests and diseases, and the importation of new and interesting plants.[53] Thus, rather than creating Repton's elegantly 'dressed' gardens, he chose to add a wide range of specialized buildings, the Camellia House, a greenhouse for 'Pelargonie', and Heath House,

John Forbes, 'The Heath House', *Hortus Woburnensis*, Plate VIII, 1833. Unfortunately, this building was demolished at the same time as the riding house, tennis court and covered walkway, but this drawing of the Heath House gives us a priceless glimpse of the complexity of these structures. Sitting partly on top of a rebuilt section of the covered walkway, the building followed the same elegant curving line and ran between the Camellia House on the left and the riding house on the right.

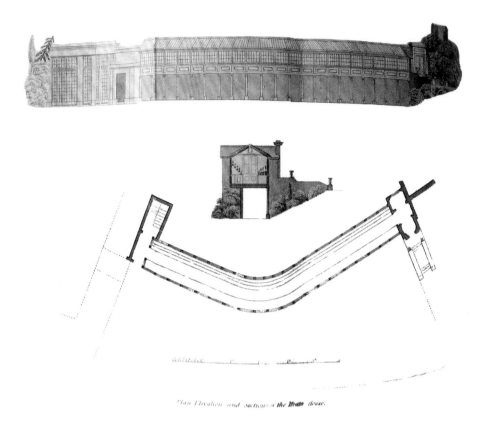

while new plantings, including a willow garden, an American garden featuring American oaks, and a pinetum, are also added. The outer areas of the gardens were then planted up with large collections of birches, alders, poplars, elms, plane trees and hollies. What is more, special beds for outdoor and hardy heathers (a particular interest of the duke's), an elaborately designed rose collection, the 'Rosarium Britannicum', and a 'Grass Ground', a carefully monitored test bed for grass varieties, were all laid out. Although some of these additions, such as the American garden, reflect suggestions made by Repton, we sense the duke was looking for a more functional and organized display of his collections than Repton had envisioned, and it was the duchess who perhaps was more in tune with Repton's 'dressed' style.

Hortus Woburnensis tells us that the new gardens 'in front of the Sculpture Gallery . . . were laid out and executed, from drawings by Her Grace, the Duchess of Bedford' *c.*1829–30, the first of a series of highly decorative and carefully designed flower gardens designed by the duchess for which she later became noted.[54] Following this, Georgina went on to create her private 'Flower Garden . . . in front of the Private Apartments' in 1822, where Forbes tells us there was 'a handsome fountain, which supplies this garden with water' standing at the centre of a circular arrangement of flower beds set within decorative iron fences and entered through elaborate

Jeffry Wyatville, *Plan of the Pleasure Grounds,* detail, 1838.
1 'New garden in front of the Sculpture Gallery', 1829.
2 'Her Grace's private Arbour'.
3 'Her Grace's Flower Garden in front of the Private Apartments', 1822.
4 'The Parterre in front of the Libraries'.
5 'The Maze'.
6 'Gardens of the Children when young, designed by Mr Repton'.

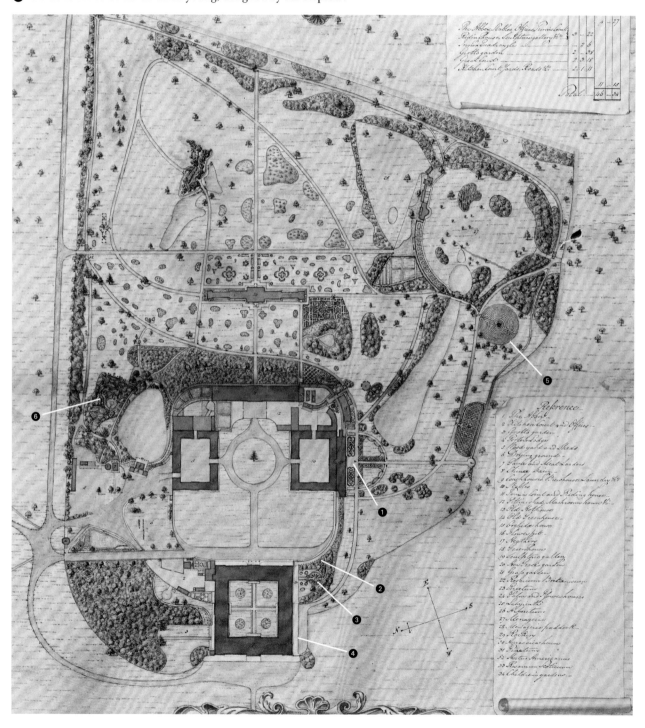

iron pergolas. Along the back of this flower garden ran 'Her Grace's private arbour, formed of open woodwork . . . with climbers'.[55] This structure was located within the first section of Holland's covered walkway and provided a secluded spot where the duchess could sit looking out over dense plantings of shrubs and trees, at the centre of which, in turn, lay an open glade with flower beds and a curving seat.

Although neither of these decorative gardens appears in detail on the 1833 plan, they do feature on the plan of 1838 and in illustrations in *Hortus Woburnensis*. Looking at them we see the development of the duchess's interest in the complex display of flowers, which culminated in the spectacular layout – considered groundbreaking in its complexity and its coordinated use of colour – she developed with the help of her gardener John Cai at Bedford Lodge, Campden Hill, in the years after the duke's death.

John Forbes, 'Parterre in front of the Sculpture Gallery', *Hortus Woburnensis*, Plate V, 1833. Georgina was clearly fascinated by both intricacy and colour, with a particular eye for free-flowing forms within a tight geometrical framework, and seems to have thoroughly enjoyed the process of designing and developing the gardens. This basic design in front of the sculpture gallery, the two rectangular beds and the semicircles beyond, had lasting appeal and is still visible in late nineteenth-century photographs of the area.

John Forbes, 'Her Grace's Flower Garden in front of the Private Apartments', & 'Parterre in front of the Libraries', *Hortus Woburnensis*, Plate IV, 1833. The small pool at the centre of the formal layout survives to this day, but the fountain and iron trelliswork are long gone.

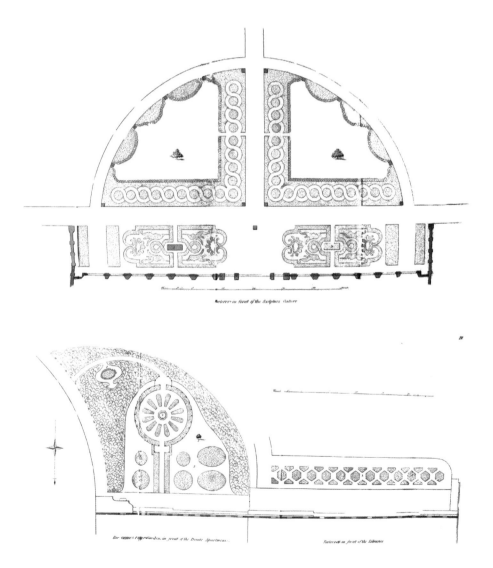

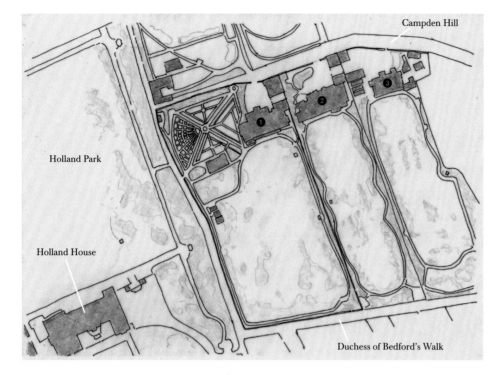

Holland Park

Holland House

Duchess of Bedford's Walk

Drawing of the gardens at
Campden Hill, *c.*1850.

❶ Bedford Lodge
❷ Holly Lodge
❸ Thornwood Lodge

Eight villas were built
along Campden Hill in the
early nineteenth century,
and Bedford Lodge (later
renamed Argyll Lodge)
was on one end next to
Holland House, the home
of the Bedfords' close
friends, Lord and Lady
Holland. The original
villa was enlarged several
times for the duke by Jeffry
Wyatville in the 1830s, and
a series of gardens were
laid out. All the houses
had extensive gardens,
large open park-like lawns,
dotted with trees and
plantings and encircled
by serpentine gravel paths
leading past small summer
houses and seats. This
uniformity is broken only
by Georgina's design, to
the left of the house, and
far more elaborate than
those at Woburn.
Other houses were Moray
Lodge, Thorpe Lodge and
Elm Lodge on the north
side of Campden Hill
and Bute Lodge beyond
Thornwood. Most of
these now lie beneath the
campus of Holland Park
School.

Beside the duchess's private garden, beyond the fence and gate,
alterations were made to Repton's terrace garden below the south wing,
when his planted soil bank was replaced by a dressed-stone wall topped
with an iron fence. The area was cleared, the wall built, the terrace laid,
and the accounts tell us that they 'cleaned and gilded' the fence, before
'setting frames for flower borders' and 'making flower baskets' to create
an elaborate honeycomb parterre of beds and baskets along the terrace in
front of the Library windows. This terrace and parterre, along with the
open lawns running off round the enclosed area of the Duchess's Garden,
formed the south front gardens until further alterations by Wyatville which
were to be completed by the 7th Duke.

Also featured on the plans of the pleasure gardens is the 'Children's
Garden', a feature for which we have no precise date, but in *Hortus
Woburnensis* Forbes tells us that it was 'executed from the designs
of the late Mr Repton'. This would suggest it was laid out after
1818, when Repton died, and before 1833, the date of Forbes's book. The
four-year gap between the births of Lady Louisa and Lord Henry
meant that in 1826, for example, there were still four children of 10
or under; this might suggest that it was part of the duchess's garden
building in the mid-1820s, as she laid out her own gardens and sought
to make the gardens more interesting and fun for the children. Also in
1826 Prince Pückler-Muskau described the Chinese dairy with its jugs
and bowls full of fresh milk and cream, in full use by the duchess and
the children.

RIGHT John Forbes, 'Gardens of the Children when Young, Designed by Mr Repton', *Hortus Woburnensis*, Plate XII, 1833.
Not included in the Red Book, this garden appears to have been a later commission. Repton may have been asked to design the garden when he was still working at Woburn, or the idea may have come up while he was creating the gardens round the house at Endsleigh in 1814, since these also included an elaborate children's garden. Designed to entertain the children with interesting shapes and little mounds, and a variety of scents and textures, the garden has now been completely restored. While this work was under way, parts of the original gravel pathways were discovered, just as they had been left when the garden fell out of use.

BELOW Anon., 'A Drawing of the Labyrinth'.
Visible on Wyatville's plan of the pleasure grounds, the Maze was added in 1833. This image of the Maze is contained in a scrapbook in the Woburn Abbey Collection and may well be the original plan brought back from Portugal by Lord George William on his return from his diplomatic posting in Lisbon. This is suggested by the fact that it does not show the Maze as completed at Woburn, with the small Chinese pavilion based on a design by Sir William Chambers at the centre, but one with a rather more fanciful structure.

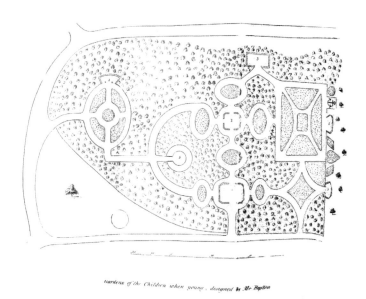

Gardens of the Children when young, designed by Mr Repton

It was a little later, but continuing this theme, that two of the most playful features in the gardens were added: a 'Swing, about 40 feet high' and a feature known now as 'The Maze', but which was originally called 'The Labyrinth'.[56] The date the swing was installed is unrecorded, but the Maze was formed in 1833 and was 'constructed from a similar one in Portugal, and the plan was brought from thence by Lord George William Russell when Ambassador to the Court in Lisbon'. It was created using hornbeam hedges, and later that year a 'Chinese Temple' was added as a destination at the centre from a design by Sir William Chambers.[57]

With the addition of these features, the pleasure grounds contained all the places of interest that caught the eye of Dr Allen Thomson, whose collection of letters to his family provide a unique eye-witness account of Woburn Abbey, its park and gardens towards the end of the 6th Duke's life. Thomson became the duke's personal doctor in 1836, living and travelling with the family until the duke's death in 1839. His accounts of the family, of life at their homes at Woburn, Endsleigh, The Doune in Scotland and Campden Hill in Kensington, are priceless, but they also provide us with a sensitive and interested personal view of the landscapes around him, and his accounts of Woburn help to bring all these developments to life.

159

In a letter of 1836, for example, we catch a glimpse of the increasingly complex pleasure grounds and the way in which they were used when he writes, 'I sauntered for 3 hours in the pleasure grounds or ornamental gardens which surrounds the house . . . the extent is about 50 acres . . . I find that every time I walk in it I discover new places and I shall not quite understand it till I see a ground plan' – something he included in his letter.[58] While not entirely accurate, his sketch nevertheless gives us an interesting glimpse of the gardens and the sense of fun and adventure, alongside serious research, which seems to have pervaded it. He continues: 'I walked about, gazed and admired, sat down and meditated. One spot I always return to with great pleasure is between 6 & 8 on a seat at the side of the pond which is before the Chinese Dairy . . . below a fine spreading oak . . . and surrounded by beds of roses, rhododendrons, azaleas, Heaths and Pines.' In 1837 he reports, 'walking with the Duchess yesterday – a thing I do nearly everyday' and 'then I saunter about . . . with a book, visit hot houses or gardens'. These descriptions make clear that the grounds had come to fulfil a number of roles for family and guests. They were more than simply a place to display the duke's plant collections, a grand setting for the Abbey, or a playground for the children; they brought together qualities of serenity and beauty which together created spaces that promoted quiet reflective thought – another, more subtle dimension of that sense of transcending the everyday which lay behind so many of the features of this garden specifically and gardens generally.

Dr Allen Thomson's plan of the pleasure grounds, redrawn from original letter of 1836. Thomson's sketch of the pleasure grounds offers us a unique insight into how the gardens were perceived at this time. Rather than recording how the garden was actually laid out, the plan seems to suggest how disorientating it felt to walk around the heavily planted fifty acres, as the long sinuous and curving paths led from one feature to another. Interestingly enough, he included in this plan what look like field boundaries out beyond the road to the kitchen garden; these may in fact indicate that the shrubberies of Parson's Wood and Somerley Grove were still in existence. Thomson's key:

1: House.
2: The Kitchen Part.
3: Lawn.
4: Stables.
5: Large building containing large riding school and tennis court.
6: Chinese Dairy & Fish Pond.
7: Children's Garden.
8: Collection of Pines.
9: Menagerie. House for Keepers & large collection of cages and houses for animals.
10: Rhododendrons, Azalias, Calmias & flowers of this description.
11: Building & ground for Heaths.
12: Garden of very rare plants before the Sculpture gallery.
13: Duchess's Private Garden.
14: Labyrinth.
15: Swing, about 40 feet high.
16: Collection of Grasses or Hortus Gramineus.
17: Fattening fish pond.
18: Ditto.
19: Large pond before the house with boat.
20: Present entrance to house and offices. The offices not seen.

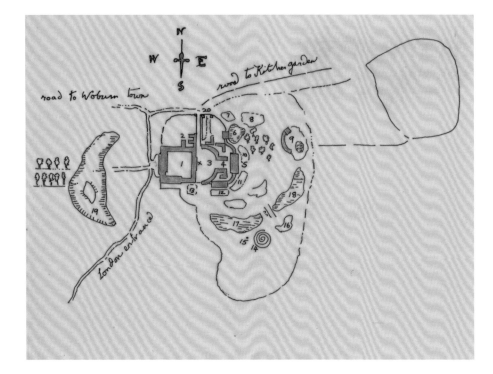

In addition to enjoying the opportunities for quiet moments of reading or meditation in the gardens, Thomson also participated in the family's use of the wider parkland. He writes: 'I have been drawing a little in sepia under the superintendence of Lady Charles and the Duchess', while 'On other days I went to fish the ponds with Lady Rachel', the youngest daughter.[59] On another occasion Thomson writes of 'collecting about 40 or 50 common plants the names of which I am teaching Lady Rachel and myself'. By this time, Lady Rachel was 10 years old, and signed off a letter to Thomson as 'your little friend'; they clearly spent happy hours in the park botanizing, fishing and riding their ponies. As with the pleasure grounds, however, he seems also to have enjoyed the park on a personal level and has left us a vivid and timeless portrait of it:

> The trees are out just now and nothing can exceed the richness of the fresh green foliage . . . the effect of which is heightened by the contrast with the fine clumps of dark pines here and there . . . I ride or walk every day . . . The grass ride round the park itself is about 12 or 14 miles long and one may ride straight forward at least twice that length without going out of the domain or going off the grass roads; every new turn presenting a varied and beautiful prospect. The woods abound with a considerable variety of plants . . . one patch is quite yellow with crowds of primroses and cowslips, another is equally blue with the squill hyacinth, Orchids, anemones, Lilly [sic] of the Valley, and wild strawberries in plenty.

In this description we see both the continuity of the experience of this parkland and some of the changes – it would no doubt be familiar to the 4th Duke, as he took his long morning walks in the mid-eighteenth century, and even to the 6th Duke and his childhood experiences in Parson's Wood with his brothers and grandmother Gertrude – yet we no longer get the sense of a park 'full of strollers from the neighbourhood' experienced fifty years before by Sir Philip Francis in the days of the 5th Duke. It had become a much more private and tranquil place. Largely it was to remain so through the nineteenth and the first half of the twentieth centuries, until visitors returned in large numbers in the 1950s.

A series of strokes through the 1820s and 1830s culminated in October 1839 when, despite the attentions of Dr Thomson, the duke succumbed to one final attack and died at The Doune in Scotland. Yet right up to the end new projects were under way both in the pleasure grounds and in the landscape beyond. In the first case, Jeffry Wyatville oversaw the construction of a series of new 'Flower Houses' between 1836 and 1838, the enormous iron and glass 'Palm and Flower House' on Repton's central terrace, and the 'Auracaria House' to grow and display the duke's expanding collections; at much the same time, a new rockery was constructed beside two ponds, as

Repton's original 'cave' designed for the Chinese Dairy Pond was finally built. It would appear that the existing spring was used to create these ponds at this time, since they do not appear on either the 1833 'General Plan' or Thomson's sketch of 1836; they are, however, pencilled in with survey points along with the new 'Flower Houses' on the undated and unfinished estate map that was used by Wyatville to plan his later additions, suggesting that they were all designed and built at the same time.[60] Finally, in 1839, a grotto was added to the children's garden, a magical place of crystals, quartzes, strange rocks and candlelight, where the children were read to and told stories. It was a feature, like the children's garden itself with all its carefully assembled scents and textures of the plants, to stimulate the imagination and provide a place of play. It would appear that this provision was of some importance to Georgina, and just as she created the garden and grottoes, swing and maze for her younger children at Woburn, so, as early as 1810, she had included a children's garden as one of the features of the house at Endsleigh. This one, overlooked by her apartments, was set in a raised curving terrace and featured an open walkway down one side, a 'Chinese Summer House', fountain and colourful flower garden, and a raised rill

The restored shell grotto and children's garden at Woburn, 2014.

Added to the children's garden in 1839, the grotto was one of the last projects ordered by the duke. Interesting rocks were brought from a number of places to create the magical interior, including the Devon estates, where a similar feature had been added to the gardens at Endsleigh House. In the 1950s when the abbey was opened to the public, the shell grotto became the location of the 'Wishing Well' attraction before falling into a long period of disrepair. It has now been fully restored and reopened and is seen today complete with the iron rose trellises added later in the nineteenth century.

Humphry Repton, 'The Children's Garden', Red Book for Endsleigh, Plate IV, 1814.
Just how much thought and effort went into entertainments for the children during this period is illustrated by the elaborate children's garden that was included in the construction of Endsleigh House. Designed by Wyatville, we see the completed garden here in Repton's image of it in his Red book for Endsleigh of 1814. The garden survives intact, replanted in the colour scheme shown here with the fountain still playing in the centre. It was placed to be overlooked by the duke and duchess's apartments so that they could keep a close eye on the children, while the little building beyond contained an indoor playroom and rooms for the nannies.

running round the low, curving outside wall along which the children sailed model boats. This garden, its plantings beautifully restored, can still be enjoyed by visitors.

Certainly, much may have been 'undone' but a great deal '[had] been done'. Between them, the two brothers Francis and John had overseen a period of intense activity at Woburn in the fifty-three years between the former's succession as 5th Duke in 1786 and the latter's death in 1839. Driven by a shared vision of 'national improvement', the Abbey, park, farms and woodlands beyond had undergone a thorough programme of modernization, changing both the appearance of the buildings and the landscape around them. Such a radical transformation, unprecedented perhaps since the days of Francis, the 4th Earl, was not to be repeated for almost 130 years, and the circumstances of this are the subject of our final chapter.

CHAPTER FOUR

'With this view, I would rather wish to restore, than to destroy the true character of the place, not to increase its importance but to preserve it, and to take such advantage of its natural situation, as neither to modernize too much, nor to neglect those improvements in comfort, convenience, and elegance, which modern times have introduced'

(Humphry Repton, *Hints, Plans and Sketches for the Improvement of Stonelands in Sussex*, 1805–6)

The nineteenth to the twenty-first centuries

Repton wrote these words as part of his discussion of the 'Character & Situation' of the house in his *Hints* for Stonelands, the childhood home of Elizabeth Sackville, wife of the 9th Duke of Bedford, and his clear and precise words seem to sum up the subsequent history of Woburn during the nineteenth and twentieth centuries.[1] They serve to frame the underlying story of this chapter, as the grand house and grounds laid out by the 4th, 5th and 6th Dukes were neither modernized too much nor increased, but preserved and then restored by successive generations of the family, a process which continues to this day.

Succeeding as the 6th Duke in 1802, Lord John had been determined to fulfil his elder brother's vision for Woburn, while also pursuing his own interests in botany and horticulture. Yet besides the practical work on the modernization of the farms and the estate infrastructure, we have seen also, particularly in the last two decades of the duke's life, the continual development of both the pleasure gardens and the park as places for the family to use and enjoy. One result of this activity was that, driven by

J. C. Bourne, *Her Majesty's Arrival*, 1842.
In his albums to commemorate the event, Bourne records the royal visit in three highly detailed images, two of which show the queen's arrival at the Abbey itself. In this picture we sense the excitement as the royal carriage is led up to the Abbey from the Bason Pond by her bodyguard of Hussars. With the exception of the group of trees on the right of the pond planted by Repton forty years earlier, which are now long gone, the view is instantly recognizable today.

his 'more romantically feudal view of his position' and his wife Georgina's 'rigidly tenacious' regard for dignity and rank, the Abbey and its setting had become altogether a self-consciously grander and expansive place, which in 1841 was ready to receive that grandest of queens, Victoria, the first monarch to visit since Charles I during the Civil War.

There was, however, one other lasting legacy of John and Georgina's enthusiasms, which sums up the importance of the picturesque aesthetic at this time: the additions they had made to the Evergreens. It is difficult perhaps for us, in an age when dark, impenetrable blocks of evergreen plantations have spread right across the countryside, to understand their impact 200

years ago, but a glimpse of the novelty and excitement that using these trees created is caught memorably in the gentle satire of Jane Austen in 1814, when she records Fanny's reaction to 'laurels and evergreens' in *Mansfield Park*: 'I am so glad to see.the Evergreens thrive! . . . The evergreen! – How beautiful, how welcome, how wonderful the evergreen! – When one thinks of it, how astonishing a variety of nature!'[2] Certainly, these trees had a lasting fascination from the 4th Duke onwards, and Repton was to describe the experience of the Evergreens at Woburn as 'a circumstance of grandeur, of variety, of novelty, and, I may add, of winter comfort'.[3]

The Evergreens Repton saw in 1805 had been substantially added to by the 5th Duke and Robert Salmon, but it was during the time of the 6th Duke and Duchess that they really came into their own.

With all the additions they made between 1802 and 1839,[4] the Evergreens became an intimate and romantic world within itself, a larger version of the fanciful, picturesque world Repton had created in the Menagerie. For us, perhaps, these final additions to the Evergreens in the years just before he died sum up the 6th Duke's legacy at Woburn. Intensely practical in so many ways – scientific and orderly, carefully monitoring and growing on all the new specimen trees and shrubs – in the Evergreens and in the pleasure grounds he and his wife nevertheless left a place sprinkled in fairy dust. Together they had created a place to be enjoyed, with a few interruptions, for generations to come.

The first glimpse we get of Francis Russell, who inherited all this as the 7th Duke, is as a 14-year-old in 1802, when he accompanied his father and brothers on the trip to Weston Park following their mother's death. Here they stayed some three weeks with their aunt Lucy Byng and her husband

George Garrard, Francis, Marquis of Tavistock, *c*.1804, detail of *The Sheepshearing* (see page 120).[5]
In this detail from Garrard's engraving of the Sheepshearing agricultural show, we see Francis, Marquis of Tavistock as a teenager, the central figure in the grey hat. The annual show was an occasion for people interested in agriculture from all over the country – including some from Europe and America – to come together to exchange information, see new animal breeds and machinery, and exchange ideas.

Orlando Bridgeman, 1st Earl of Bradford. The boys took full advantage of their time: 'The boys have all been hunting this morning and have had good sport,' and it is clear that hunting was to remain one of the central interests of the 7th Duke's life.[6]

After graduating from Trinity College, Cambridge, in 1808, Francis married Anna Maria Stanhope,[7] and the couple moved into Oakley House, living there until he inherited the dukedom in 1839. Francis wrote later, 'I know that the happiest years I have passed were at Oakley, free from all the cares which have since fallen on me,'[8] and it seems clear that life at his childhood home suited both of them. One of his first actions was to take over as Master of the Oakley Hunt in 1809, and Anna Maria's 'Pocket Books' indicate that this was a shared passion.[9] The diaries start in 1838, and entries for 1839 tell us that in January they were hunting daily throughout the month, with many 'good runs'; in March they hosted the Oakley Hunt Ball. Clearly, the hunt and its social world were very much a part of life at Oakley for the family, as they had been indeed for Francis's father and uncle.

Following his marriage and move to Oakley, Francis, at this time Marquis of Tavistock, became a Member of Parliament, but unlike his younger brother Lord John, who went on to be Prime Minister in the mid-nineteenth century, he seems to have had little enthusiasm for the world of politics or serving in government. Anna Maria's diary confirms this: 'he has no ambition for it.' Other than his public duties, we know that the years at Oakley were his 'happiest', and while, as Georgiana Blakiston tells us, he may have 'lacked his father's happy enjoyment of a variety of interests',[10] it is clear that in addition to hunting and horse racing, both he and his wife took an interest and some pride in the gardens at Oakley, and subsequently at Woburn. His father and mother, expecting to live at Oakley for many years, had developed significant flower gardens there before 1802 that had matured by the time Francis and Anna Maria arrived six years later, and we soon see them making improvements of their own.

Due to her mother's position as Lady of the Bedchamber to Queen Charlotte, it is quite possible that Anna Maria, as a companion to the young princess Victoria, will have been familiar with many of the developments the queen initiated both at Kew Palace and the botanical gardens, and her private flower gardens at Frogmore House, Windsor, so it is not surprising that just a year after they arrived at Oakley, Humphry Repton was consulted on improvements. His subsequent 'Minute' to the Oakley gardener in 1809, effectively giving orders for certain jobs to be carried out following his visit, covers plantings for the flower beds in front of the veranda, a side path down towards the river, a bridge over the 'Spring', and the treatment of the 'Entrance' through the gardens.[11] In addition, a further image also survives in the archives, and although unsigned and undated, it is captioned in what appears to be Repton's handwriting, 'This hint for a Cottage at the Entrance of the Grounds near Oakley House'.

THE EVERGREENS, 1802–39

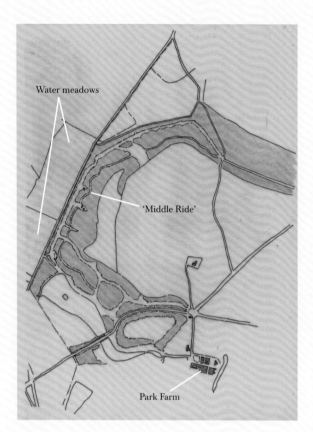

Water meadows

'Middle Ride'

Park Farm

LEFT Plan of the extended Evergreens and Middle Ride. This plan indicates the location of the 'Middle Ride' added by the 6th Duke following the completion of new plantations *c*.1805. Wide enough to accommodate a donkey cart, the ride ran along the contours, looping in and out of the small valleys running down towards Drakeloe Pond. It was also just high enough up the slope to permit wide views over the park wall to the water meadows in the valley and the plantations on the Wavendon ridge beyond. Today these views are essentially unchanged, as the experimental farm occupies the meadows and the woodlands still stretch up to the horizon.

BELOW LEFT H. W. Burgess, *Donkey Cart in the Evergreens*, 1837. In *Fragments on the Theory and Practice of Landscape Gardening* (1816) Humphry Repton described the Evergreens as 'a circumstance of grandeur, of variety, of novelty', and here Burgess catches the scene in the heart of the Evergreens soon after the Middle Ride was created. In this image we see the duchess seated in the cart being driven down one of the large open rides from the slopes above.

BELOW RIGHT H. W. Burgess, *Shelter Hovel*, 1837. The Shelter Hovel as seen by Burgess some two years after it was constructed. It must have been a most spectacular place to visit, with open views in a wide arc out in front of it. The Crawley road is seen in the distance, but Husborne Crawley church on the horizon is obscured by the needles of the dark pine tree down the slope. The site was recently rediscovered; the dilapidated remains of the structure were recognizable as late as the 1950s, but today its location is only discernible by the line of the stone foundation. On the right, the track still runs down the gap in the bank, before zigzagging its way to the Log Cabin.

RIGHT Plan of Upper Ride, Shelter Hovel and views over surrounding countryside.

This plan shows the Evergreens after the new additions were made by the duke and duchess in the 1820s and 1830s. The plantations were extended to the top of the slopes and spread east across the old Warren site. Along the top of the slope the new Upper Ride, laid out *c.*1826, ran north to the small promontory where the land starts to fall away sharply on all sides. At the end of the ride the Shelter Hovel was built in 1835 as a destination with extensive views. Finally, in the wide valley below, the Log Cabin was added in 1839. With these additions the Evergreens reached their final form, by now a maze of tracks and rides running through the extensive plantations with a series of buildings and outlooks to add further interest.

BELOW LEFT J. C. Bourne, *Ruins from Ridgemont House*, 1842. Bourne shows the Colonnade below the Arch, and by this date both structures have become considerably overgrown. The structure was still standing in the 1990s, but appears to have been knocked over by a falling branch from a nearby cedar tree.

BELOW RIGHT J. C. Bourne, *Log Cabin*, 1842. The Log Cabin in the Evergreens can still be seen looking just as it does in Bourne's painting. The biggest difference, perhaps, is that many of the trees are now fully grown, in particular the redwoods seen in the background, which now tower over the scene and give it a suitably North American feel.

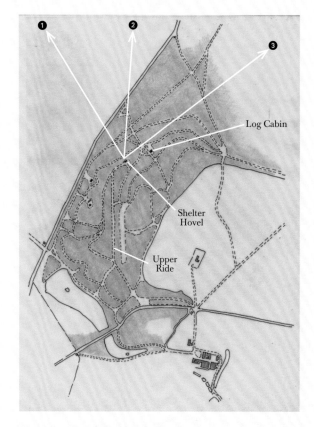

Log Cabin

Shelter Hovel

Upper Ride

Views from the Shelter Hovel:
❶ Possible view to Aspley Guise church.
❷ View to Husborne Crawley church tower.
❸ View to Ridgemont church spire.

Attributed to Humphry Repton, 'This hint for a Cottage at the Entrance of the Grounds near Oakley House, is proposed as in a style not too rude, nor too architectural for the Character of the House', *c.*1809.

This design would seem to date from Repton's visit in 1809, when he was still in the middle of completing the Menagerie at Woburn. It is not likely to be the present entrance to the house, and may well have been down by the bridge where the road from both Bedford and Woburn still crosses the river Ouse.

Neither 'too rude' nor 'too architectural', it seems to be very much in the decorative picturesque style Repton had so successfully produced for the 6th Duke and Georgina at Woburn at this time. That this style also very much suited the taste of Anna Maria is suggested by another drawing of a decorative feature at Oakley, this time a substantial Gothic folly, dated to 1816 and captioned, 'Oakley House July 18th 1816 – Design for Dairy'.[12] If this was built, it no longer survives today, but the unusual design of one of the old estate cottages on the driveway today could suggest the subsequent conversion of this dairy into a cottage.

Putting these clues together we can perhaps better imagine the gardens Anna Maria developed at Oakley and whose taste her only son, William, 8th Duke, would later define as 'the grouping [of] the most beautiful flowers in nature, with the prettiest patterns and the most beautiful masses of colour'.[13] Although largely quiet about Oakley itself, Anna Maria's Pocket Books provide two vivid images of their life there. In October 1838 she writes that 'the Weather is very warm – charming for sitting under the Verandas', and in September 1839 that it is 'A lovely day – our Garden in great beauty'. In addition, knowing of her parents' 'sempiternal occupation of tea-drinking', we can perhaps also imagine that, beyond admiring the beauty of the gardens, the family were also sipping tea as they sat under the verandas, just as they were later to do at Woburn where, as duchess, she is credited with having introduced five o'clock tea.

Unfortunately, just a month after she reports on the peace and quiet of the 'lovely day' in their beautiful gardens in 1839, Anna Maria writes, 'Lord

J. C. Bourne, *Oakley House, c.*1840s, showing the family out in the gardens. The gardens of Oakley House, following development by the 6th Duke and his first wife, Georgiana, and by Francis and Anna Maria. Although it is undated, the image shows circular flower beds surrounded by basketwork in front of the house very similar to those proposed by Repton in his 'Minute' of 1809. The road running in from the right-hand background would have led to the house from the entrance shown in Repton's drawing.

T[avistock] has had an alarming account of the Duke of Bedford having had an apoplectic fit at The Doune'; the next entry tells us that 'dear Tavistock [is] quite cast down by the poor duke's death.' Following the duke's funeral at Chenies, they 'went to church at Woburn – All the church in mourning for the Duke – so touching', and when Francis succeeded as 7th Duke they moved from Oakley to take over the Abbey.

Splendid though the park, farms, gardens and Evergreens created by the 6th Duke and Duchess may have been, they, like his brother before them, had also enormously overspent. Once again, the estate finances were in disarray, and such were the 'debts and encumbrances' he inherited that Francis found 'It will be necessary to shut up the old Abbey for a time' since it 'must be my part . . . to repair the breaches that have been made, or the family importance and influence in the Country will sink into ruin'.[14] Although he seems to have been determined to complete those projects started by his father – the development of the Evergreens and the Abbey gardens, especially the South Terrace Garden and further enlargement and deepening of the Bason Pond – he instigated very tight budgets, focusing expenditure on investment in the estates: repair, maintenance and improvement of the infrastructure and facilities. Typical of his priorities is the fact that, although he saw through the completion of Wyatville's new

LEFT Attributed to A. Dunn, *Anna Maria Stanhope, Duchess of Bedford* (1783–1857).
While as duchess she supported the temperance movement and was patron of the Bedford Infirmary, this portrait catches something of her artistic side, expressed in her interest in planning and planting flower gardens in a style her son, William, described in a letter as 'grouping the most beautiful flowers in nature, with the prettiest patterns and most beautiful masses of colour'.

BELOW J. C. Bourne, *The Conservatory*, 1842.
Bourne's image of the conservatory, also referred to as the Orchid and Palm House, gives some idea of how the pleasure grounds at Woburn looked after all the developments undertaken by Wyatville for the duke's father and at the time that Victoria and Albert visited. Although Repton had designed a conservatory and greenhouses for his grand terrace, it was Wyatville's structure which finally occupied it. This view shows the building as it was seen walking up into the gardens from the Abbey.

RIGHT Stephen Pearce, *Francis Russell, 7th Duke of Bedford* (1788–1861), 1859.
Both Francis and and his wife, Anna Maria, were avid fox hunters like his grandfather and his uncle, the 5th Duke. Throughout his life, Francis remained deeply committed to his role as both landowner and employer, and Woburn's place at the centre of local life.

THE DEVELOPMENT OF THE SOUTH TERRACE GARDEN, 1830s–1900

Anon., Post-Repton South Terrace Garden, watercolour. Although undated, this image appears to show the south front of the Abbey after alteration by Repton and just before Wyatville's design for a series of terraces was adopted in the 1830s. Certainly, the ground has been excavated below Repton's terrace and the retaining wall built, and looking further out Repton's alterations to the Bason Pond and his plantings round the edges have been carried out. In addition, as he predicted, the deer are now seen roaming right up to the Abbey, animating the scene outside the Dining Room and Library windows.

Jeffry Wyatville's proposal for the new South Terrace Garden, undated but probably late 1830s.
Although not all the details in this drawing were adopted, the basic layout is what we see today, with the ground partially filled back in to carry the extended lower terrace. The upper parterre terrace survives below the windows, while the lower garden features a new fountain. Wyatville also seems to be proposing decorative architectural additions to the Abbey itself, which were certainly not adopted.

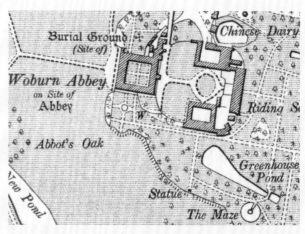

Edward Adveno Brooke, 'The Terrace Garden, Woburn Abbey' (chromolithograph after original watercolour) from *The Gardens of England*, published by T. McLean, London, 1857. With the construction of Wyatville's new terrace and the laying out of these gardens, the area took on the look and style that it has retained to this day. Additional tree planting means that the south court is no longer visible in the background, but the fountain, walks, urns and other ornaments, including the astrolabe, still feature in the gardens.

Woburn Abbey and gardens, detail of Ordnance Survey map of 1902, Bedfordshire, Sheet XXIV, SE.
The layout of the South Terrace Garden can be seen here as it was at the end of the nineteenth century. The central path runs down from the upper terrace, round the fountain and out to meet the ha-ha looping round the end of the terrace. The area of the Duchess's Garden has remained untouched, but a long east–west path runs from the new gardens, out past the sculpture gallery, past the site of the Menagerie (long gone by 1902), to the garden's boundary. The layout is much the same today.

flower houses and the Log Cabin, when a disastrous hailstorm smashed all the glazing in the grand Orchid and Palm House in 1844, the duke gave the orchid collection to Queen Victoria (who in turn presented it to Kew Gardens). Although the glazing appears to have been repaired, the building was not restocked and it was later pulled down.

Nevertheless, before necessary economies could be made, there was one more glorious occasion to be organized: the visit in 1841 of the newly-wed Queen Victoria and Prince Albert. As a lady-in-waiting and friend of the queen, Anna Maria hosted the pair at Woburn for a couple of days, and judging from Bourne's images of the visit, it must have been quite a show, the gardens, park and Evergreens providing a suitable backdrop to the drama and pageantry of such an event.

After the excitement and activity (and expenditure) of both his father and stepmother's time at Woburn and the visit of Victoria and Albert, a different sort of energy took over which, in its way, also changed the face of the estates. While Anna Maria was involved with the temperance movement in Bedford and became patron of the Bedford General Infirmary, the 7th Duke developed a passion for better standards of estate housing and community facilities, and not just in and around Woburn but also at Thornhaugh, Thorney and as far away as Tavistock. Typical of his interests

J. C. Bourne, *The West Front of the Abbey*, 1842. Here the royal couple alight under the awnings set up at the main door, while the crowd lines the slopes on either side. The Abbey is seen in all its mid-nineteenth-century splendour. Repton has added the small service building on the near end of the west range, and Flitcroft's north court fills the background behind the Abbey, all coming together to create a most impressive series of structures.

and reflecting his practical, thorough approach, the duke not only built new estate housing, he also went on to produce a small book of the designs and added comments that he hoped would be of use to other landowners seeking to improve the housing and therefore, he thought, the standard of living and morals of their agricultural labourers and their families.[15]

Published with the snappy title *Plans and Elevations of Cottages for Agricultural Labourers, designed for and executed on the Duke of Bedford's Bedfordshire Estate: with Bills of Quantities of Materials Required in their Construction,*

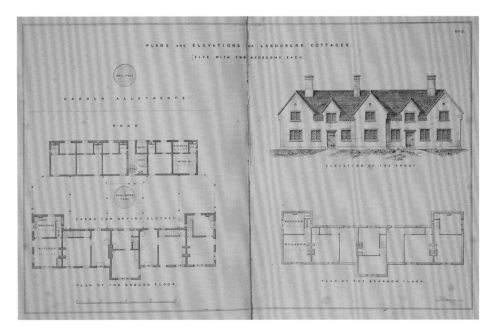

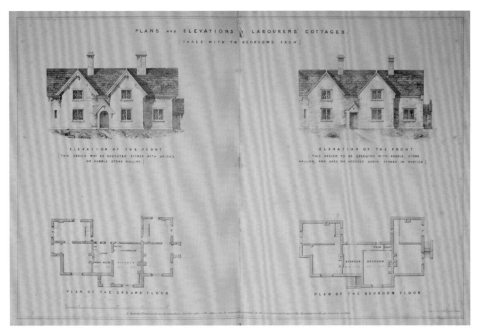

Cottages for Agricultural Labourers, No. 2: 'Plans and Elevations for Labourers' Cottages' (five houses with two bedrooms each). In addition to the cottages themselves, the duke and his surveyor also provided extra facilities in an attempt to create self-sufficient units of housing. With their fronts facing the road, at the back was a carefully laid out outdoor space complete with neatly divided up 'Yards for drying clothes', a central rain water tank, and a range of outbuildings containing a communal bakehouse, as well as a woodshed, pigsty and toilet for each house. Behind this ran an access road with the families' allotments behind.

Cottages for Agricultural Labourers, No. 7: 'Plans and Elevations for Labourers' Cottages' (five houses with two bedrooms each, and ideas for ornamentation). Allowing a small budget for extra ornamentation, the cottages were otherwise entirely utilitarian in design, with space pared down to a minimum. Nevertheless, they were built to a very high standard, and it is perhaps no surprise that they stand today, still sought after as housing, having been modernized during the 1980s by Robin and Henrietta, 14th Duke and Duchess.

Labourers' cottages: the development of the settlement along the road between Crawley Lodge and School Lane.
Typical of the development of small communities of labourers' cottages around the Woburn park wall in the nineteenth century is that along the Crawley road (A4012) from Woburn village. The cottages were largely built by Francis, 7th Duke, and all are occupied and in good repair today. The addition of the Reading Rooms on the corner opposite the pub on School Lane by Herbrand, 11th Duke gave the community a central focus.
Date key for the cottages:
green: 1850; blue: 1852; yellow: 1853; red: 1854; brown: 1856; purple: 1894.

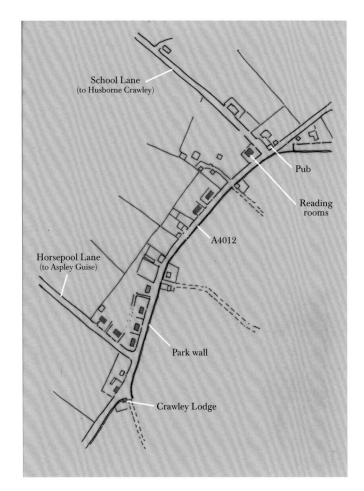

School Lane
(to Husborne Crawley)

Pub

Reading rooms

A4012

Horsepool Lane
(to Aspley Guise)

Park wall

Crawley Lodge

the book eventually ran to two editions. In it the duke writes that new cottages are needed because, first, many of the existing ones 'are deficient in requisite accommodation as to be inadequate to the removal of that acknowledged obstacle to the improvement of the morals and habits of agricultural labourers, which consists in the want of separate bedrooms for grown up boys and girls, and, second, the practice of taking in lodgers had led to still further evils.' Another consideration is that 'improved methods of cultivation . . . and the conversion of wood-land into tillage' have increased the demand for labourers, so good new cottages are needed to meet this demand. To this end the book includes some seven designs for houses of two or three bedrooms, and while the style and design of the buildings are largely severely practical in the interests of economy, he would not have been his father's son if there was no possibility of some ornamentation. This appears at the end of the book, where we find some suggestions as to how these plain brick buildings could be given a lift and 'ornamented' with the addition of 'rubble stone walling', 'axed or dressed quoin stones in rustics', projecting string courses under the eaves and decorative barge boards on the gables.

The blocks of cottages can still be seen as you drive round the outside of the park wall; some of those built by the 7th Duke between 1850 and 1856 are neatly lined up along the roadside outside the park gates at Crawley and on Leighton Street, Woburn, while a number by the 11th Duke can be seen in the villages of Ridgemont[16] and Woburn, each with its date stone alerting us to when they were built. Similar survivors can also be seen in and around the village of Thornhaugh, where, in addition to cottages, the wonderful Post Office building still survives as a private residence set back from the road in its neat garden, the duke's initials 'FB' visible above the front door. This building, with its blend of the practical with elements of the fanciful picturesque aesthetic that was so much a part of his father's life, represents a utilitarian but decorative addition to the village, and is one which in many ways seems to sum up both the interests and the legacy of the 7th Duke and Duchess. Their legacy was to spread as far afield as Tavistock, where between 1845 and

RIGHT Old Thornhaugh
Post Office, 2104.
Typical of the good state
of repair of the buildings
built by the Bedford estate
in the nineteenth century
is the surviving Post Office
building, now a private
house, outside the village
of Thornhaugh. Unlike
the utilitarian, red brick
buildings which were to
follow, the 7th Duke added
a touch of the picturesque
whimsy he had grown up
with at Woburn to the
houses he created.

OPPOSITE George
Richmond, *Hastings Russell,
9th Duke of Bedford* (1819–
1891), 1869.
This portrait shows
Hastings as the capable
and committed manager
of the estates that he was,
someone who took his
responsibilities as duke
very seriously, while also
following a keen personal
interest in experimental
agriculture.

1866 some 300 cottages were built by the duke and his surveyors, primarily for mining families, and many are still extant.[17] His statue, erected in Tavistock by public subscription in 1864, stands today in front of the market and town hall complex which he created and which still provides a thriving focal point in the centre of the town.

With the death of the duke in 1861, however, after the long years of stability, Woburn's future suddenly seemed less assured. Anna Maria had died in 1857, and the duke was to be succeeded by their depressive, hypochondriac only child, William, who had spent most of his life living alone behind the closed shutters of his parents' London house in Belgrave Square; even the thought of a visit to Woburn, let alone living there, appears to have been a form of torture to him. Blakiston, who provides us with a wonderful portrait of the unfortunate heir, quotes his reasons why he found Woburn so unpleasant: 'By long experience and the exercise of ingenuity I have found ways of passing the day [in London] without it seeming long. But in the country [at Woburn], as I can, owing to my lameness, neither take a walk in the garden, nor owing to the weakness of my sight, avail myself of a library . . . I find by experience that I am quite without resource in the country, and without any sort of pleasure or amusement, and bound hand and foot the victim of ennui.'[18]

Given these circumstances, many at Woburn must have wondered what the future held in the hands of the 8th Duke. In the event, the answer came swiftly. While his father was alive, William had continued his sad, reclusive life in London, and on his death, unable even to contemplate taking on the responsibilities coming his way, he immediately handed over management

Richard Buckner, *Elizabeth Sackville-West, Duchess of Bedford* (1818–1897). Wife of the 9th Duke and mother of the 10th and 11th Dukes, Elizabeth was at the centre of family life during the height of Woburn's Victorian pomp and prosperity, and her influence on how it was run and how it appeared to the world lasted until her son Herbrand's death in 1940. Thanks largely to the interest in photography of her daughters Ela and Ermyntrude and her own prolific diary writing, we are able to recapture something of the splendour of her time at Woburn.

of the Bedford estates to his cousin, Hastings Russell, the 43-year-old son of Lord George William and Elizabeth Russell.

Hastings, who eventually inherited as 9th Duke on his sickly cousin's death in 1872, was to prove a capable manager for the estates. With his wife, Elizabeth Sackville-West, he was to fill the Abbey again with the bustle of family life as they raised Sackville (later 10th Duke), Ela, Ermyntrude and Herbrand (later 11th Duke), the first Russell family whose life at Woburn we can come to know through photography.[19] Besides routine estate management, Hastings went on to develop and alter the park in line with his own personal interests, which included experimental agriculture, in the cause of which he became President of the Royal Agricultural Society, and as a keen naturalist he expanded the existing deer herds with the introduction of new species. During his time and that of his son Herbrand, Woburn became renowned for its collections of animals, a tradition that is maintained to this day in the form of the Safari Park.

After a childhood spent travelling in Europe with his parents, who by this time were estranged and living apart, Hastings Russell had returned to England in 1839 when he joined the Scots Fusilier Guards as a lieutenant. With limited prospects of promotion, he left army life in 1844 when he married Elizabeth Sackville-West, and the couple settled at Bourn Hall in Cambridgeshire. Unfortunately, his mother formed an implacable dislike of his bride, a situation which caused a permanent rift between mother and son, and broke his heart. Reading what he went on to write to his father, '[my mother's] dislike to my wife, which is consummate, tho' not unexpected as you know, forbids my looking forward with much pleasure to anything', suggests that it had also broken his spirit.[20]

A rootless, peripatetic childhood on the Continent, the estrangement of his parents, his disappointment in the Army, and now his mother's relentless hostility to his wife, all seem to have come together to turn Hastings into an introverted, solitary man who, although entertaining lavishly as duke, pursued his interests alone, detached emotionally from his family. In later life he became increasingly obsessed by money and his children's prospects, cynical and irritable. In 1891, faced with increasing illness, he shot himself.

While we know that the 9th Duke liked nothing better than time spent out in the park, studying and becoming something of an expert in the natural history of his deer herds and other animals of interest, it does not appear that he engaged in any meaningful way with the gardens and pleasure grounds. His wife, however, is a different matter. The daughter of George, 5th Earl de la Warr and Elizabeth Sackville, the young Elizabeth spent her childhood as part of a large and close family. Her diaries, kept between 1834 and 1876, give an interesting account of life at the family home of Buckhurst Park in East Sussex, an estate set in rolling countryside near Tunbridge Wells.[21]

HUMPHRY REPTON, *HINTS, PLANS AND SKETCHES FOR THE IMPROVEMENT OF STONELANDS IN SUSSEX*, 1805–6

Repton suggests that the house at Buckhurst Park (which he knew by its earlier name of Stonelands) be considered as a 'hunting seat, or lodge, on the verge of the ancient great park of Buckhurst, with the annexed lands and interest in the vast forest of Ashdown to which it is in a manner attached'. He goes on: 'With this view, I would rather wish to restore, than to destroy the true character of the place, not to increase its importance but to preserve it, and to take such advantage of its natural situation, as neither to modernize too much, nor to neglect those improvements in comfort, convenience, and elegance, which modern times have introduced. Those I think may be grafted on the old stock of its ancient character, without rooting it out entirely to plant a new one.'[22]

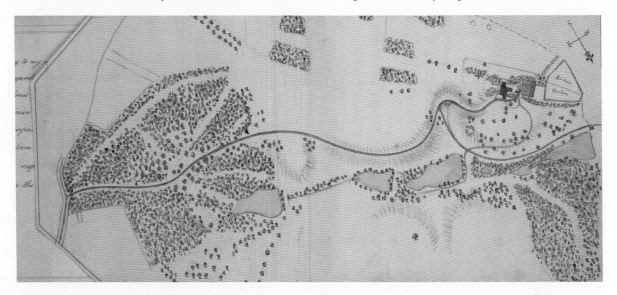

ABOVE Plate I: 'Plan of Improvements'.
Buckhurst Park, set in the East Sussex countryside near Ashdown Forest, as it was when Elizabeth Sackville was a young girl. In Repton's plan of the site, which includes his ideas for alterations, we see the gardens around the house where she spent much of her time. Also visible are the plantations to which she loved to walk, the approach roads down which the family travelled, and the lakes on which she sailed and fished with her brothers.

BELOW LEFT Plate II: 'View from the House to the South-West (After)'.
The millpond seen to the south-west of the house. This was another favourite destination for Elizabeth and where she went 'out in the punt before breakfast with Reggie [one of her brothers] to take up the Trimmers [a kind of fishing line]' and caught two pike. On another occasion, she tells us that 'We went out in the garden and planted the Princess's acorns in the ground near the Mill Pond.' The princess was Victoria, Elizabeth's childhood friend whom she went on to serve as a lady-in-waiting. Perhaps the oaks that grew can still be found. Repton shows us how he would alter the view to improve the picturesque qualities of the composition. How he did this was typical of his approach, screening the unsightly barn which dominates the centre of the view above the pond, while opening up the trees on the near shore to reveal the much more interesting mill itself. He then wraps new woodland round the far end of the pond, running the belt of trees up the hill behind, framing the pond in a long elegant wooded curve that follows the shape of the ground. He also suggests bringing an overall uniformity and cohesion to the scene by converting the arable fields on the far side of the pond into open parkland.

An 'Entrance Lodge' is recommended to be built in the 'style and date of those old cottages on the borders of a forest', and to be designed – as Aspley Lodge at Woburn was to be five years later and Purrett's Hill Lodge in the 1830s – 'by a nice observance of the costume, forms, and construction, of such buildings as actually existed in the days of Queen Elizabeth'.

The top picture below shows the house as Elizabeth knew it, and it is still largely recognizable today. It would seem that some of Repton's ideas were adopted, particularly the new style of chimney, but not the new 'arcade' and tower along the main front.

ABOVE Plate III: 'Entrance Lodge' to the park (shown on the left of his plan), to be built in the style of an Elizabethan era 'Woodman's Cottage'.

LEFT Plate VI: 'The House, Before'.
Repton seems to have found the house rather plain and forbidding, and as will be seen in the next plate (after), he proposed adding a number of more decorative features which 'may be adopted or omitted without injury to the rest'. These were to include an 'arcade' along the ground floor which 'may be open in Summer, and glazed in Winter', a higher and grander central tower, and a new design for the rather dumpy chimneys.

LEFT Plate VI: 'The House, After'.
The house as Repton imagined it with new flower beds in the walled garden in front. Again, this design for the garden is very reminiscent of his design for the 'Dressed Garden' at Woburn. Following his discussion of the house, Repton goes into a long 'Digression' on the 'necessity of nice attention to the minutest detail in imitating the character of different dates'. Clearly, the 6th Duke of Bedford's comments about the necessity of authenticity was something that preoccupied both Repton and his son John Adey at this time.

LEFT Paris House, 1878.[23]
One significant
contribution by the 9th
Duke to the park as we
know it today was the
Paris House. Its proximity
to the Milton Gate in
the park wall, seen in
the background on the
right-hand side of this
photograph, led to it
playing an important role
in the wartime activities of
the secret services during
the Second World War. It
is now a restaurant.

RIGHT Lady Ermyntrude
standing in front of the 'Ivy
Window', 1882.
The 'Ivy Window' is the
opening amongst the ivy
that appears in several
family photographs,
in this one over Lady
Ermyntrude's shoulder.
Behind it is the passage
from the sculpture gallery
to the Camellia House, and
it seems to have been a
favourite place for people
to sit to look out over the
Sculpture Gallery Garden.
The opening still exists
just above the point where
the grass bank runs down
to the terrace, but it has
since been fitted with a
window frame and glazed.
The large urn also survives,
but has been moved round
to the central path of the
gardens running up to the
central terrace.

Reading the diaries, we follow her life as she works in her garden most
days for an hour or so before breakfast, practises piano and singing, helps
her mother entertain visitors, visits London and Tunbridge Wells, stays
with her Sackville cousins at Knole, accompanies her father to inspect
the bullocks or to watch him shoot, sits 'under the trees all afternoon
drawing', strolls in the gardens or sits reading there on long summer
evenings, and, above all, takes long daily walks or rides to every corner
of the estate and neighbouring countryside: she walks to the 'Plantations',
the cascade and the hop garden, fishes in the millpond, sails on the
lake with her brothers, rides to the 'five hundreds'. What makes these
diaries particularly interesting, however, is the fact that the landscape,
gardens and some of the features around Buckhurst she describes had
been recorded for us by Humphry Repton (who knew the property by the
earlier name of Stonelands) in his Red Book for Stonelands some thirty
years before.[24]

And it was not only at Buckhurst that Elizabeth came to know Repton's
work, since by the time her husband took over responsibility for the Bedford
estates from his ailing cousin in 1861 and the couple moved into the Abbey,
they had been living at Bourn Hall in Cambridgeshire, another property
where Repton had offered 'hints'. Owned by her parents from around 1803,
the house had picturesque grounds, part of which included the ruins and
'raised earthwork of the old castle'.[25] Repton advised on the grounds, the
route of the driveway approach and the design of the ornamental gardens
c.1815, before his son, the architect John Adey Repton, enlarged the house
between 1817 and 1819.

As we know from her diaries that Elizabeth was interested in gardens and gardening from an early age, and came to know the landscapes at both Buckhurst and Bourn intimately, we can imagine her interest on discovering the Red Books for both Woburn and Endsleigh in the Abbey library. Since her husband's interests lay in the practical and scientific worlds of agriculture and natural history, during their time at the Abbey from 1872 to 1891, it is likely to have been Elizabeth who was responsible for the continued upkeep and development of the gardens, the pleasure grounds generally, the Duchess's Garden and the formal layouts of the South Terrace Garden and the Sculpture Gallery Garden, overlooked by the 'Ivy Window'.

These gardens, and the pleasure grounds beyond, went on to survive in all their complexity until at least the 1930s, when landscape designer Percy Cane was called in with the specific brief of clearing and simplifying them in order to cut the number of gardeners needed and to generally

LEFT Sculpture Gallery Garden, *c.*1910. A view over the Sculpture Gallery Garden some twenty years after Ermyntrude posed beside her urn. The urn itself is visible at the point where the ground levels out in this photograph. The plants of the parterre gardens had changed since Georgina had designed this layout in the 1830s, but the scene would have been as immediately recognizable to her as it is to us today. One intriguing question about this photograph is the identity of the little girl sitting sedately beside the hedge on the left. She appears in a number of photographs of this time, clearly under strict instructions to keep still, but is never named.

lower maintenance costs. In one sense this move reflects the necessity of economy in the face of the new realities of the inter-war years, but it also reflects the fact that neither the 11th Duke nor his wife was particularly interested in the gardens.

On his father's sudden death Sackville Russell, Marquis of Tavistock, became the 10th Duke in 1891. Although he had become a barrister and served as a Member of Parliament, Sackville suffered persistent ill health, largely due to diabetes, and he was to die just two years after becoming duke, aged 37. So it was that, although he could not have foreseen the possibility, these two deaths meant Sackville's younger brother, Colonel Lord Herbrand Russell, unexpectedly succeeded as the 11th Duke in 1893. As the second son of the 9th Duke, Herbrand had found a career for himself in the Army, serving in Egypt before becoming an aide-de-camp on the staff of Lord Dufferin, Viceroy of India, in 1884. Judging from the photographs that survive of his time in India, images of the young colonel as part of the vice-regal staff posed amidst the extraordinary grandeur of imperial architecture and the luxurious garden parties in Barrackpore and Simla, it would seem that this was a world in which Herbrand was entirely comfortable. It suited not just his sense of self but also his talents, as he 'applied to the duties of organizing the vice-regal establishment the same qualities as he brought to the estate management', a combination which provided the pattern for the rest of his life.[26]

Government House, Barrackpore, India, 1887. A wonderful photograph which causes the viewer to look twice and wonder about the house and where it is. The grand house, with sweeping grassed parkland, lake and towering trees, looks very familiar; but it is not Woburn or indeed any other country house in England. It is, in fact, Government House at Barrackpore. The picture is interesting because it indicates the luxurious and apparently timeless setting in which the Viceroy of India and his staff lived and worked at the height of the British empire, a setting that remained a part of Herbrand's vision of himself and how Woburn should be run.

Writing of his grandfather, whom he first met as a teenager in 1933, John Russell (known as Ian), who became 13th Duke in 1953, says, 'I think he knew he was a survivor from another world and wanted only to live out his time.'[27] That other world was not just Edwardian England but also British imperial India. John goes on: '[He] lived an extraordinary life . . . completely isolated from his contemporaries and the affairs of his time.' Surviving through the turmoil of the First World War and the Depression, the 11th Duke appears as a solitary, somewhat melancholy man, who saw it as 'his job to continue the traditions of the past', and was determined to maintain the Abbey and the estates in the form in which he found them.

This assessment of the 11th Duke by his grandson is supported by others. Christopher Trent, for example, writes, 'Duke Herbrand . . . projected the traditions and image of the 19th century Dukes far into the 20th with an unflagging determination.'[28] In 1897, Herbrand published *The Story of the Great Agricultural Estate,* in which he advocated the importance of maintaining tradition. In it he outlines his belief that 'the system of land tenure which allows a great estate to descend unimpaired from one generation to another, secures to those dwelling on the soil material and moral advantages greater than any that are promised under any alternative system', and this appears to have remained his conviction regardless of the speed at which the world was changing around him. His grandson sums things up: 'He regarded himself as something of an innovator in agriculture and forestry . . . [but] otherwise Woburn was run exactly as it had been since the 18th Century.'

Given these circumstances we should not look at this time for innovation, new gardens, new ideas or new designs. Rather, the changes that came at the Abbey and in the park of his day reflected above all Herbrand's interest in pheasant shooting, on the one hand, and zoology and the Zoological Society, of which he served as president between 1899 and 1936, on the other. His long presidency of this society was one of the few public forums in which he continued to participate.

While in India he had met and married Mary Tribe, daughter of the Archdeacon of Lahore, in 1888, and on their return to England that year, while based in London, they soon began to spend an increasing amount of time at Cairnsmore, a shooting estate in Galloway on which they took a long lease. Life at this 'hunting lodge', beneath the windswept fells of Cairnsmore of Fleet, seems to have suited both of them. Herbrand sought to improve both access to the moors with a new road and the grouse habitat and to introduce new species of game birds. Mary herself was a crack shot and confirmed outdoor person, and their only child, Hastings, the future 12th Duke, was born at Cairnsmore and remembers their life being spent between the three estates of Woburn, Cairnsmore and Endsleigh.

Meanwhile, as duke, Herbrand immediately began to add to the animal collections at Woburn, notably in 1895 when he added Père David deer from China, and in 1896 we get a vivid image of the park at the turn of the century.

George Reid, *Herbrand Russell, 11th Duke of Bedford* (1858–1940), 1903. Although he had exchanged his military uniforms for 'morning coat and striped trousers', Herbrand continued to see the world through the lens of vice-regal splendour. His grandson Ian, later 13th Duke, remembers that on journeys to London you 'never travelled with your suitcase . . . it had to come in another car, so you had a chauffeur and a footman with yourself, and a chauffeur and a footman with the suitcase . . . This régime went right on until my grandfather died in 1940.'

Lady Abercromby, *Mary Tribe, Duchess of Bedford* (1865–1937), the 'Flying Duchess', 1906.
This portrait of Mary is one of the very few images of her in which she is not dressed for some outdoor pursuit. More often than not, she is canoeing, shooting, sailing, riding, hiking, fishing, bird watching on a Scottish island, wrapped up in her leather flying gear or in her nurse's uniform. Hers was a busy, active, adventurous life, often spent far from Woburn and not at the heart of the household or developing the gardens.

In the October edition of *The Zoologist*, Richard Lydekker describes 'the naturalist's paradise' he found in the Woburn 'Menagerie' that year:

this extensive and beautifully-timbered domain contains . . . a collection of wild animals which in this country can be rivalled only by the well-known gardens at Regent's Park. Instead, however, of being cooped up within the narrow limits of small paddocks . . . [the animals] are allowed room to roam under conditions more or less resembling those of their native lands . . . perhaps the most marked and interesting instance is afforded by the Elks, of which there are several. On most days these huge ungainly ruminants may be seen standing belly-deep in one of the lakes, lazily cropping the water-plants . . . or a party of three or more Sable Antelopes [may be seen] feeding among a mass of bracken in a secluded glen.[29]

Also present were bison, wild horses, wallabies, cavys, a 'unique collection' of swans, and multitudes of game birds. Of the last Lydekker writes: 'Wandering through the well-kept coverts [the Evergreens], one may be startled by the flashing metallic tints of a cock Monal (*Lophophorus impeyanus*) as it dashes in head-long flight; while the next moment a Tragropan (*Ceriornis*) struts by in all the glory of its scarlet plumage and blue neck-frill . . . Considering that the coverts are regularly shot, one wonders how all these lovely birds escape destruction; till one is told that those in which the exotic forms are chiefly kept are shot over only by the Duke and Duchess, who fire only at *Phasianus colchicus*.' Completing his picture of the late nineteenth-century park, Lydekker tells us: 'that the ordinary public are not debarred from participating to a certain extent in the delights afforded by the collection is clear from the fact that on the August Bank Holiday the entire park and grounds are thrown open to all who care to come. Since, moreover, the park is crossed by a public road, the pedestrian or cyclist has any day of the year an opportunity of seeing such of the animals as happen to be grazing or wandering within sight of the track.'

This account is really very interesting, and not only enables us to imagine the park as it appeared some hundred years ago, but also tells us that the deer park had finally completed its centuries-long conversion from a place of hunting deer and game to one of their ornamental display, that the trees of the Evergreens, once the centre of attention themselves, were now seen as

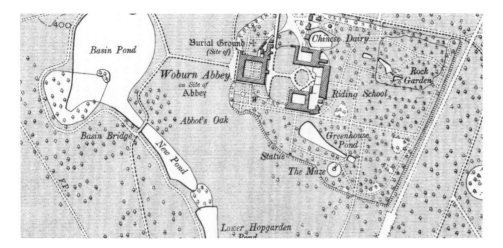

Ordnance Survey map of 1902, Bedfordshire, Sheet XXIV, SE, detail of Bason Pond and Menagerie area. In addition to the layout of the South Terrace Garden, two other details are very interesting. First, we see that the Bason Pond has been divided up into separate enclosures to keep various water bird species apart. It is also evident from this map that many of the flower beds in the pleasure grounds have been replaced by grass, although some caution is needed in taking the map too literally since photographs indicate that the Sculpture Gallery Garden, not shown here, was most certainly there at this time.

providing 'well-kept coverts' for pheasant shooting, and that the Menagerie, once a discrete area of the pleasure grounds, was now seen to extend across the entire park. Indeed, by the 1880s, Repton's Menagerie of 1808 appears to have been totally dismantled. The look and atmosphere of the park will also have changed, divided in places with fenced enclosures, including around sections of the Bason Pond itself. It also seems clear that from the time of Lydekker's visit in 1896 until the duke's death in 1940, although the numbers of animals steadily declined from the late 1930s, the look and uses of the park itself remained essentially unchanged from that described by Dr Thomson in 1838.

The duke and duchess's son, Hastings, later 12th Duke, also grew up with a deep interest in natural history, and in his memoir of 1949 he tells us that the collections had begun about 1895, with his father adding, seemingly quite randomly, an enormous variety of new species, some of which thrived but many of which did not. Some, like the wild horses, failed because 'Little trouble was taken by my father to breed them properly and the herd gradually faltered.'[30] Others, such as the tahr goats, proved too aggressive towards other species to be kept in the open park, while many, such as the giraffes, fell victim to the wartime lack of fodder, both in 1914–18 and 1939–45, that decimated the deer herds and those of other large ruminants such as the eland, kudu and gnu. Wartime rations also fatally reduced the bison herd, but a number of species had only ever been marginally successful since the grass at Woburn simply did not suit their needs, and the lack of specific nutrients led to many developing rickets and other diseases.

And so, in spite of the bucolic outward appearance of things as described by Lydekker, all did not continue well for the park full of animals. Hastings goes on to explain, 'My father, though keenly interested in the animals and most knowledgeable, displayed in certain directions a strange carelessness, combined with an unwillingness to take suggestions or advice.' Thus, when Hastings, as 12th Duke, resumed some kind of control after the war, the great collection had been reduced to the red, roe, fallow and Père David deer herds, and a few other stray survivors, notably the rheas and wallabies.

While the collections of animals and participation in the Royal Zoological Society were largely due to Herbrand, Duchess Mary shared many of these interests and became well known in ornithological circles for her researches in the new science of bird migration. Of her other interests, some left an enduring legacy to the history of Woburn, including her establishment of a military hospital at the Abbey during the First World War, her creation of a groundbreaking surgical hospital in the village of Woburn, and her passion for flying. The role played by Duchess Anna Maria at the Bedford General Infirmary had been that of patron and fundraiser; Duchess Mary's interest in the hospitals she founded and at which she worked long shifts was different. Her involvement reflected a lifelong interest in nursing, and she participated as both administrator and trained nurse, not just on the wards but also in surgery. Any traces of the military hospital which occupied the riding school were swept away with the building itself, but outside the village of Woburn, after requisition during the Second World War by the secret services and life in the 1960s as an adult education centre, her Marylands Hospital survives today as private housing.

In 1925, Mary turned with typical enthusiasm to a new interest when she started to learn to fly. Over the years that followed she became a national figure as the 'Flying Duchess', making a series of record-breaking flights with one of her instructors, Captain Barnard (to India in 1929 and South Africa in 1930), but mostly she flew for her own pleasure. A typical flight is recorded by the *Glasgow Herald*, which in September 1926 reported in its 'Social

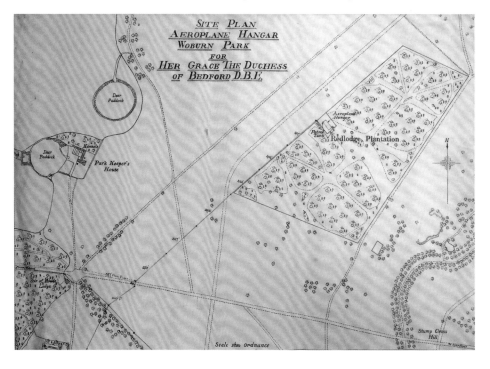

'Site Plan: Aeroplane Hangar Woburn Park'. Recently rediscovered in a storeroom in the Bedford estate offices, this map finally solves the puzzle as to exactly where the hangar for the Flying Duchess's planes stood. We see it here set amongst the trees of the Red Lodge plantation, complete with petrol tank.

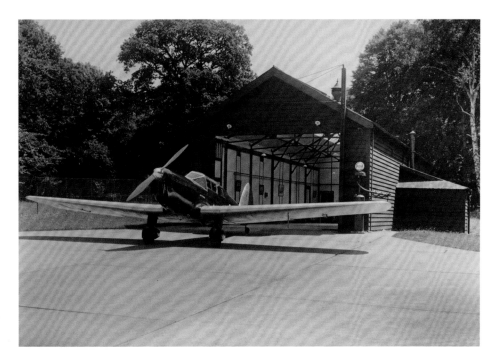

and Personal' column: 'The Duchess of Bedford travelled from Woburn Abbey to Cairnsmore, the Duke of Bedford's estate in Kirkcudbrightshire, yesterday in a de Havilland Moth aeroplane piloted by Capt. Board. The machine made a perfect landing.' In order to make it possible to fly in and out of Woburn, in 1928 the duchess had a section of the park levelled sufficiently to act as an airstrip, and built a small hangar and workshop amongst the trees of the Red Lodge plantation. The exact location of her landing strip is not recorded, but it was almost certainly incorporated into the much longer one created by the Air Ministry a few years later during the war. Audrey Taylor, daughter of the duchess's mechanic, J.W. Dodd, tells us that 'Mary, Duchess of Bedford, had a lovely hangar . . . It was painted in her favourite colours, green and white, accommodating two aircraft, a Gypsy Moth and a Puss Moth. She herself had a very pleasant office there on the left and to the rear was my Father's workshop. To the right at the front was a petrol pump. There was also a windsock. Many species of deer, llama and rhea wandered in the Park and my father had to clear the runway both for take-off and landing, by riding along on his bicycle.'[31]

While the animal collections may already have diminished, Mr Todd must have cut quite a figure shooing animals away while pedalling furiously across the park ahead of the aircraft. The other figure those passing along the road to Froxfield in winter may have caught sight of at this time was that of the duchess herself, scarf flying, as she circled her special outdoor ice rink in the park. Today, the site of the rink is one of the more ephemeral reminders of her use of the park, and it is at Endsleigh, rather than Woburn, that we catch more certain glimpses of her interests and the kind of person she was.

Once again, Hastings points the way when commenting on his mother's skill as a canoeist, an interest she pursued on the Tamar at Endsleigh. 'Canoeing in the Rob Roy canoes was a pastime in which my parents and their guests indulged regularly in their younger days . . . It required considerable skill, as the Rob Roy is an unstable craft and the Tamar is full of rocks and rapids.' He adds, 'My mother, always brilliant at

LEFT 'Rob Roy' canoes on the Tamar, early twentieth century. We know from his mother's diaries that Herbrand was something of an expert in these canoes, and Mary may well have been 'hardly ever unshipped', but their instability was a cause of constant hilarity to the family as yet another hapless visitor was flipped into the water. Fishing is too important a business these days for any such disturbance of the river.

The 'fishing cottage' at Endsleigh.
The fishing cottage mentioned in Elizabeth's diaries was often used in the late nineteenth century as a place to visit for tea. It sat in complete isolation beside the river Inny as it flowed down to join the Tamar below Castle Head. To reach it, the family crossed the Tamar below the house, and took the carriage along a narrow riverside path as it looped round the bend, following the river upstream beneath the steep wooded slopes of Wareham Woods. Outings like this remained central to their holidays at Endsleigh right up until the Second World War.

The family at Weir Cottage 'tea house'.
Other trips took the family downstream, again following the path beside the river. In this case they are visiting the 'tea house' beside the river at Weir Cottage, some way downstream from Horsebridge. At least three of these little cabins were built: one on Castle Head, now in ruinous condition, one high up in Wareham Woods, still standing, and this one, preserved today exactly as it looks in this picture. We also catch a glimpse here of the duke and duchess, on what looks like a more formal outing, and their son, Hastings, standing behind them.

every sport or more serious enterprise she turned her hand to, was hardly ever unshipped, and my father was always very good in a canoe.'

While at Endsleigh at least three 'tea houses' were built, little was added to such facilities at Woburn. The Thornery and the Log Cabin in the Evergreens continued to be used, and the dairy at Park Farm was restored and possibly enlarged around 1900, but many of the park buildings, such as Purrett's Hill Lodge, were long gone and not replaced. By 1902, most of the buildings, tree plantings and formal flower beds shown east of the stable blocks on the 1838 plan of the pleasure grounds had also gone, and this process of simplification was further advanced by Percy Cane's work in the 1930s when the high-maintenance plantings and formal border layouts were removed. Repton's children's garden seems also to have gone out of use at around this time.

In 1939, as war was declared, Herbrand was 81, living alone in the Abbey in increasing ill health, in mourning for his wife, who had died two years before, and estranged from his son, whose pacifism during two wars caused a lasting rift. It was truly the end of an era, and when Herbrand died the next year, everything changed at Woburn. While during the period that followed we cannot trace interesting developments in new gardens, new buildings, or the arrival of new animals in the park, it is nevertheless

Dairy at Park Farm, 2015.

crucial to the history we are following, since the changes that occurred were responsible, in many important ways, for how the house, park and gardens look today.

In 1940, following Herbrand's death, the Abbey, the estate and a number of properties in Woburn, Aspley Guise and Milton Bryan were all requisitioned for the war effort, which saw the arrival of staff from various divisions of the secret services and Bletchley Park between 1940 and 1942, and staff and equipment from the Air Ministry from 1943 to 1948. To those in the secret services who took over the Abbey, it became 'CHQ' (Country Headquarters), to the Wrens from Bletchley billeted there it became part of 'HMS Pembroke', while to pilots the park became 'SLG [Satellite Landing Ground] No. 38'. With extraordinary suddenness, the long continuity of occupation and identity we have been following was broken as the family were replaced by secret service personnel.

Most of these were connected to PWE (Political Warfare Executive), a highly secretive division formed in 1941 to disseminate 'black propaganda'; this was largely in the form of radio broadcasts, but also included newspapers and leaflets for air-drops into Germany. PWE's director, Dennis Sefton Delmer, describes his aims as trying out 'a new type of "Black Radio" on the Germans . . . one that undermines Hitler not by opposing him, but by pretending to be all for him and his war . . . a super patriotic platform . . . to get across all manner of subversive material under the cover of nationalistic patriotic clichés.'[32] Broadcasting from a purpose-built high-powered transmitter at Milton Bryan (which still stands in the woods on the edge of the village), this format was then extended to broadcasts aimed at specific audiences, such as German U-boat crews in the Atlantic and German troops in northern Europe.

Although these operations were largely going on out of sight, they filled the quiet villages around Woburn with an unprecedented number of new arrivals. As Sefton Delmer explains: 'My team had expanded so rapidly that we had been forced to requisition extra houses in Aspley Guise . . . the villagers were much intrigued by the mysterious foreigners who strolled through their narrow lanes and village streets. No one knew who or what they were.' This influx anticipated the years of tourism that were to follow, and was part of the sudden changes that affected not just the Russell family and the Abbey at this time, but also the tempo and nature of life of those living around it. The outside world burst in on the quiet, self-contained continuity of Herbrand's dukedom and the communities within it, and it was here to stay.

For others, the Abbey took on another identity altogether. The 'bombes' used to decipher German codes at Bletchley were each staffed twenty-four hours a day by Wrens whose life, as naval ratings, was regulated by naval tradition, and whose posting at Bletchley was codenamed 'HMS Pembroke'. About 200 Wrens, whose unit was HMS Pembroke V, were billeted at

Woburn Abbey, either in the house itself or in two prefabricated huts outside in the east court. Whether they were in the attics or the huts, 'we were given, not rooms but cabins', while another also remembers that 'We had to speak Navy talk all the time, so we had cabins, and a forecastle, and we ate in the galley'; in a fascinating and unique switch of viewpoint, 'when we went out the front door, we were said to have gone ashore.'[33]

In the Abbey we are told 'there were no carpets and no heating, it was always bitterly cold' and 'they had taken out all the furniture, all the carpets and all the pictures . . . My cabin was up in the attic . . . and it was bitterly cold in winter, freezing, and diabolically hot in summer. They could just about fit four double-decker bunks in each cabin so there were 8 of us squashed in . . . The cabin became our little social group.' A number of the Wrens also recall the park itself, through which they had to walk to and from the village, on their way to the pub or a cup of tea in the NAAFI, and march through in uniform to church on Sundays. One describes the Abbey as 'a lovely place to be; it had a beautiful park and I remember the barking of the deer in the rutting season . . . We were free to walk in the entire park.' Another recalls: 'In summer we could sleep in the Park, taking care not to disturb the rhododendrons!'

By 1943, the Air Ministry in its turn had become interested in the park itself, and part of it was requisitioned to become No. 38 Satellite Landing Ground, a storage and maintenance facility for the No. 8 MU (Maintenance Unit) based at Little Rissington. Chris Gravett, the curator at Woburn, tells us that by June 1943 there were some thirty-six aircraft based at Woburn, including Tiger Moths, Spitfires, Hurricanes, Wellingtons and Lancasters, parked amongst the trees of Red Lodge plantation behind the Flying Duchess's hangar.[34] Beyond this, her airstrip was extended to run from the edge of the trees, across the road and up the rising ground above the Bason Pond; barbed wire fences were erected to keep the deer herds off it. By April 1944, the number of aircraft in the park had increased substantially as 200 Stirling bombers arrived to be converted to tow gliders in preparation for the Normandy landings, after which some of the Stirlings 'returned to Woburn [and] were broken up on site'.[35]

While the last of these planes were finally disposed of by 1948, the large-scale smoothing out of the ground for the extended airstrip represents, perhaps, the last great alteration to be made to the landscape of the park that we now see, the end of a process begun all those years ago by the 4th Duke when he ploughed out the last of the medieval ridge and furrow fields below the Serpentine Terrace. It is a legacy of which no doubt the Flying Duchess herself would have been proud, and has continued into modern times with a series of air shows featuring her favourite planes, the Gypsy Moths.

As with so many places across Europe, at the Abbey and in the grounds these war years were the moment when countless intricate and often unnoticed layers of accumulated material and human history were stripped away and lost as the house and grounds were relentlessly modified to meet the needs of conducting a war. Indoors, as the Abbey and the buildings around it were steadily taken over, the family's possessions and furniture were packed up and stored in one wing, the bare rooms broken up by partition walls into warrens of small offices, conference rooms and canteens. Outdoors, in the park, trees were taken down, undergrowth removed, roads laid, fences erected, huts built, rubbish buried, and the deer herds thinned not just by a lack of food, but also, as Hastings tells us, by 'the park gates being left open' and the 'reckless driving [of ministry officers] which killed and maimed many of the deer'.[36]

Of course, following the war, repairs were made to the buildings, while in the park the fences were removed and the grass grew again, but something had been lost – the Abbey, park and gardens would never look, and perhaps feel, the same again. What had been lost is hard to describe, since it represents as much as anything else an intangible quality of association, for, however good the repairs, the ephemeral patina of age and memory was gone. Making it possible for this to form again, and providing the right kind of surfaces on which such phenomena can form, has been the post-war challenge and provides the deeper narrative of the current restoration programme.

Though the war ended in 1945, not until the end of 1948 were the Abbey, park and grounds fully handed back to the family, and for a number of

The east entrance just before demolition, c.1949. A last look at Henry Holland's grand east entrance to the Abbey shortly before the post-war demolition began. The photograph gives a vivid impression of just how the building had deteriorated with broken balustrades, boarded up windows and a general air of abandonment. Today this wing is completely gone and steps run down into the remaining east court.

Porter's lodge and the road over the bridge to the east front.
Built in the 1830s by Wyatville, the porter's lodge survived the demolition and still stands today. This photograph shows the entrance road to the Abbey passing through the gates to the right and straight on down over the bridge to the east entrance. It also shows the porter standing at his post resplendent in top hat and brass-buttoned jacket, a sight that could be seen at all the lodges round the park. Today, the lodge provides offices and mess room for the Abbey's gardeners.

reasons the house was not lived in again until 1953. When Herbrand died in 1940 he had been succeeded by his son, Hastings, as 12th Duke of Bedford, but the new duke and duchess, Louisa Jowitt Whitwell,[37] were never to move back to the Abbey. Having spent most of the war living in London, in 1945, estranged from his wife, Hastings prepared to move back to the Abbey where he hoped to 'restore in some measure the zoological treasures'.[38] At Woburn, however, he 'found that the hush-hush people who had taken over part of Woburn refused to have him anywhere near the place in view of the reputation as a security risk he had gained for himself'. Faced with this situation, Hastings retired 'to the shooting estate [his father] had always rented in Scotland'.[39]

Four years later, the secret services and the Air Ministry had finally left and Hastings ordered a survey of the Abbey to assess its condition. Apart from anything else, the survey discovered extensive dry rot which led to the demolition of the entire east wing and the adjoining parts of the north and south wings between 1949 and 1950; given the financial situation, with death duties of some £5,000,000 due following his father's death, this was perhaps inevitable. Also demolished, although for less clear reasons, were the riding school and tennis court complex,[40] and with these went the Heath House and the covered walkway. While the riding school and tennis court were certainly quite a loss, the removal of the walkway broke that crucial connection between the house, the sculpture gallery, the Chinese dairy and the children's garden and grotto beyond, which had for so long provided not

just the underlying sense of cohesion of the idea of the pleasure grounds, but also the unity of the physical layout.

Due partly to the scale of the demolition project, but also to the difficulties of obtaining building licences and materials for work on private houses in the immediate post-war period, the rebuilding work was still under way in 1953, the year Hastings was found shot dead at Endsleigh. The circumstances surrounding his death remain unclear, whether the gunshot which killed him was an accident or not, but the result was another severe financial blow for the estate. Following the death duties already incurred, Hastings in turn died before measures taken to avoid further duties came into force; the result was a further bill of £4,500,000 and a complex problem for the new duke John, known to the family as Ian, as to how to save the Abbey from being either sold, gifted to the National Trust, or demolished.[41]

Although Ian was not told that he was the grandson of the Duke of Bedford until he was a teenager and was 16 the day he first set eyes on Woburn Abbey in 1933, when he suddenly found himself duke in 1953, he seems scarcely to have hesitated in making his decision. Despite having no memories of the place, no emotional attachment to it, and little chance it seemed of ever being able to enjoy it, he insisted that the Abbey and parkland should not be sold or given to the National Trust. Instead he was determined to restore and live in the Abbey, while raising funds to do so by opening it to the public. He tells us in his book *A Silver-Plated Spoon* that he 'had realized from the beginning that the only way of financing the reopening of the house was to follow the tentative example of other families in our position, and allow the public to see it in return for an entrance fee'.

'A shattering experience' was how Ian described his first sight of the Abbey after the war in 1953, and his account of what he saw gives us a clear picture of the legacy of war and the demolitions:

> The Abbey looked as though a bomb had dropped on it. The Riding School and Tennis Court building had disappeared; so had the whole of the east front, together with at least a third of the north and south wings where it had joined them. There were piles of stones and building materials lying in haphazard fashion all over the place, the courtyard in the centre of the house was full of Nissan huts. There were only one or two workmen around, but otherwise the place was deserted. A troop of Alsatian dogs, chained on to long wires, kept watch at most of the gates . . . the interior was freezing cold and desolate . . . and reeked of damp. It looked as though no maintenance work had been done at all.[42]

Ian's first wife, Clare Holway,[43] had died in 1945, and it was with his second wife, Lydia Yarde-Buller,[44] that he set out on the daunting task of proving the Trustees and other doubters wrong, by making a financial success of opening the Abbey. As one era was about to begin, however, others were

Henry Graves, *Lady Ela Russell* (1854–1936), 1874.
Although her sister, Ermyntrude, had married in 1885, Ela remained a spinster, and was remembered as a somewhat eccentric great-aunt by the 13th Duke writing his memoir in 1959. Here we see her, however, as a 20-year-old in 1874, and it is interesting that she should have chosen Endsleigh as the background for her portrait. She is known to have been very fond of the house and continued to visit before her death in 1936. Indeed, it is quite possible that she is the elderly figure seated in her Bath-chair in the background of the photograph of the family canoeing (see page 193). The image also serves to emphasize the enduring importance of Endsleigh to successive generations of the family.

ending, and nowhere was this more true than in the wider Bedford estates. In order to proceed with the new plans, money needed to be raised, and during this period two of the iconic Russell estates were sold: Chenies in 1953 and Endsleigh in 1956. The former, Anne Sapcote, 1st Countess of Bedford's old childhood home beside the church and family mausoleum, had not been the family's primary residence since the 1630s, but Endsleigh had remained treasured for carefree family holidays, and was used consistently by successive generations from the moment it was built in 1814 right up until Hasting's death there in 1953.

After the war, however, things had changed, emotional ties had broken, and when Ian returned to Endsleigh from his home in South Africa for the inquest on his father's death it was as a stranger, since he had never holidayed there. When he later described it as 'a hideous Victorian house standing in the middle of our Tavistock estates', and said that he 'could not have cared less' what happened to it or Tavistock,[45] we can tell the spell woven so long ago by John and Georgina, the 6th Duke and Duchess, had finally broken. The sale of much of the land went ahead in 1956, with the house, gardens and fishing rights being run as a hotel by the Trustees of the Bedford Estates until 1962, when the remainder was all sold to the Endsleigh Fishing Club. It is now run as a private hotel, and much of the garden has been beautifully restored. On a summer's evening, sitting on the terrace as the swallows graze the lawn and the woods stretch away on all sides, it is still possible to recapture something of the qualities that made the place so special.

Back at Woburn, two years of hard work repairing, cleaning and decorating the Abbey, unpacking, washing, selecting and arranging furniture, china, pictures and ornaments, meant that a series of rooms were ready for visitors. Central to this process were Duchess Lydia and her sister Denise, Lady Ebury, who had come to live at Woburn with her children, and who was tasked, amongst other things, with cleaning the grotto – washing every shell and pebble with a cloth, soap and warm water – before acting as one of the guides.[46] With the guidebook written, the Abbey opened in April 1955, and as Ian makes clear, this was a huge step into the unknown. The entrance fee was set at 2/6d for adults and 1/6d for children, but on opening day 'We had no idea what to expect: half a dozen people on bicycles or a queue of cars as far as Dunstable.'[47] As it turned out, the venture proved a great success: 181,000 visitors came in 1955, 234,000 in 1956, 372,000 in 1957, with the half-million mark being reached in 1958, sufficient to solve the immediate financial crisis and provide a viable future for the Abbey into the twenty-first century.

Outside the Abbey the effect was as dramatic as within. By opening day, a plan for traffic circulation had been established, the internal park roads resurfaced, a visitor's car park created, ticket offices and gift shop built, and a restaurant set up in the south stable block, but this was only the beginning. As he warmed to his role as Woburn's Salesman-in-Chief, Ian was full of bigger plans. He tells us that prior to opening he had 'paid a couple of incognito visits to other houses open to the public', and had come away convinced that people must be made to feel welcome, of the need to 'make [visitors] enjoy themselves, give them service and value for money and make sure they come back again'. In an echo of the 5th Duke's attitude to the park and gardens, Ian states, 'I really discovered the enormous amount of pleasure and satisfaction there is in giving other people happiness . . . We keep no part of the Park to ourselves.'[48] In a mere fifteen years the park had gone from the private seclusion of Herbrand's time to a place where the Wrens could walk, march and even sleep out, and then to be entirely open to all for the price of a ticket.

To fulfil his vision, apart from opening the Abbey itself, Ian also introduced new elements which have since come to dominate the tourist experience – outdoor attractions. He had realized that although the 'actual contents and layout of the house cannot be altered to any major degree, the amenities of the park are capable of infinite variety'.

The 13th Duke and Duchess Lydia with the duke's second son, Rudolf (far right), and an inhabitant of the children's zoo, 1964.
Suddenly, almost shockingly, the world of Herbrand, Mary, great-aunt Ela and the top-hatted porters is gone, swept away by the war and the subsequent changes in the family's fortunes. A new duke in a sharp pinstripe suit and the world of modern tourism have both arrived at Woburn. In a photograph typical of the time, we see John, 13th Duke and Duchess Lydia greeting visitors in the Abbey's Petting Zoo, as the success of the opening of the house secured its future.
Images from the guidebooks tell the interesting story of how the attractions initially fitted into the surviving fabric of the buildings and gardens, before steadily expanding in a variety of new custom-built buildings and structures which, at the height of the 13th Duke's developments, came to dominate the entire area. Subsequently, changing tastes and an increasing emphasis on the history of the Abbey and its gardens have led to a new balance being established with a focus on the Abbey's past.

WOBURN OPENS TO THE PUBLIC: GUIDEBOOK MAPS

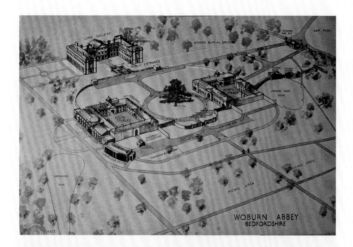

Site map from the first guidebook, 1955.
In this image, space is allotted for playgrounds and picnic areas, the grotto features as a wishing well, and the restaurant has opened in the south court, but little else has changed. The porter's lodge still dominates the entrance, and the bridge leads visitors over to the house, which is entered from the east court.

Site map from guidebook, 1964.
By 1964 we get the first indications of change. Little has changed around the Abbey itself (the entrance has been moved to the north front), but around the north and south courts new attractions are changing the layout. Although the bridge and road to the east court are still there, the new entrance leads to a 'Pet's Corner' and additional conveniences, a new garden laid out beside the north court, and catering facilities including a new restaurant and a milk bar. As visitor numbers rapidly rose, attractions were now being added beyond the Abbey itself, and the guide indicates the way to the boating ponds. The open spaces of the park, advertised here as 'Britain's most beautiful private park', were starting to be exploited.

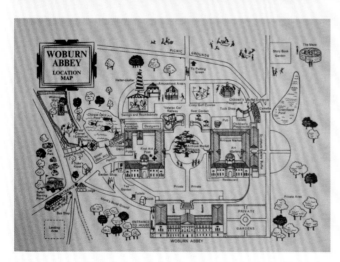

Site map from guidebook, 1969.
Five years later, as visitor numbers continued to grow, the attractions were now starting to dominate the gardens. A look at this plan reveals that new animal houses, an aviary, shops (selling 'film etc'), a pottery, garden shop, and tea garden have been added to the entrance area. Beyond that, round the north and south courts, an aquarium, a fun fair, 'Veteran Car Railway', crazy golf, pub (the Duke's Head) and beer garden, an antiques market, and a 'story book' garden have all been added, while the sculpture gallery is now a 'buffet'. Outside, in the park, there is now a coach park in addition to the car park, a landing area for helicopters, and 'Safari Rides' round the park are being offered to see the deer. In addition, the bridge has finally gone, and all trace of the grand approach to the entrance in the east front has gone with it, leaving challenges to access and visitor flows which persist to this day.

WOBURN OPENS TO THE PUBLIC:
PHOTOGRAPHS OF ATTRACTIONS

Steam rally in the park, 1958. This remarkable photograph captures not just the simplicity of fun in the 1950s, when visitors were happy to paddle round the empty ponds, but also, as the black smoke of the steam engines billowed across the park, scenes which would have been unimaginable just eighteen years before, as Herbrand lived out his last days in the Abbey alone in another world.

Caravan Club in the park, 1962.
On what had been the Flying Duchess's landing strip are the central marquees of this enormous gathering, with several thousand caravans stretching out over the park in every direction, an early indication of how opening the Abbey altered the uses of the park. In fact, this area has remained a focus of activities to the present day, since the land in the middle distance – beside the Red Lodge plantation (which had housed the hangar) – and all of that in the top right-hand corner have become the site of the Safari Park.

The duke at the gift shop, 1966.
A picture of the duke in his element, engaging with the children who were still very much the focus of the attractions. It seems to have been assumed that the adults would spend their visit walking round the Abbey, while the children were entertained by teams of attendants on the outdoor attractions. The gift shop sold Triang and Hornby trains and Revell kits of aeroplanes, while a sign points to the entrance to Kiddies Korner, which included a model railway layout that had opened in 1964 and, as the sign on the left proudly announces, had been 'seen on T.V.' Taking the entrance money, selling the models and kits, and charming visitors was all in a day's work for the duke.

The Fun Fair, 1970.
A corner of the gardens had become the 'Fun Fair'. With the 'Veteran Car Railway', helter-skelter, carousel and sideshow arcade, along with a ghost train, dodgems and swing boats, this picture captures the end of an era. By the early 1970s, the first generation of large custom-built amusement parks were opening to the public, offering the kind of high-velocity, thrilling rides that steadily replaced the more sedate ghost trains and swing boats. Within a few years all this was gone from around the north and south courts as interest in the historic Abbey and grounds started to reshape the visitor experience.

Initially there were 'two or three attractions I had thought of . . . a children's zoo, a playground of swings and see-saws with attendants, a boating lake, with boathouse and paddle dinghies', and a 'milk bar' fitted with espresso coffee machines and a juke-box, 'decorated in sky blue tiles', a wonderful echo of the 5th Duke's ceiling of the lost tennis court, which had been 'painted to represent a clear sky'.[49] Later additions were an aquarium, fun fair, carriage and horse rides, model village, 'story book' garden, crazy golf, antiques market, model village built on the Rockery, and even the 'Duke's Head' pub and beer garden.

In 1960, following his divorce from Lydia, Ian married Nicole Milinaire, who matched his interest in, and flair for, publicity.[50] Over the next thirteen years, the duke and duchess turned Woburn into an international success, publicizing it not just not at home but in America and Canada, and as far away as Australia. Some indication of the reach of this publicity drive is indicated by the fact that on a cattle ranch in the hills outside Wagga Wagga, New South Wales, this writer was shown a Woburn guidebook, signed by the duke and duchess on their Australian tour.

As Ian had rightly predicted, the 'amenities of the park are capable of infinite variety', and during the late 1950s and 1960s, as well as playing host to nudist camps, steam rallies and caravan clubs, in August 1967 the true spirit of the 1960s wafted in across the park, enveloping it in clouds of incense, love and music, as the three-day 'Festival of Flower Children' got under way.[51] This was followed the next year by the slightly scaled back two-day *Melody Maker* 'Woburn Music Festival'. The one-off music festivals aside, in terms of the park as we see it today, 1968 in fact turned out to be a watershed year, due largely to the hiring of the first general manager for the Abbey, Ray Barratt. Up to this point, most of the events and activities were held in existing buildings or in the open spaces of the park and gardens as they were, but with the arrival of a manager the development of the commercial side of the business started to impact on the park and grounds. One development in particular was to bring the old park into the world of modern mass tourism.

One day in the summer of 1969 an unusual procession of vehicles pulled slowly out of the depths of a small sandstone quarry deep in the West Sussex countryside. Leading the way was a vintage, open-topped Bentley followed by two straining low-loader lorries, both laden down with assorted sandstone rocks. As they wound their way through the narrow Sussex lanes, the sound of straining engines was accompanied by the strains of Mozart emanating from the truck cabs. Neither of the lorries was much accustomed to long-distance road trips, but this time, instead of delivering machinery to a local job site, they were bound for distant Woburn Abbey. It was a trip full of incident, due partly to the persistent rain and partly to the need to stop in the rain to change blown tyres. The novelty of this journey somehow epitomizes the novelty of the project of which it was one element.

A significant part of the park at Woburn was about to undergo some of the biggest alterations it had seen for over 150 years: not simply in the way it looked, but also in the way it was used. The age of the modern theme park had arrived.

Barratt tells us: 'One day I had a call from Jimmy Chipperfield asking if I thought the duke would be amenable to having a safari park at Woburn.' At this time, Chipperfield was just completing a novel new attraction at Longleat, the drive-through Lion Enclosure, where work had been going on since 1966. Woburn already offered its own 'safaris', rides round the park in an open-topped vehicle to see the deer, and while at first the duke seems

Woburn Park Zoo, proposals for the central area.
Woburn Park Zoo, now known as the Safari Park, one of the first generation of such attractions, was seen as the real future of tourism at Woburn, and the designers seem to have been given carte blanche to take as much space as they deemed necessary. Had these proposals gone ahead, the look and atmosphere of park and Evergreens would have radically changed. The new roads in from Ridgemont and Crawley Lodges would have had four lanes, coaches would have had access throughout, and the Froxfield road would have had new, larger junctions, controlled by traffic lights. Red Lodge plantation was completely subsumed into the design, with new concrete roads winding through the thinned out trees.

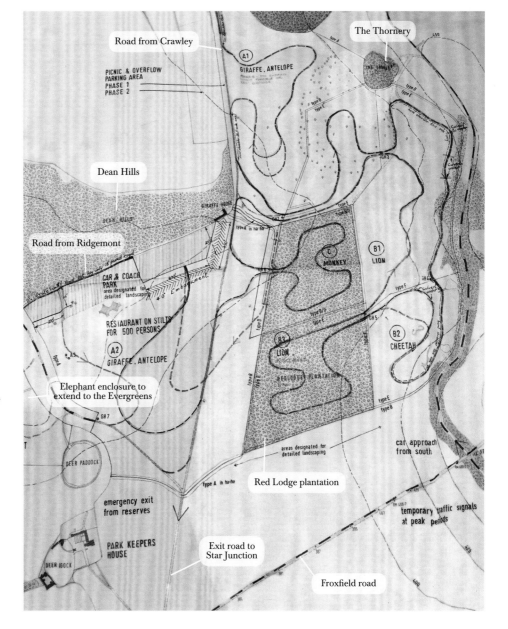

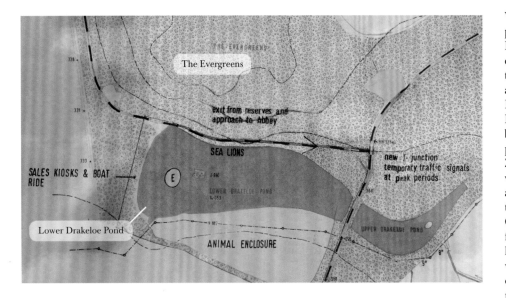

The Evergreens

exit from reserves and
approach to Abbey

SEA LIONS

new T- junction
temporary traffic signals
at peak periods

SALES KIOSKS & BOAT
RIDE

LOWER DRAKELOE POND

Lower Drakeloe Pond

UPPER DRAKELOE POND

ANIMAL ENCLOSURE

Woburn Park Zoo, proposals around Drakeloe Pond area, showing new coach and car access road, traffic management, shops and kiosks.
In the new plans, Lower Drakeloe would have become an important part of the Woburn Park Zoo. A new, wider road would have brought cars and coaches round from the restaurant area and Crawley Gate to the pond, from where they would have exited to the Abbey via a new traffic-light-controlled junction. The pond itself was to be a home for sea lions and boat rides, while a row of sales kiosks and a ticket office would have lined the dam. These developments did not go ahead, but in 1972 a major new attraction was added, the 'Cableway', then known as the Jungle Cabin Lift'.

to have been uncertain, encouraged by Nicole and Barratt he eventually agreed on the condition that the new facility 'should not dominate the Abbey'. With this in mind, plans went ahead on a site 'in a different part of the estate some distance away', using the civil engineer Peter Barber, who had also designed the Longleat enclosure. The place chosen for the 'Woburn Park Zoo' was tucked out of sight in the open valley running north, below the old Serpentine Terrace and the Thornery, from the Red Lodge plantation, last used some twenty years before to park aircraft, up to Crawley Heath Farm.[52]

The plans demonstrate clearly the extent to which this project was seen, at least by its planners, as the most important priority in the long-term future of the park, and had they been fully implemented, the impact on the landscape of the park of the Phase 1 main complex and its infrastructure of roads and traffic lights would have been enormous. Phase 2 would then have seen the addition of an extensive elephant enclosure.[53] In the event, both phases were scaled back, but other later additions had an impact of their own.

The civil engineering of the roads and enclosures was under way by late 1968, and it was at this moment that the procession arrived from West Sussex. Anthony Archer-Wills, then 23 and at the beginning of his acclaimed international career creating ponds, pools and waterfalls, was the driver of the Bentley, and his commission was to create something interesting at the point where water was to flow between two pools in front of the restaurant before carrying on down the slope in a series of falls through Pet's Corner.[54] Presented with a selection of rocks one might have used to construct a small garden rockery, Anthony sensed that this unique setting required something much more dramatic, grander and more imposing, and the hunt for such rocks had led him to the quarry in Sussex.

TOP RIGHT Boating Lake Falls, waterfall installation at Woburn, spring 1969. The completed Boating Lake Falls used a number of the large sandstone slabs that had been transported up from Sussex to create a feature that matched the scale of its setting. Water flowed over these falls until 2014, when the area was redesigned using a form of artificial rock.

TOP FAR RIGHT Pet's Corner, installation of the stream. Anthony Archer-Wills at work on constructing the stream from the Boating Lake Falls down the slope to Pet's Corner. The sloping site and limited equipment available meant that smaller stones were used for this, but it was still being completed when the animals began to arrive.

BOTTOM RIGHT Pet's Corner stream today. Part of the Pet's Corner stream, seen here in the process of being cleaned out and repaired. Its large terminal waterfall has been built on, but it is still possible to see much of the stream, which it is hoped will survive for another forty-five years.

Despite an initial lack of equipment and the early arrival of animals – with white rhino roaming the enclosure, the Bentley was soon switched for a Land Rover – work went ahead on the main fall and pools, with Anthony still hard at work completing the Pet's Corner watercourse as the 'Wild Animal Kingdom' opened its doors to the public in late spring. The immediate success of the new attraction, and the central role of the motor car in the experience of it, meant that it was not long before a new problem began to strain the relationship between the Abbey and those living nearby, as the village and the roads around it became regularly choked with unprecedented volumes of traffic, which arose largely from the timing. Projected visitor numbers had been based on places like Longleat and facilities provided accordingly, but Woburn's proximity to

The Jungle Cabin Lift' over Drakeloe Pond, 1972. With a curious sea lion looking on, an acrobat performs during the opening of the newly constructed Jungle Cabin Lift, designed to whisk visitors up through the Evergreens and on to the Safari Park.

the newly extended M1 motorway, and its rapidly increasing popularity for recreational outings, made it uniquely accessible to London and the novelty of the new animal theme park ensured it early success. It took time and lengthy consultations to ease the problem, but things in Woburn would never be quite the same again.

Nor would they in the park, where the site for the Safari Park, chosen because it was 'some distance from the Abbey', also happened to be one of considerable historical significance. The valley it occupies, and the view beyond this to the Dean Hills and what was the open landscape of the Warren, was once considered to be one of the prettiest areas of the park. From at least the mid-eighteenth century, the valley was the focal point for an overlook designed as one destination along the tree-lined avenue: the 'Serpentine Terrace' which ran along the ridge above it from Stump's Cross. This is also the same overlook from which Arthur Young was to enjoy his 'vast prospects' (see page 111), and a close look at Repton's plan on page 134 shows that, in turn, he chose the same location for his *cottage orné*, the Thornery, drawn as others before had been by the views.

Almost certainly the needs of the Safari Park could have been met by other, less significant sites, but by the mid-twentieth century the importance of this ridge and valley as one of the special places of the park had been lost; the continuity of awareness of its decorative importance had been broken. Although the Safari Park was initially seen as a temporary tenant, projected to be removed by the 1980s, its continued popularity has meant that today the Abbey and its gardens and the Safari Park, on what has by now become its own part of the estate, operate as both individual and complementary twin attractions. It will take a significant shift in taste and values, and the subsequent development of some new use for a landscape whose only asset is that it is 'picturesque' to look at, before the Abbey could ever claim back this part of its historic park.

There are two other significant aspects of the impact of the construction of the Safari Park attractions: on the trees of the Evergreens and the 'Chinese' temple on the island in Drakeloe Pond. In the first case, the construction in the early 1970s of the cable car ride up from Drakeloe Pond, through the heart of the original Evergreen plantation to the Safari Park, necessitated the felling of a large number of trees as a wide corridor was cut straight up and over the hillside, and the construction of a series of pylons erected on large concrete foundations. No record was made of what was cut down, but certainly trees from the original plantings were included, and today, while the ride itself proved to be a short-lived economic failure, the loss of the trees remains a permanent legacy, as are the concrete foundations.

It is not entirely clear what happened to the temple on the island, but it would appear that the existing structure was severely damaged by the inhabitants when it became 'Monkey Island' in the early 1970s and was

The temple on the island at Drakeloe Pond.
The temple as we see it today. Erosion over the years has made the island itself considerably smaller than the one on which the original 'Chinese' temple was created in 1749. The temple itself has also changed a number of times since then, but exactly how many is unclear.

at some point extensively repaired, if not entirely rebuilt. The structure visible today dates from this period and was repainted in the 1970s and 1990s. Whether this structure replaced that shown by Dodd in his guide to Woburn of the early nineteenth century, or whether something else had already replaced it, is equally unclear, but certainly any remains of the original eighteenth-century wooden structure shown by Repton are long gone.

These reservations aside, the opening of the Abbey and the development of the Safari Park were a continuing success, and in 1973, after being in charge for twenty years, the duke and duchess handed over responsibility to his eldest son, Robin, and retired to the Continent. Ian's enthusiasm and unflagging commitment had secured Woburn as the family home, in much the same way as Francis, 4th Earl and John, 4th Duke had done. For Robin and his wife, Henrietta Tiarks – or Lord and Lady T as they were known until his father's death in 2002 – the task was now to consolidate and build on what had been achieved.[55]

Having lived initially in Boston, Massachusetts, where Robin was studying across the Charles River at Harvard, and where Andrew, the present duke was born, Lord and Lady T lived first at Chevington Grove, near Newmarket, while he worked as a stockbroker in London. Following his father's retirement, Robin travelled back and forth to Woburn, before moving the family there in 1974. Taking stock of the situation, he soon realized that the determined focus on making a success of opening the estate to the public during Ian's time had left other pressing issues unaddressed. In the Abbey itself, there were problems ranging from the plumbing and wiring to repairs of the structure both inside and out, which included

Robin and Henrietta, with Andrew, Robin and Jamie. With their parents are Robin Russell (b.1963) and Andrew, 15th Duke of Bedford (b.1962) on Henrietta's left and right respectively, and Jamie Russell (b.1975) on his father's lap. Robin and Henrietta's time running the estates after his father retired in 1973, and then briefly as duke and duchess, was one of rationalization – particularly in the administration of both the household and the commercial activities – investment in the infrastructure and assets of the estate, and development of long-term, sustainable businesses based around the Abbey, Safari Park and golf courses.

everything from fixing the crumbling external stonework to replacing the leaking windows in the grotto.[56] All the things, in fact, which had been left undone when the contents of the rooms had been laid out for opening to the public. In addition to this, as Henrietta points out, they had to deal with some four hundred estate cottages that had never been updated, with 50 per cent of them lacking running water, proper bathrooms, inside toilets or insulation.[57]

Equally pressing was the necessity to create a modern management structure to run the various new departments, and now that outside contractors (rather than the army of estate staff available before the war) were required to do the work, they needed to recruit staff who had experience in pricing, negotiating and managing such contracts. There was also a need to rationalize the sprawl of attractions and their high staffing levels. More fundamentally, the tourism market was changing rapidly. Simple pleasures of the immediate post-war era such as swings and see-saws, roundabouts and paddle-boats were beginning to look distinctly dated. Decisions had to be made on what could provide a longer-term, more sustainable basis for the business.

These issues were to preoccupy Robin and Henrietta for the next twenty-five years, as they sought also to make Woburn a home for their family, which by 1975 included Andrew, Robin and James. With such family considerations and so much else to concentrate on, Robin and Henrietta were concerned to redefine priorities, to play a less high-profile role in the visitor experience and limit the impact of visitors on the family. Thus, while Ian had been happy to personally greet and talk to visitors and 'keep no part of the Park to ourselves', they chose to play a more administrative role and to limit public access in those areas of the park immediately around the Abbey itself.

With a focus on those areas which represented business opportunities in their own right – the Flying Duchess tea rooms, the pottery, the antiques centre, the sculpture gallery as events venue and so on – the attractions were trimmed of the playgrounds, fun fair, model railway and model village, aquarium, story book garden, paddle-boats and carriage rides, (and, indeed, the pub), while a new gift shop and ticket office were opened at

Peter Beadle, ONZM, *A Scene on the Marquis Course, Woburn Golf Club*, oil sketch on board, 2005. A new generation of waterfalls are created at Woburn, this time as part of the construction of the Marquis golf course in 2000. The three courses at the Woburn Golf Club make full use of the woodland settings of Little Brickhill, parts of which were first planted during the forestation of Old and New Wavendon Heaths and this area to improve the view from the Evergreens in the late eighteenth century.

the visitor entrance gate. Beyond such rationalizations, Robin also focused on the creation of the world-class Woburn Golf Club, with the opening of three courses, the 'Duke' and the 'Duchess' courses in 1976, and the 'Marquis' course in 2000, amidst the beautiful mixed woodland of Little Brickhill. Andrew has written of his father's development of these courses: 'I would say my father's great legacy to Woburn was having the foresight and imagination to create the three outstanding golf courses which we have at the Golf Club.'[58]

The other great legacy of this period was the conversion of Park Farm, where the buildings took on a new lease of life as the administrative office for the Bedford estate, complete with a new, custom-built muniment room for the family archives, and the stable complex for the Bloomsbury Stud. As Henrietta remembers, when the stud took over some of the old barns, carriage houses and stables of the farm in 1966, there was still a dairy herd of Jersey cows and some Aberdeen Angus beef, but farming operations, kept alive by Hastings, the 12th Duke, were rapidly winding down. Francis, 7th Duke had maintained an interest in horse racing and breeding, working with Admiral Rous, the distinguished trainer and racing administrator, but on his death the 5th Duke's racing colours had lapsed. These were re-registered by Robin and Henrietta, and with the purchase of an unfancied mare, Mrs Moss, in 1975, the foundations of the stud's success were laid. This remarkable mare proved an 'inspired purchase' and is remembered today in the life-size bronze statue that looks back towards the Abbey, ears pricked, from beside the Bason Pond: the only piece of statuary on the estate outside the Abbey gardens.[59]

After suffering a major stroke in 1988, Robin stepped back from the responsibilities of running the estate and all the new enterprises, and

Bedford estate office, Park Farm, and Park Farm dairy, 2015.
Park Farm dairy and the buildings of the old Park Farm, those used as stables in the centre and those now occupied by the Bedford estate offices on the right, as seen from the entrance to the park. These buildings provide many visitors with their first glimpse of the history of the park at Woburn Abbey, and they capture for us something of the interests and optimism of the great period of development during the late eighteenth and early nineteenth centuries as the 5th and 6th Dukes put their 'plans for national improvement' into action.

these were largely devolved to Henrietta, who managed also the house and forty-two acres of grounds, and to their son Andrew, then Lord Howland, who took on management of the wider Bedford estates. The rewards and challenges of this period in the Abbey's life were memorably caught in the television documentary *Country House* recorded over three series from 1999.[60] After running Woburn for so long as the Marquis of Tavistock, Robin briefly became 14th Duke of Bedford on his father's death in 2002, before his own death in 2003, at which point Andrew succeeded as the 15th Duke.

As one commentator has put it, the post-war introduction of government grants, the custodial role of the National Trust and the opening of country houses to the public meant that a 'reinvention of the purpose of the aristocracy was taking place, aristocrats as the guardians of our national heritage',[61] and, of course, this reinvention of purpose included not just their owners, but also the houses, gardens and parklands themselves. No longer simply a setting for family life and reflecting the interests of family members, these places now had to meet the interests of the paying public, while also becoming repositories of national history and heritage to be displayed in the picture galleries, libraries and rooms of the interiors, as well as in the look and features of the exterior landscapes. Making this history and heritage as it applies to Woburn Abbey accessible to as many visitors as possible, whether they are there for a day or are pursuing longer term specific interests, is very much the aim of the present duke and duchess. While the demanding schedules of maintenance and repair continue as they have since the 1950s, additional work is also being carried out in order to refresh the presentation of the Abbey and its history, to add to the visible layers of history, and to make the experience of visiting both inside and outside the house more stimulating and interesting.

To this end, a series of five-year plans for the development for the Abbey and the gardens have been put in place, including indoors a fresh look at the layout of the visitor experience and the presentation of a number of the rooms and an updating of displays. Outdoors they have concentrated on creating gardens that are worthy of a stand-alone ticket price: offering both beautiful gardens and an environment where history is on display, as it is in the house.

As Louise has recounted in the Foreword to this book, her interest in the gardens was not to commission new designs but rather, inspired by the

Louise in the Sculpture Gallery Garden. Louise's passion for the gardens at Woburn Abbey led to her promotion of the ongoing programme of restoration; the ideas, interests and commitment of her predecessors are once again visible in the gardens. This picture reflects the spirit of the new gardens: on the one hand, the setting would still be immediately recognizable to Lady Ermyntrude and even John, the 6th Duke, both of whom we have seen in this location, while, on the other hand, the sculpture gallery itself has new uses and the Ivy Window (seen over Louise's shoulder) has lost its ivy and is no longer open.

The family at the Log Cabin in the Evergreens. Andrew and Louise visit the Log Cabin with Alexandra (b.2001) and Henry (b.2005). For many years in the twentieth century it acted as the venue for shooting parties, but as the park and Evergreens continue to evolve in the twenty-first century, it has regained the importance it had for earlier generations as a destination in its own right, one visited for the pleasure of enjoying its unique location (see also page 169).

discovery of Repton's Red Books in the Library, to reinstate those outlined by him, which had made up the pleasure grounds during their heyday in the time of the 6th Duke and Duchess. She has attempted to recapture something of the magic woven by Holland's Chinese dairy, Repton's Menagerie, children's garden, pavilions and rockery, and Wyatville's rockery, conservatory (Orchid and Palm House), grotto and paths, and to allow this atmosphere to provide the background theme for thoroughly modern gardens capable of hosting events such as the annual garden shows, displays of modern sculpture, the winter light fantasies of the Luminaries Woburnensis, horticultural workshops and historical study days.

Further work on the fabric of the Abbey and associated buildings began as early as 1989, with repairs to the stable block south court, before moving on to the Abbey itself.[62] Here, amongst other things, extensive stonework repairs were carried out on the length of the west front, the east court, the South Terrace Garden and its retaining wall. Beyond this in the park, the London entrance, long superseded in importance by the entrances nearer the M1 motorway, was repaired, and Chambers's bridge/Repton's viaduct was substantially rebuilt between 1990 and 1993. At much the same time, the failure of the 'wharfing' round the New Pond above the viaduct meant that erosion of the banks had reached the first line of trees on the east side.

New edging was installed and backfilled to stabilize the banks, but this means that the shape of the pond on that side today is not exactly Repton's original. The 'Arch' designed by the Marquis of Tavistock in 1756, however, still stands at the top end of the pond and awaits restoration. These projects, running from 1989 until 2007, have turned the neglected buildings of the post-war era into what we see today, and have animated the views across the park with a new lease of life, while the clearance of the aggressively invasive *Rhododendron ponticum* has done the same for the Evergreens.

Until the 1980s, the Evergreens had continued to be leased out for pheasant shooting, with up to 30,000 birds a year being raised in extensive rearing pens fenced off amongst the trees, while the Log Cabin acted as the assembly point from which the main drives started and to which people returned for lunch. Encouraged as habitat for the pheasants, where cover was essential, the *ponticum*, a Victorian favourite in its own right and considered the best rootstock for many of the hybrid rhododendron species, gradually began to choke the spaces beneath the trees and the rides, overwhelming the less vigorous species, and blocking all the historic views that had been such a part of the original Evergreen experience. As the clearance

The Abbey and Repton's viaduct.
This timeless view of the Abbey and Repton's viaduct seen from over the Bason Pond differs only from the scene painted by Barratt in the 1770s (see page 107) in that Chambers's original bridge has been replaced by Repton's viaduct dam. In it we are sharing the vision for this area of John, 4th Duke of Bedford, who, working with his son Francis, Marquis of Tavistock, between 1755 and 1760, updated the pond originally created by his father, Wriothesley, 2nd Duke, working with George London around 1710.

proceeded, it revealed the full layout of the rides, the sites of lost structures, the views from them, and the planting plan which lined the rides with highly decorative hybrid rhododendrons and azaleas, set against the darker *ponticums*, and the patterns of significant trees set at the mouth and at the top of each of the side valleys. For the first time in several hundred years it is possible to appreciate the unique nature of these plantations, and how they provided such a special experience, re-establishing the importance of this place. No one remembers the square temple in the Evergreens as anything other than roofless and derelict, but both Henrietta and Lady Kiloran Grosvenor remember that the 'Colonnade' shown by J. C. Bourne in 1842 was still standing in the 1950s. It appears to have been knocked down by a falling cedar tree sometime in the 1980s, while the Arch above it was long lost in the undergrowth until the pile of stones was recently uncovered during the clearance programme.

Following the appointment of Martin Towsey as Estates Gardens Manager in 2004, work began on drawing up the first of the five-year plans in 2005. Between 2005 and 2010 they concentrated on refurbishing the existing gardens, including the clearance of sites, repair and restoration of the surviving structures, along with both new plantings and the restoration of some of the historic designs. This work included refurbishment of the Chinese Dairy Pond, Camellia House, stone temple, Rockery and Maze, reclamation of the original Menagerie site, the creation of a new bog garden and perennial borders, the recreation of the 6th Duke's 'Heathland' garden, and installation of new drains, signage and paths. The culmination of this work was the opening in 2010 of the first Woburn Garden Show and, the same year, the invitation to become a 'partner garden' of the Royal Horticultural Society.

With the basics of infrastructure, repaired buildings and new plantings in place, a new interest from visitors, and the recognition of the RHS, the project moved into its second five-year plan, this time focusing firmly on bringing the historic gardens back to life. Initially, Humphry Repton's Aviary, central to his Menagerie design, was reconstructed from surviving images, along with repairs to the tunnel in Wyatville's Rockery. The next year, Repton's children's garden and the rose arbours attached to the shell grotto were restored, and his design for a small Chinese pavilion was implemented on top of the Rockery. This work was followed by the reconstruction of Repton's Pine Cone Pavilion in the Menagerie, and the simulation of a section of his 'rustic fence'. With these in place, it is now possible to catch a glimpse of some of the features of the pleasure grounds as they looked by the end of the 1830s, and more will be added in the future. Today's restorations are carried out in much the same spirit as that outlined by Repton quoted at the start of this chapter, and thus provide a sense of continuity to the vision of Woburn.

Further recognition of both the purpose and quality of the work undertaken came with the 'Hudson's Heritage Award for New

RIGHT The stone temple today.
Amongst the features visible in the gardens today is that known as the stone temple. The exact history of this building is not clear, but there are indications that it is the 'small temple' shown on the 1833 plan of the pleasure grounds from *Hortus Woburnensis* (see page 154) and in the background of Repton's view from the Chinese dairy (see opposite below). If it is the same structure, it would appear that it was moved to its present location by John, 6th Duke, and re-erected as a memorial to his brother Francis, the 5th Duke. This is suggested by the fact that, when it was restored as part of the first five-year plan, it was noticed that the back wall of the building showed evidence of having had a plaque of some sort attached to it. The subsequent discovery of an identically shaped plaque in storage in the Abbey which carried a profile of Francis and a dedication to his memory, and the key location of the temple today at the top end of the central axis of the gardens, strongly supports this supposition.

RIGHT Humphry Repton, detail of 'The Chinese Dairy Pond' (after), Red Book for Woburn, Plate XXX, 1805.
In this close-up of Repton's drawing of the Chinese Dairy Pond, we see what may be the stone temple (centre background); given the angle of Repton's view in this picture, the temple has to be in the location indicated on the *Hortus Woburnensis* plan of 1833. What remains unclear at present, however, is whether this structure was originally built by Francis, the 5th Duke, or whether it dates all the way back to the temples built by John, the 4th Duke.

The reconstruction of Repton's Aviary. The magnificent Aviary designed and built in 1808–9 by Humphry Repton as the centrepiece for his Menagerie has been carefully restored on its original site using information from surviving plans and drawings. Although the two keepers' cottages on either side and the curving wall of the bird cages are missing, it helps re-establish the cohesion of the carefully designed layout of the upper gardens.

The reconstruction of Repton's Pine Cone Pavilion. The restoration of the Pine Cone Pavilion allows visitors to experience the Menagerie area as the family would have done when it was first built. Entered from the Doric doorway immediately behind it (and soon to be restored), the pavilion exemplifies Repton's vision of the decorative picturesque, a structure to transport those entering it from their everyday world to a place of fantasy and whimsy. The design of every aspect of the Menagerie beyond, seen from the pavilion across the pool – from the swags of cones hanging above them to the Aviary, the twig-work on the range of bird boxes, the exotic plumage of the birds, and the rough posts and netting of the surrounding fence – was designed to surprise, amuse and then enchant.

LEFT The reconstruction of the Chinese pavilion on the Rockery.

Elegantly perched once again on top of the rock grotto, the Chinese pavilion first proposed by Repton in his Red Book adds interest and colour to the upper gardens, as well as restoring the third focal point of the original layout. The restoration of the pavilion is based on Repton's image. Although he suggests that 'to the top of the cave may be removed the Chinese building from the Drakelow pond', it is clearly not the same structure as the one he shows on Drakeloe. Perhaps, in the end, that building was simply too plain for the pleasure gardens.

BELOW The central lawn indicating the sight lines to the Rockery, the stone temple and the Aviary.

Although tree branches now obscure the Chinese pavilion on top of the Rockery, restoration of this building and Repton's Aviary allow us to understand the layout of the upper garden much better. As family and visitors left Wyatville's conservatory a panorama opened up and the destinations available became clear: straight ahead to the centrally located stone temple, to the left to the Rockery, and to the right to the Menagerie.

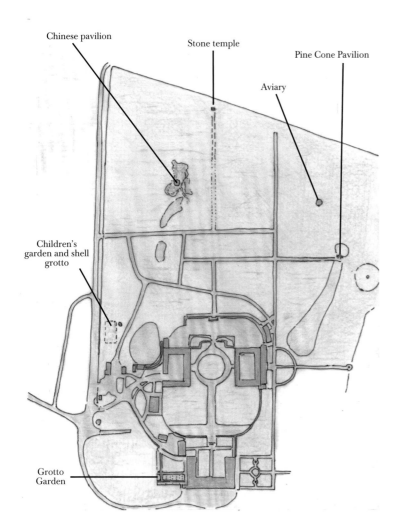

Chinese pavilion

Stone temple

Pine Cone Pavilion

Aviary

Children's
garden and shell
grotto

Grotto
Garden

Plan of gardens today
showing the modern path
layout and the locations of
the restored structures in
the Abbey Gardens, and
the new Grotto Garden
outside the Abbey.

Commission' for the Chinese pavilion on the Rockery, and the 'Georgian Group Award for the Best Restoration of a Georgian Garden or Landscape' for the restorations as a whole. Further projects under way as part of the third five-year plan include a modern garden outside de Caus's grotto in the Abbey, designed to be sympathetic to the style of the time when it was built, and thus to improve both the setting from the outside and the view from the inside; and the conservatory arbour project, designed to replicate the size and shape of Wyatville's Orchid and Palm House. With these additions, the Abbey Gardens and the educational programmes associated with them are set to join the Abbey, Safari Park, Golf Club and Woburn Hotel in providing the long-term foundation of Woburn Enterprises and the future of the family home at the Abbey.

From monastic estate to hunting park, the land beyond the Abbey which had been of 'pasture and arable land' had for so long protected and

The landscape at Woburn Abbey today, from the house itself in the background on the extreme right, round to the Evergreens above Drakeloe Pond on the left. We cannot be sure how many of the earls and countesses, dukes and duchesses or their family members that we have met during the telling of this story would recognize the landscape, but with the interest and dedication of Andrew and Louise, the story of this landscape and the individual contributions of their predecessors to what we see today are becoming increasingly clear and better understood.

sustained life at the Abbey. Worked on by successive generations of Russells, with help from a variety of designers and architects, the park had become a place of recreation, a source of aesthetic pleasure for family, friends, the 'quality of the area' and mushroom pickers. After becoming home to an extraordinary collection of animals, airplanes and sleeping Wrens, it has now found a role in the twenty-first century, a flavour of which is summed up in the 1967 guidebook: 'the tranquillity and beauty of the Abbey's 3,000 acres of parkland . . . are a paradise for nature lovers and a sanctuary for many varieties of animals.'[63] Created by the Russell family and supported now by interested visitors, this enduring landscape is defined by both its history, much of it still visible today, and its extraordinary ability to adapt. Its continuing popularity as a place to visit would seem to suggest not only that it is still of importance and interest to many people, but also that its future relevance and survival are secure.

NOTES AND REFERENCES

ABBREVIATIONS
WAC: Woburn Abbey Collection
BLARS: Bedford & Luton Archives and Record Office
NRO: Northamptonshire Record Office

INTRODUCTION

1   Survey of Berwick Manor, Swyre, Dorset, dated 1583. Gladys Scott Thomson, *Family Background*, London, Jonathan Cape, 1949, gives a detailed account of John Russell's background and circumstances. Additional notes by Scott Thomson can be found in WAC BE-AD2 GST 316.

2   Image of Berwick Farmhouse, from John B. Knight, *Some Account of the Dorset Estate of the Duke of Bedford, consisting of the Manors of Swyre, with Berwick and Kingston Russell*, 1850. Leather-bound volume, with text and watercolour images: WAC HMC 158.

3   Jeremiah Wiffen, *Historical Memoirs of the House of Russell*, 2 vols, London, Longman, 1833, vol. 1, p. 181.

4   John Leland visited *c*.1544, and described it in his *Itinerary*: John Chandler, ed., *John Leland's Itinerary: Travels in Tudor England*, Gloucester, Sutton, 1993, pp. xxx–xxxii.

5   See *Chenies Manor, Chenies, Buckinghamshire: An Archaeological Evaluation of a Tudor Manor House and Assessment of the Results*, Wessex Archaeology Report, January 2005. This report records the excavation and post-excavation work of the archaeological evaluation by Time Team, Channel 4 Television, 2004.

CHAPTER ONE

1   Jonas Moore's survey of the Woburn estate, 1661 (WAC WE-P900).

2   Dianne Duggan, 'Woburn Abbey: The First Episode of a Great Country House', *Architectural History*, 46, 2003, p. 69.

3   These plans and the annotation on them are based on those in Duggan, 'Woburn Abbey', in which the author gives a full description of the monastic layout and its sequential adaptation by the 4th and 5th Earls, and the 4th and 5th Dukes, to become the house that survived until the 1950s. Today the north, west and south wings remain.

4   For detailed information on this see Duggan, 'Woburn Abbey', p. 77, n. 10.

5   Description of Nyn Hall is based on that by Oliver Harris, 'Nyn Hall, Hertfordshire: An Alternative History', *Hertfordshire Archaeology*, 13, 1997–2003, p. 99.

6   British Library Add. MS 32467, fol. 242.

7   Catalogue for 'Sale by Auction' of the Thornhaugh estate at the Angel Hotel, Peterborough, October 1931 (private collection).

8   John Bridges, *The History and Antiquities of Northamptonshire compiled from the manuscript collections of the late learned antiquary John Bridges, Esq., by the Rev. Peter Whalley, late fellow of St. John's College, Oxford*, 2 vols, Oxford, 1791.

9   The map was surveyed in 1729 but not drawn until 1751 (NRO, ref: Map 6403).

10   English Heritage listing for the site: 'The farmhouse at Home [now New] Farm was rebuilt by the 3rd Duke of Bedford, on the site of a former hunting lodge of Lord William Russell, 1st Baron of Thornhaugh.' See https://historicengland.org.uk/list, accessed 30 July 2015. Listing details: 5141. Thornhaugh. Wansford Road (north side) TF 00 SW 8/618 Home Farmhouse.

11   Thornhaugh, tithe map, 1838 (NRO, ref: T198).

12   See Dianne Duggan, '"London the Ring, Covent Garden the Jewel in that Ring": New Light on Covent Garden', *Architectural History*, 43, 2000, pp. 140–61.

13   Warwick Draper, *Chiswick* (1923), London, Philip Allen, 1970, pp. 44–5.

14   Roy Strong, *The Renaissance Garden in England*, London, Thames & Hudson, 1998, p. 121.

15   For a very useful discussion of the attributions for Twickenham Park and Moor Park see Sally Jeffery, 'The Formal Gardens at Moor Park in the 17th and early 18th Centuries', *Garden History*

(Journal of the Garden History Society), 42: 2, 2014, pp. 157–77.

16   For a detailed history of Burleigh House gardens, see Paula Henderson, *The Tudor House and Garden*, New Haven and London, Yale University Press, 2005.

17   Household accounts (WAC 4E-18, 1628–9).

18   Alnwick Castle Collections and Archives Department.

19   Dianne Duggan, 'Isaac de Caus: Surveyor, Grotto and Garden Designer', *Studies in the History of Gardens and Designed Landscapes*, 29: 3, 2009, p. 154. The survey is one of the plans that Duggan unearthed during her researches into the grottoes and gardens at Bedford House and Woburn and on which the following descriptions are largely based.

20   Thomas Colepeper, 'Grotto in Bedford Garden', *c*.1705 (British Library Harley MS 7593, fol. 104).

21   See Duggan, 'Isaac de Caus', p. 157. Duggan also writes: 'Under strong magnification Hollar's bird's-eye view shows what seems to be an arched doorway in the staircase leading into and under the terrace, and the western apse-shaped "platform" protruding on to the Piazza fits in with the similarly shaped far end of Colepeper's plan. It can be confidently suggested that a tinted drawing in the Victoria and Albert Museum of a grotto interior … and almost certainly by Isaac de Caus, actually depicts this feature at Bedford House.' She goes on to say that 'Roy Strong nominates this drawing as the Bedford House garden grotto because of its similarity in style to the Woburn grotto' (pp. 155 and 167, nn. 32, 34).
Roy Strong describes the Bedford House grotto as 'The Diana and Callisto Grotto' and adds: 'the ribs of the vault are accentuated and the ceiling between ornamented with characteristic arabesque patterns; the walls are divided into arches and small niches for fountains and statuary. In the centre of the ceiling four putti bear crowns, conceivably a hydraulic mechanism which could rise and descend. The sources of the grotto would seem to prove beyond a doubt that Isaac, like Salomon [de Caus], had studied in Italy and at Pratolino in particular. The group of Diana's nymphs discovering Callisto's unchastity … reflects a grotto on the same subject at the Pratolino' (Strong, *The Renaissance Garden*, p. 141).

22   Since so much of the west, south and east ranges of the Abbey had survived, it is likely that the church itself had suffered most in the earlier fire, and had been subsequently demolished.

23   This summary is based on Duggan's analysis of the building programme and her observation that 'Jonas Moore's survey, *c*.1661, also shows what appear to be classically laid-out, walled gardens to the north, west and south of the abbey, and there can be little doubt that Bedford's plans would have included a complementary garden for those architectural elements which were closely related to garden settings, namely the grotto, and the loggia.' Duggan goes on to note, 'it is perhaps relevant that there is depicted on Moore's naïve view something which appears to be a domed, pedimented banqueting house-type building at the eastern end of the southern garden. This is similar to that which had been designed by Isaac de Caus for the terrace-walk just a couple of years before at Bedford House' (Duggan, 'Woburn Abbey', p. 68). This banqueting house may well have been a conversion of the existing building shown on the monastic plan.

24   This interpretation is suggested also by Duggan, who comments that on Moore's map the area 'directly in front of the grotto in the north wing appears to depict slim cypress, a popular Mediterranean tree used by Jones [in his masque backdrops], and at Danvers House, Chelsea' (Duggan, 'Isaac de Caus', p. 159).

25   Sir Henry Wotton, *The Elements of Architecture* (1624), quoted in John Dixon Hunt and Peter Willis, eds, *The Genius of the Place: The English Landscape Garden 1620–1820*, Cambridge, Mass., MIT Press, 1988, p. 48.

26   See Duggan, 'Isaac de Caus', p. 167, n. 50, and Hunt and Willis, *The Genius of the Place*, p. 48.

27   Celia Fiennes's description of Somerhill, Sussex, 1697. See Celia

Fiennes, *The Journeys of Celia Fiennes*, ed. Christopher Morris, London, Cresset Press, 1947, p. 137.

28 Quoted from Emma McFarnon, 'Bad Sports? Puritan Attempts to Ban Games in 17th Century England', 2013, History Extra website, www.historyextra.com, accessed 4 July 2014.

29 Quoted in Georgiana Blakiston, *Woburn and the Russells*, London, Constable, 1980, p. 57.

30 John Dixon Hunt, *Garden and Grove*, Princeton, N.J., Princeton University Press, 1986, p. 135.

31 Duggan, 'Isaac de Caus', p. 157.

32 Although there was clearly contact between the families when in Chiswick, the Bedfords' disapproval of the marriage was due to the events which led up to the marriage of Anne's mother, Frances Howard, to Robert Carr. These involved the scandal of her divorce from her first husband, the Earl of Essex, the poisoning of Sir Thomas Overbury, Howard's imprisonment in the Tower in relation to this, and her subsequent marriage to Robert Carr, a favourite of James I.

33 It appears that William and Anne's religious beliefs were a cause of suspicion throughout his career, both at court and in Parliament, and created real problems when Anne was briefly arrested in 1675 for attending a conventicle, an informal religious meeting of lay people which had been outlawed following the 'Conventicle Act' of 1664.

34 For the 1643 campaign against the Parliamentary stronghold of the city of Gloucester, William is likely to have stayed at his mother's old home of Sudeley Castle, which Charles had chosen as his headquarters. The castle had been briefly occupied by Parliamentary cavalry in early 1643, who had stabled their horses in the church and destroyed many of the Chandos memorials, and further destruction followed when it was refortified for Charles, at which time gun positions were set up in Grey Brydges's magnificent gardens. Sir William Waller attacked Sudeley in 1644, and its garrison of 300 Royalist Foot surrendered after an intense initial bombardment: 'Waller faced the castle, and brought his heaviest guns to bear on it: a shot beheaded their gunner, and so discouraged the garrison that the fortress was surrendered at discretion.' See Rev. John Webb, *Memorials of the Civil War in Herefordshire*, 2 vols, London, Longmans, Green & Co., 1879, vol. 2, p. 42. The destruction of the Countess of Bedford's childhood home was completed after the war, following the family's opposition to Parliament.

35 Anne Clifford quoted in Gladys Scott Thomson, *Life in a Noble Household*, London, Jonathan Cape, 1950, p. 69.

36 The complex division of loyalties that occurred during this time in the immediate Russell family is apparent when one realizes that while William initially supported the Parliamentary side, his mother's family, the dukes of Chandos, held Sudeley Castle for the Crown, his two elder sisters were married to husbands on different sides, Katherine's husband Robert Greville was a leading Parliamentarian general, while Anne's was George Digby, 2nd Earl of Bristol, whose family home at Sherborne Castle was destroyed after a long siege by Parliamentary forces. His younger brother, Colonel John Russell, was a Royalist cavalry officer under Prince Rupert, while his sister Margaret was married first to James Hay, 2nd Earl of Carlisle, a Royalist Colonel of Horse, and second to Edward Montagu, 2nd Earl of Manchester, who had been a Parliamentary general, and finally his youngest sister Diana married Francis Newport, an ardent Royalist, who was away campaigning when Diana and the children were besieged in his family home at High Ercall in Shropshire. William, as we have seen, found himself on first one and then the other side as circumstances changed.

37 See John Harris, *The Artist and the Country House*, London, Philip Wilson Publishers for Sotheby Parke Bernet, 1979, p. 61, where he describes the walled formal garden as 'of the Jonesian/de Caus type'.

38 Epsom Downs appears to have been a location for horse racing from at least 1625, and was well established as a venue for racing by the time of the Civil War, the races largely run as a result of extravagant wagers between wealthy enthusiasts.

39 See letter from William Morley to Thomas Coke at Melbourne Hall, August 1701. Historic Manuscripts Commission (HMC) 12th Report Appendix, Pt II, 1889: *Earl Cowper, Melbourne Hall, Derbyshire*, 3 vols, vol. 2, p. 433. Report held at the Muniment Room, Melbourne Hall, Derbyshire.

40 Scott Thomson, *Life in a Noble Household*, p. 390.

41 The arrival of John Field was particularly significant since he was one of the leading plantsmen of his time, and in 1681 became a partner in the Brompton Park Nursery alongside George London, Moses Cook, gardener at Cassiobury, Roger Looker, the queen mother's gardener at Somerset House, and Henry Wise. These connections placed Field at the centre of the most important commercial nursery operation of the time and provided him with connections across the country. Both Charles Bridgeman and Stephen Switzer, who went on to become leading garden designers, were apprentices at the nursery.

42 WAC 5E-A3-2-5 (1672).

43 WAC 5E-A3-2-4 (1669–70).

44 WAC WE-P905. In 1738 the 4th Duke of Bedford commissioned a new survey of the Woburn estate from Thomas Browne. The original map, 'A Plan of the Manor & Parish of Woburn ...', 'surveyed and delineated by Thomas Browne, Blue Mantle Pursuivant of Arms', can still be seen at Woburn today and in the present book is referred to as 'Browne's 1738 map', to distinguish it from what appears to be a later copy of the map, though dated 1738, from Browne's survey, held at Bedford and Luton Archive and Record Office (BLARS R1-237) and referred to here as 'Anon. 1738 map'. Some confusion has arisen in the past about the dating of features shown on the latter because it has been assumed to be a contemporary copy of the former and, therefore, that features shown on it date from or before 1738. Closer examination, however, reveals that in fact it has to be a later version, based on the original Browne 1738 survey but 'delineated' by someone else and with significantly later features shown on it that had been added in the meantime. Comparison of the known dates of some of the documented additions to the Abbey, park and gardens during the time of the 4th Duke that appear on the Anon. 1738 map and those that do not would suggest that it was created *c*.1755, and that its specific purpose was to record, in the same way Moore's 1661 map did, what existed and who the tenants of farmland were in preparation for the further expansion of the park planned at this time.

45 Fiennes, *The Journeys*, p. 343.

46 Henry B. Wheatley and Peter Cunningham, *London Past and Present: Its History, Associations and Traditions*, 3 vols, Cambridge, Cambridge University Press, 2011, vol. 2, p. 292.

47 Scott Thomson, *Life in a Noble Household*, p. 245.

48 12 November 1671. The date that the gatehouse was finally removed is not recorded, but the fact that work was being done on it as part of the 'new model' might suggest that the earl intended keeping it for some time. It seems most likely that it was eventually demolished either as part of developments planned by Wriothesley, 2nd Duke of Bedford *c*.1710, or as part of the general removal of all the garden walls suggested by Charles Bridgeman in 1733 and carried out by John, 4th Duke over the next few years. Either way, it is gone by the first 1738 map (WAC 5E-A3-2-6, 1671).

49 'Sludge' in this context is most likely to refer to the puddled clay liner used to seal these new ponds (WAC 5E-A3-2-16, 1671–87).

50 Fiennes, *The Journeys*, pp. 119–20.

51 The connection between these two sites can be understood from Browne's 1738 map, in which 'The Straits', or the 'Strait Spiney' as it is labelled on the map, is shown adjoining the kitchen gardens (WAC 5E-A3-2-6, 1671).

52 Fiennes, *The Journeys*, p. 116.

53 WAC 5E-A3-2-6 (1671–2).

54 Fiennes, *The Journeys*, p. 120.

55 Fiennes, *The Journeys*, p. 119.

56 See Scott Thomson, *Life in a Noble Household*, p. 79.

57 Fiennes, *The Journeys*, p. 342.

CHAPTER TWO

1 By this date William was, of course, on the throne of England, but 'he normally spent the winter months ... in London, and until 1697 he spent the campaigning season in the summer fighting

against the armies of Louis XIV in the southern Netherlands.' See K. H. D. Haley, 'For Profit and Ornament: The Function and Meaning of Dutch Garden Art in the Period of William and Mary, 1650–1702', in *The Dutch Garden in the Seventeenth Century*, ed. John Dixon Hunt, Washington, DC, Dumbarton Oaks Research Library and Collection, 1990, p. 9. In 1697, William was also overseeing the completion of his gardens at Het Loo, and gardens in or around The Hague that William would have known well were Honselaarsdijk (built by his grandfather Frederik Hendrik, 1630s) and Sorgvliet (built 1675 by his friend Hans Willem Bentinck, who became the Earl of Portland and Superintendant of Royal Gardens in England).

2   Gladys Scott Thomson, *The Russells in Bloomsbury 1669–1771*, London, Jonathan Cape, 1940, p. 87.

3   Scott Thomson, *The Russells in Bloomsbury*, p. 120.

4   For a useful short biography of Dr William Sherard (*c*.1659–1728) see Miles Hadfield, Robert Harling and Leonie Highton, *British Gardeners: A Biographical Dictionary*, London, Zwemmer, 1980, p. 260.

5   Charting the duke's continued interest in horticulture, Wiffen goes on to recount the following anecdote: 'In one of his letters to Sir Hans Sloane, in 1709, he seeks to tempt that philosophic virtuoso and amiable man to Woburn, by stating that he was receiving "a great number of rarities, and particularly a large collection of ranunculi from Canada, such a one as he believes has never been seen in England."' Jeremiah Wiffen, *Historical Memoirs of the House of Russell*, 2 vols, London, Longman, 1833, vol. 2, p. 327.

6   William Bray, ed., *The Diary of John Evelyn Esq.*, London, Chandos Classics, Frederick Warne & Co., n.d., p. 303.

7   For Switzer's family tree and a detailed account of his connections to East Stratton and subsequent career, see William Alvis Brogden, 'Stephen Switzer and Garden Design in Britain in the Early 18th Century', Phd thesis, Edinburgh College of Art, 1973, vol. 1 (text), PDF on Edinburgh Research Archive website, http://hdl.handle.net/1842/6979, accessed 24 July 2014.

8   Stephen Switzer, *Ichnographia Rustica*, 3 vols, London, 1718 and 1742, vol. 1, p. x.

9   Switzer, *Ichnographia Rustica*, vol. 1, chapter 1, 'The History of Gardening', p. 66. The opening to volume 3 is quoted from John Dixon Hunt and Peter Willis, eds, *The Genius of the Place: The English Landscape Garden 1620–1820*, Cambridge, Mass., MIT Press, 1988, p. 152.

10 Browne's survey of Stratton Park, 1729–30, Hampshire Record Office 92M95/F8/5/1.

11 Quoted in Marie Draper, 'The Houses of the Russell Family', *Apollo*, CXXVII: 316 (new series), June 1988, p. 388.

12 Although much survives at Stratton Park, 'Love Walk' appears to have been lost when the M3 motorway was created along the route of the old turnpike.

13 'Inventory of Bedford House', 1700: WAC 5E-25 (1700).

14 Much of the appeal of Chippenham Park to the admiral appears to have been its proximity (three miles) to the fashionable racing venue at New Market Heath. The admiral had been created Lord Orford in 1697, following his crushing victory over the French fleet at La Hogue, an event which made him briefly a national hero. The admiral had been close to his uncle William, 5th Earl of Bedford, and was with him as part of the delegation to The Hague to invite William and Mary to take the throne of England in 1688. Following the death of Wriothesley's father in 1683 and his grandfather in 1700, he seems to have become close to the admiral, who was married to his aunt Margaret Russell, and who seems to have considered it his role to keep an eye on the young duke, while delighting in advising him on the development of Woburn, something he considered himself to be an expert in. See letter to Lady Rachel, 1708, in Wiffen, *Historical Memoirs*, vol. 2, p. 306.

15 Quoted in Wiffen, *Historical Memoirs*, vol. 2, p. 306.

16 Accounts from Brompton Park Nursery are for plants supplied, but sometimes include the words 'for the use of my masters', suggesting they may also have both visited and perhaps supplied drawings, since similarly worded invoices are found at Melbourne Hall, where we know London and Wise not only supplied trees but also made site visits and drew plans. For example, 'Dec 21st 1710: Joseph Carpenter [of Brompton Park Nursery] bills for £30: "Account for trees and for the use of my masters George London and Henry Wise."' For 2nd Duke of Bedford garden accounts, see WAC 2D-A3-2 (1702–11). For details of accounts at Melbourne Hall, see X94 Lothian Box 219 Melbourne Hall Muniments.

17 See WAC GST28–GST42.

18 See WAC GST28–GST42.

19 Originally a part of Crowlands Abbey, the house and estate had been radically improved by the flamboyant courtier Humphrey Weld of Lulworth Castle *c*.1670. Having already laid out extensive new grounds at Lulworth, Weld went on to enlarge the house at Dry Drayton and create new access and gardens. Unfortunately, his free spending on both properties meant that Weld died heavily in debt in 1685, and the property was acquired by Elizabeth Howland's father, John Howland, as principal mortgagee. After his death in 1687, we can catch a glimpse of the house and grounds in an inventory taken at the time when the estate passed to his widow, Elizabeth Howland, and then to their daughter on her marriage to the 2nd Duke in 1695. (Inventory for Dry Drayton: WAC 5E-23 (13.6.1687). Quoted from A. P. M. Wright and C. P. Lewis, eds, *A History of the County of Cambridgeshire and the Isle of Ely, Volume 9*, Oxford, Oxford University Press, 1989, pp. 74–7.) Elizabeth retained Dry Drayton as Dowager Duchess after the death of her husband, and it passed on her death to her younger son, Lord John Russell (later 4th Duke of Bedford). Until this point it appears that the house was kept up as an occasional family home, but after it was devolved to the 4th Duke's son Francis, Marquis of Tavistock, who appears to have had no interest in it, the house became sufficiently rundown for Francis, 5th Duke to sell the property in 1795. It was demolished *c*.1817.

20 Draper, 'The Houses of the Russell Family', p. 390.

21 Georgiana Blakiston, *Woburn and the Russells*, London, Constable, 1980, p. 95.

22 Draper, 'The Houses of the Russell Family', p. 387.

23 See E. W. Brayley, *A Topographical History of Surrey*, London, 1912, vol. 4, p. 77, accessed at British History Online: www.british-history.ac.uk/vch/surrey/vol4/pp78-83.

24 Quoted in Gladys Scott Thomson, ed., *Letters of a Grandmother 1732–35*, London, Jonathan Cape, 1943, p. 35. The letters of Sarah, Duchess of Marlborough contained in Scott Thomson's book can be found in WAC HMC 205.

25 Draper, 'The Houses of the Russell Family', p. 387. 'The Downs' in this case were Banstead Downs, just to the south of the village, and these, along with Epsom Downs to the west, formed a huge area of open down land stretching along the chalk ridge. Long popular for 'Horse Matches', which later became organized race meetings, the downs and their network of paths provided miles of excellent rides with wide views across the Thames Valley. Even fifty years later, as shown on John Carey's *15 Miles Round London* of 1786, Banstead Downs were still broad open down lands cut through with rides which linked them to Epsom.

26 Draper, 'The Houses of the Russell Family', p. 387.

27 In the Wilton gardens, de Caus's elaborate parterre gardens on the south side of the house, built 1632–4, were totally eradicated, and the whole area laid to open lawns running down to the river Nadder. In its turn the river was dammed to increase the body of water and decorated by a Palladian-style bridge; the result is essentially unchanged today. As was to be the case at Woburn, de Caus's Italianate gardens, complete with elaborate grotto, slowly passed out of fashion, were altered and simplified, before being removed entirely as the changes hinted at by Switzer and others developed into the 'English' style.

28 Scott Thomson, *Letters of a Grandmother*, p. 54.

29 Scott Thomson, *The Russells in Bloomsbury*, p. 169.

30 Draper, 'The Houses of the Russell Family', p. 390.

31 Draper, 'The Houses of the Russell Family', p. 390.

32 Quoted in Scott Thomson, *The Russells in Bloomsbury*, p. 352.

33 Scott Thomson, *The Russells in Bloomsbury*, p. 352.

34 The 'Red Plan' of Bloomsbury is undated, but Montagu House had become the British Museum in 1759, and Bedford Square was laid out 1775–83, so the plan must date from between 1783 and

1800, when Bedford House was demolished by the 5th Duke.

35 These Memorandum Books, which the 4th Duke kept assiduously between 1736 and 1769, are actually small, leather-bound annual almanacs called *Rider's British Merlin*, an interesting mixture of agricultural almanac, monthly horoscopes and social events. The duke's notes are jotted down on blank pages, often running over into spaces between the text and images, and many of them are then crossed out and annotated 'Done' after he had taken appropriate action. Clearly, the size of the books and their robust leather bindings made them ideal for him to carry round on his walks, but it is not known why he did not simply buy similar notebooks with blank pages. The answer may well be that he liked to have the day by day and seasonal information on hand as a reference point for his own observations, and being able to put his notes into this wider context outweighed the inconvenience of having to write where he could find sufficient space. Touchingly, he kept these notebooks right up until his eyesight and health simply failed, and the entry on the last page of the last book becomes an illegible scrawl that trails down the page and fades out unfinished. There are thirty books altogether in WAC HMC 58, 1740–70.

36 WAC HMC 58, 1736–7.

37 John Sanderson, *Designs for Woburn Abbey*, 1733 (WAC HMC 151).

38 WAC HMC 58, 1736–7. John Sanderson and Charles Bridgeman both appear in the Memorandum Book for 1736–7, and the 'Evergreen Walks' and miscellaneous 'Evergreen' entries in the books for 1741 and 1742.

39 Robert Salmon, *Woburn Plantations in & about the Park in 1808*, survey and drawings 'made in the year 1802', no. 14, 'Old Evergreens' (WAC HMC 119).

40 Draper, 'The Houses of the Russell Family', p. 391.

41 The Dilettanti Society was founded in 1736, and each year in his Memorandum Book the duke records paying his annual fee. It was a society which originated in a group of people who had shared the experience of the Grand Tour, and who wished to further their interests in art, architecture, archaeology and, if Horace Walpole is right, 'being drunk'. How involved the duke was in the club's activities, drinking or otherwise, is not clear, but he seems to have met like-minded people such as Thomas Anson and Sir Francis Dashwood, amongst others, who were also developing gardens and plantations at this time. Anson lived at Shugborough in Staffordshire with his brother Admiral Anson, who had just returned from his trip around the world, and Dashwood at High Wycombe in Buckinghamshire.

42 Peter Collinson, *'Forget not mee & my garden': Selected Letters 1725–1768*, ed. Alan W. Armstrong, Philadelphia, American Philosophical Society, 2002, letter no. 136.

43 Specific cricket matches noted in HMC 58, 1740, 1743 and 1744.

44 This short account of the Abbey as it existed in 1733, the demolition work of 1751 and the subsequent rebuilding programme 1752–c.1755 is based largely on Dianne Duggan's account in 'Woburn Abbey: The First Episode of a Great Country House', *Architectural History*, 46, 2003, pp. 57–80.

45 Henry Flitcroft (1697–1769) had been working for Gertrude's family at Trentham Hall, Staffordshire, where he remodelled the house for the 4th Duke's brother-in-law, the 2nd Lord Gower, 1737–8.

46 WAC 4D-C3-12-2-8 (1750).

47 Duggan, 'Woburn Abbey', p. 69.

48 WAC WA-P182.

49 WAC 4D-C3-12-2-8 (1750).

50 See Memorandum Books, WAC HMC 58, 1742 (greenhouse) and 1747 ('new' garden and orangerie).

51 WAC 4D-A2-11-159-172 (1749–61).

52 Rather than referring to all comers as today, the 'public' referred strictly to the 'quality', to 'society', to gentlemen and their families, often being shown around when the family were not there.

53 4th Duke's Memorandum Book (WAC HMC 58, 1749).

54 For details of work on 'The Chinese Temple for the Pleasure Grounds', see WAC 4D-GP3-1.

55 WAC 4D-A2-11-159 and 4D-A2-11-181.

56 WAC 4D-C3-12-2-8 (1750).

57 WAC 4D-A3-72.

58 WAC HMC 58, 1753.

59 Philip Miller to the Duke of Bedford, February 1755: 'Manuscript Letters 1755: Volume XXXI for period of the 4th Duke, fol. 24' (WAC HMC 8-31).

60 WAC HMC 58, 1757.

61 WAC 4D-A3-72.

62 The *OED* tells us that 'La Folie' was 'widely used as a name for houses and gardens', and that 'the Folly' was widely used in England as late as the nineteenth century to describe 'pleasure gardens or the like'. It seems likely, then, that the name 'Lady's Folly' was used as a suggestive, exotic name rather than describing a specific use. An area of woodland labelled 'Lady's Folly' does appear on a late nineteenth-century map of the estate, but it is not clear whether this was the same place or simply a reuse of the name.

63 WAC 4D-A3-72. The 'Spring Well': two main springs still exist in the Abbey gardens today, one in the centre of an area which in 1756 appears to have become the New Pheasantry and subsequently developed into the Menagerie, and the other (perhaps a more likely candidate) some way north of this on a spot marked today by the two ponds overlooked by Repton's Chinese pavilion atop its rock grotto.

64 WAC HMC 58, 1759.

65 WAC HMC 58, 1764.

66 WAC HMC 58, 1768.

67 WAC Butcher Correspondence.

68 WAC 4D-A1-2-35-10.

69 WAC 4D-A2-11.

70 WAC HMC 58, 1742.

71 Daniel Defoe, *Tour through Great Britain*, 4th edn, 4 vols, 1748, vol. 3, letter 1, p. 52 (sourced from https://books.google.co.uk).

72 WAC HMC 58, 1755 and 1756.

73 Francis Russell, Marquis of Tavistock (1739–1767): in 1760, after leaving Cambridge, Russell 'joined the Bedfordshire Militia, telling his parents he had a "rage for everything that has a connection with military life ... I am more militia mad than ever."' In 1761 he set off to Italy, from where he described to friends his 'awakening interest in art and architecture', and where he also started buying art. He then joined his parents in Paris in 1763, and there returned again on his own next year: 'Here he spent a week at the I'lle Adam, Prince Conti's country house,' and Blakiston goes on to imagine him deep in conversation amongst the 'striped pavilions and pedimented temples' (Blakiston, *Woburn and the Russells*, pp. 130–35). In 1764 Tavistock married Elizabeth Keppel, and the pair made their home at Houghton House, Bedfordshire, bought by his father in 1738. Here he settled down to country life, 'mad' now for hunting rather than the military and continuing to give his father 'advice about laying out the garden'. It is very interesting to imagine what kinds of gardens Lord Tavistock might have gone on to develop had he not died so young. Something of his taste is perhaps visible in both the Batoni portrait and his design for the Arch, and this suggests that his gardens would have been somewhat different perhaps to those his more practical sons Francis and John were to produce.

74 WAC HMC 58, 1753.

75 WAC 4D-A3-72.

76 See John Phibbs, 'Landscapes attributed to Lancelot "Capability" Brown', *Garden History* 41: 2, 2013, p. 275.

77 Gertrude's nieces were Mary and Betty Wrottesley, daughters of her sister Lady Mary Wrottesley, and Lady Mary Fitzpatrick.

78 Blakiston, *Woburn and the Russells*, p. 143.

79 Arthur Young, *A Six Month Tour through the North of England ...*, 2nd edn, 4 vols, London, 1770–71, vol. 1, pp. 40–42. It should be noted that the Chinese temple that Young catches sight of at the end of the 'great glade' is the same building as the 'elegant and light' Chinese temple he later sees on the island of Drakeloe.

CHAPTER THREE

1 John Martin Robinson, 'Estate Buildings of the 5th and 6th Dukes of Bedford at Woburn 1787–1839', *Architectural Review*, November 1976, p. 276 (BLARS CRT 130 Woburn 29).

2 See Account Book (WAC 5D-A1-2-42-62).

3   As detailed in the 'Agreement' with 'Thomas Walker of
    Woodstock, Oxfordshire and Joseph Farrington of Great Russell
    Street', these sales included the Manor of St Giles-in-the-Field
    and 'All of the Messuage of Mansion House called Southampton
    House [Bedford House]' in London, while, further afield, estates
    sold included 'The lands and rights of the Honor and Manor
    or Lordships' of Tooting Bec, part of Streatham, Chesham,
    Rotherhithe, Raines, Eaton Socan (plus all the tolls of navigation
    on the Ouse between Erith and Bedford), Ampthill, part of
    Houghton, Maulden, Flitwick and Silsoe, Thorney, part of Dry
    Drayton, Bedford House in Exeter, and a number of farms in
    Devon and Cornwall (WAC 5D-TDI). Further sales were to follow
    at the turn of the century as expenses continued to grow, and
    included the house and park at Dry Drayton, Cambridgeshire,
    in 1795, further land at Houghton Conquest in 1800, followed
    by the remainder of the Streatham estate and the entire estate
    at Stratton Park, Hampshire, in 1801; 155 years after it became
    the family's principal home, Woburn was now, with the later
    exception of Endsleigh House in Devon, the sole focus of major
    capital expenditure.
4   Letter from 6th Duke of Bedford to Arthur Young following the
    5th Duke's death (Georgiana Blakiston, *Woburn and the Russells*,
    London, Constable, 1980, p. 173).
5   Henry Holland (1745–1806) had been working since 1775 with his
    father-in-law, Capability Brown, at Trentham Park, Staffordshire,
    for Granville Leveson-Gower, 1st Marquis of Stafford and brother
    of Gertrude, Dowager Duchess of Bedford. He had then been
    commissioned in 1776 to build the new building for Brooks's
    club, whose members included both Francis Russell, his brother
    William, and George, Prince of Wales, before going on to work
    for the prince at Carlton House in 1785. In working for the
    Prince of Wales, Holland pursued his interest in Chinese design,
    creating the Chinese Drawing Room at Carlton House, a theme
    he was to use again at Woburn Abbey for the Chinese Dairy in
    1787.
6   *Sporting Magazine*, February 1795 (BLARS CRT 130 Woburn 5).
7   C. Bruyn Andrews, ed., *The Torrington Diaries, Volume 4: A Tour of
    Bedfordshire, 1794*, London, Methuen & Co. Ltd, 1970, p. 48.
8   *Sporting Magazine*, February 1795 (BLARS CRT 130 Woburn 5).
9   *Woburn Abbey* guidebook, 2013, p. 63 (WAC).
10 John Farey (1766–1826), born in Woburn, was an outstanding
    mathematician who became a civil engineer in London until,
    in 1792, he was hired by the duke to return to Woburn to help
    organize and implement his ideas. Working alongside Salmon
    and Cartwright and subsequently with William Smith, he oversaw
    much of the work running operations in the park, and by 1798
    he had completed the drainage of 200 acres of land 'on the edge
    of Crawley bog' (David Brown, 'Reassessing the Influence of the
    Aristocratic Improver: The Example of the Fifth Duke of Bedford
    (1765–1802)', *Agricultural History Review*, 47: 2, 1999,
    p. 190). Learning rapidly from the people he worked with, Farey
    eventually moved back to London in 1803 to work as a consultant
    surveyor and geologist. He succeeded Arthur Young as Secretary
    of the Smithfield Club.
11 Robert Salmon (1768–1821) arrived at Woburn initially as Henry
    Holland's Clerk of Works. His abilities were soon recognized by
    the duke, who in 1794 hired him as the Steward at Woburn and
    Controller of Woods at Chenies. It was Salmon who went on to
    design and build the innovative Park Farm complex from 1795,
    organize many of the stock breeding and new crop management
    programmes, and become an award-winning inventor of new
    farming machinery. He was also behind the installation of the
    new steam engines for the mill and the highly detailed surveys
    of the plantations and woodlands at Woburn, which formed
    the basis for the future development programmes. He became
    one of the key figures at Woburn and a respected friend of
    Humphry Repton after working with him on his programme of
    improvements, and remained on the estate until his death. He is
    memorialized with an elaborate plaque on the wall in Woburn's
    old parish church.
12 Dr Edmund Cartwright (1743–1823) was a clergyman and poet,
    hired to advise on experimental farming and cultivation techniques.
    Inventor of the 'Spinning Jenny', the first powered loom, he joined

    Salmon in 1801, expanding the range of experiments in everything
    from soil chemistry, innovative crop rotations, new seed types and
    stock breeding programmes to new machinery. In 1804, he went on
    to become tutor to Lord John Russell.
13 William 'Strata' Smith (1769–1839?) was a pioneering geologist
    who, in 1815, produced *A Delineation of Strata of England and
    Wales with part of Scotland*, the 'first true geological map produced
    anywhere in the world'. In recognition of his growing 'reputation
    for canal-making, his expertise in farming ... and the draining
    of fields', Smith was elected a member of the Royal Bath and
    West of England Society in 1796, at whose meetings he met the
    Duke of Bedford and other agricultural improvers and like-
    minded scientists, including Thomas Coke, Sir Joseph Banks and
    Humphry Davy. He was hired by the duke in 1801 to conduct
    a mineral survey of the Woburn estate and start the process of
    draining its marginal land (Simon Winchester, *The Map that
    Changed the World*, Harmondsworth, Penguin, 2002, pp. 2, 128).
14 Winchester, *Map that Changed the World*, p. 212.
15 T. Batchelor, *A General View of the Agriculture of Bedfordshire*,
    London, 1813, pp. 484–90.
16 Brown, 'Reassessing the Influence of the Aristocratic Improver',
    p. 190.
17 John Farey, Account Books and Memorandums (WAC
    uncatalogued). A particularly thorny problem Farey had to
    contend with at this time seems to have been the reallocation
    of tithe entitlements following the enclosure of various pieces
    of land. Although the commoners simply lost out with no real
    redress, a number of the larger tenant farmers, and a few of the
    parish vicars, were not happy with what they were offered in
    compensation for the loss of traditional rights and challenged
    the settlements suggested. Although the 'Sheepshearings' were
    undoubtedly a social success and did much to promote new
    ideas, the rapid implementation of some of the duke's ideas on
    the Woburn farms caused lasting tension and were by no means
    guaranteed to make the tenants more, or even as much, money.
18 WAC uncatalogued.
19 Robert Salmon, *Woburn Plantations in & about the Park in 1808*
    (WAC HMC 119).
20 Accounts for building the Cold Bath (BLARS R5/1348, 1802–4).
21 J. Parkes and H. Merivale, eds, *Memoirs of Sir Philip Francis*, 2 vols,
    London, 1867, quoted in Blakiston, *Woburn and the Russells*, p. 166.
22 C. Bruyn Andrews, ed., *The Torrington Diaries, Volume 2: A Tour of
    the Midlands, 1789*, London, Methuen & Co. Ltd, 1970, pp. 125–7.
23 Blakiston, *Woburn and the Russells*, pp. 154 and 168.
24 Blakiston, *Woburn and the Russells*, p. 169.
25 Blakiston, *Woburn and the Russells*, p. 169.
26 Diary of Lord John Russell, January–March 1802 (WAC
    uncatalogued). The diary is an account of a trip taken by Lord
    John following the death of his wife Georgiana Byng a few months
    before, during which he visited Georgiana's sisters, staying
    first at Weston Park, Shropshire, with her sister Lucy Byng and
    her husband Orlando Bridgeman, Lord Bradford, and then
    at Longleat, home of Isabella Byng and her husband Thomas
    Thynne, Marquis of Bath. Both men shared Lord John's interest
    in landscaping and improving agriculture and, while staying at
    Weston, they visited various estate farms, including Pattshull
    Hall, Staffs, Somerford Hall, Brewood, Staffs, and Freeford
    Manor near Lichfield. While at Longleat they visited Stourhead
    to view the house, gardens and new water meadows, before
    John had to hasten back to Woburn. His three boys (14, 12 and
    10) travelled with him to Weston, and enjoyed 'good sport' on a
    hunting trip, before returning to school in London.
27 From letters of Dr Allen Thomson, 1837 (WAC Ph-MSS-35-33).
    Thomson became the duke's personal physician following his
    series of strokes, and from 1836 until the duke's death lived and
    travelled everywhere with the family. In long letters to his family,
    particularly his sister, he recounts life at Woburn, in London,
    Scotland and Ireland in fascinating detail.
28 Letter from the Duke of Bedford to Arthur Young, quoted in
    Blakiston, *Woburn and the Russells*, pp. 172–3.
29 Quoted in Blakiston, *Woburn and the Russells*, p. 190. In 1798
    Charles Abbot had published *Flora Bedfordiensis*, 'Comprehending
    such plants as grow wild in the County of Bedford', a book which

developed his earlier work of 1795, the *Catalogus Plantarum*, a list of 956 such plants according to the Linnaean system. A note on *Flora Bedfordiensis* in the *Gentleman's Magazine* describes him as wishing 'to promote the knowledge of botany among the ladies ... [and he] introduce[s] a most affectionate remembrance of his wife's talents in this line' (*Gentleman's Magazine*, 70, 1800, p. 360, https://books.google.co.uk, accessed 8 November 2014). It would seem that Abbot may have inspired the interest of not just Lord John but also his first wife, Georgiana, in botany and the natural world, and, as duke, John went on to emulate Abbot's work with his own series of publications.

30 See Robinson, 'Estate Buildings of the 5th and 6th Dukes', pp. 276–81.

31 Derek Linstrum, *Sir Jeffrey Wyatville: Architect to the King*, Oxford, Clarendon Press, 1972, p. 88.

32 Diary of Lord John Russell.

33 *Stourhead Landscape Garden*, National Trust, 2000.

34 See http://www.bedfordshire.gov.uk/CommunityAndLiving/ ArchivesAndRecordOffice/CommunityArchives/Woburn/ TheRoundHouseWoburn.aspx, accessed August 2015. See also 'Plan and Elevation for Cottage to be made from lower part of Woburn Windmill, over the lower rooms are to be two Bedrooms. 1805' (BLARS R3/2114/530–531). The top of the windmill was removed; the resulting cottage fell into disrepair in the mid-twentieth century and was renovated in 2006.

35 Humphry Repton, Red Book for Woburn, 1805, pp. 4–5 (WAC 7427).

36 Repton's career was to pick up again, but never to the numbers of the late eighteenth century, and following a serious injury to his back in a carriage accident in the winter of 1810, which made travelling very painful for him, it slowly fell away, with two or three commissions a year until he decided to retire in 1816 to concentrate on his writings. He died two years later. For a useful chart of the number of Repton's commissions between 1788 and 1818, see Stephen Daniels, *Humphry Repton: Landscape Gardening and the Geography of Georgian England*, New Haven and London, Yale University Press, 1999, p. 40.

37 Repton, Red Book for Woburn, pp. 10–23.

38 Paul Smith, 'The Landed Estate as Patron of Scientific Innovation: Horticulture at Woburn Abbey, 1802–39', Phd thesis, 1983, p. 115 (BLARS CRT 130 Woburn 47).

39 Some idea of just how ornamental this building is can be gained from its description in the English Heritage listing: 'Pavilion in the form of small picturesque cottage ... Squared clunch with hipped thatched roof. A small square single-storeyed building. Gable to centre of each elevation. Deep eaves on all sides, supported by pine tree trunks retaining bark. Gables have barkwork bargeboards. Round-arched doors ... diamond pane window glass.' Interior design includes: 'Walls and ceiling have painted decoration of bamboo trelliswork covered with a variety of plants and birds', while outside 'Ground drops sharply immediately west of the Thornery, and set into bank below it is a vaulted serving room. Its entrance is of coursed ironstone ... with cambered-arched entrance ... Lower parts of the door and panels below windows have rustic twig and barkwork decoration' (see https://historicengland.org.uk/list, accessed 30 July 2015, list entry number 1158441).

40 Personal letter from Marie Draper, then Woburn Abbey archivist, to 'Miss Bell', September 1980 (BLARS CRT 130 Woburn 33, 7661).

41 Repton had been heavily criticized in a very public way by two individuals in particular, Richard Payne Knight and Uvedale Price, for what they considered to be his erroneous understanding of what the picturesque in both painting and landscaping actually implied. Defending himself vigorously in his book *Sketches and Hints on Landscape Gardening* (1794), Repton was nevertheless hurt both personally and professionally by the criticism, but retained his faith in what he saw as the decorative and ornamental qualities of the picturesque and the romantically rustic architecture associated with it. See Richard Payne Knight, *The Landscape, a Didactic Poem*, 1794, and Uvedale Price, *An Essay in the Picturesque, as Compared with the Sublime and the Beautiful; and, on the Use of Studying Pictures, for the Purpose of Improving Real Landscapes*, 1794.

42 Quoted from Reverend John Evans, *The Picture of Bristol*, 1818, by Nigel Temple, *John Nash and the Village Picturesque*, Gloucester, Alan Sutton, 1979, p. 33.

43 WAC HMC 58, 1744.

44 James Forbes, *Hortus Woburnensis*, 1833, p. 285 (WAC).

45 Letters of Dr Allen Thomson, Woburn Abbey, 1836 (WAC Ph-MSS-35-10).

46 John Farey, Accounts and Memorandums, 1809–10 (WAC uncatalogued).

47 Prince Pückler-Muskau's description of the Chinese dairy quoted in Patrick Connor, *Oriental Architecture in the West*, London, Thames & Hudson, 1979, pp. 106–7.

48 Humphry Repton, *Fragments on the Theory and Practice of Landscape Gardening*, London, 1816, quoted in Daniels, *Humphry Repton*, p. 179.

49 Aspley Lodge was a house for the keeper at the Woburn Sands entrance to Aspley Wood. Stephen Daniels sums up the historic references the Reptons used: 'the design was made up of "some curious specimens of timber buildings", printed in *Archaeologia*, the journal of the Society of Antiquities ... The ornaments painted on posts and rails were taken from a portrait of Henry VIII ... [and] the design of the garden and the selection of flowers were taken from details in portraits in the gallery at Woburn' (Daniels, *Humphry Repton*, p. 181).

50 The Round House (*c*.1805), now with a single-storey extension; the Thornery (1808), recently restored; Aspley Lodge (1810), now screened by trees; and Ivy Lodge (1825), altered and extended.

51 Fortnightly Account Books (BLARS R5/1357 and 1358, 1834–5).

52 Fortnightly Account Books (BLARS R5/1357 and 1358, 1834–5).

53 This summary of the duke's interest in arboriculture and scientific methods is based on that by Smith, 'The Landed Estate as Patron of Scientific Innovation', p. 10.

54 Forbes, *Hortus Woburnensis*, 1833, pp. 245 and 242. The basis of this garden remains today and the area is known as the 'Duchess's Garden'. The water source for the fountain may well be the same spring around which the 'Temple in the Lady's Folly' was constructed in the time of the 4th Duke.

55 Forbes, *Hortus Woburnensis*, p. 287.

56 As the information board at the Maze explains, 'Although called a "Labyrinth" at the time of the 6th Duke, it is really a Maze': the difference being that a labyrinth should have only one path, while in a maze there are choices of pathway to be made.

57 Under Wyatville's direction, Richard Peake Nixon was paid 'for building a Chinese Temple' after a drawing by Sir William Chambers in his *Designs of Chinese Buildings*, 1757. See Account Book (BLARS R5/1127).

58 Quotations from Dr Allen Thomson's letters taken from WAC Ph MSS-35-10, 15, 16, 18 and 25. His plan of the Abbey pleasure grounds can be found in WAC Ph-MSS-35-10.

59 Lord Charles Russell (1807–1869), the duke and duchess's third child, was one of the local MPs for Bedfordshire and he and his wife, Isabella Clarissa Davies (d.1884), lived at what is now Bedford Lodge in Woburn. Thomson goes on to tell us that 'Lady Charles draws trees both in pencil and sepia in the very best style. The duchess knows a good deal about the art but does not execute much.' Lady Rachel Russell (1826–1898), the Bedfords' youngest child, went on to write historical romances. Thomson also mentions the prominent role Lord Charles played in the running of the estates at this time, a situation which elicited the following comment from Francis, Marquis of Tavistock to his brother George William: 'Charles has now management of everything; the shooting, stable department, and the invitations, and it is curious to see how completely he rules my father. He seems to do everything very well, with the exception of being a little too selfish and arbitrary' (Blakiston, *Woburn and the Russells*, p. 188). There were clearly still considerable tensions existing between the duke's three eldest sons, who had never lived at Woburn, and their stepbrothers and sisters of the 'Gordon crop'.

60 See map BLARS R1/238.

CHAPTER FOUR

1 Humphry Repton, *Hints, Plans and Sketches for the Improvement of Stonelands in Sussex*, 1805–6, a fourteen-page Red Book now in the

collection of the Beinecke Rare Book and Manuscript Library, Yale University, New Haven (GEN MSS VOL 221).

2 Jane Austen, *Mansfield Park* (1814), London, Oxford University Press, 1970, p. 188.

3 Humphry Repton, *Fragments on the Theory and Practice of Landscape Gardening*, 1816, quoted in Stephen Daniels, *Humphry Repton: Landscape Gardening and the Geography of Georgian England*, New Haven and London, Yale University Press, 1999, p. 178.

4 BLARS R5/1358: 1835–8.

5 The individuals around Francis, Marquis of Tavistock include Sir John Foster (1740–1824), Irish lawyer and MP and improving landowner; Rev. Bate Dudley, JP (1745–1824), known at this time for his determined suppression of anti-enclosure demonstrations in Essex – he also chronicled the life of Gainsborough; Sackville Tufton, Lord Thanet (1769–1825), Whig politician, Hereditary Sheriff of Westmoreland; and Dr Edmund Cartwright.

6 Diary of John, 6th Duke of Bedford, 1802, entry 26 January (WAC uncatalogued).

7 Anna Maria Stanhope (1783–1857) was the daughter of General Charles Stanhope, 3rd Earl of Harrington, and Jane Fleming. Her father served in the American Revolutionary War as aide-de-camp to General Burgoyne, seeing action at Saratoga, while her mother, Jane Fleming, was a Lady of the Bedchamber to George III's wife, Queen Charlotte of Mecklenburg-Strelitz, between 1794 and 1818. Interestingly enough, Charlotte was a keen amateur botanist who encouraged the development of Kew Gardens and worked with Capability Brown. 'Queen Charlotte ... was an avowed miniaturist, loving her botany and flower paintings, and eventually her private gardens at Frogmore, Windsor, where only her friends were allowed' (Jane Brown, *The Omnipotent Magician: Lancelot 'Capability' Brown 1716–1783*, London, Chatto & Windus, 2011, p. 154). Anna Maria's parents were noted for their 'sempiternal occupation of tea-drinking ... neither in Nankin, Pekin nor Canton was the teapot more assiduously and constantly replenished' (entry on Jane Stanhope, Countess Harrington, https://en.wikipedia.org/wiki/Jane_Stanhope,_Countess_of_Harrington, accessed February 2015).

8 Georgiana Blakiston, *Woburn and the Russells*, London, Constable, 1980, pp. 195, 196.

9 Three 'Pocket Books' survive, dating from her appointment as a lady-in-waiting to Queen Victoria in 1838, and while they are mostly concerned with her schedule for 'Waits' or 'Waiting', they also contain some details of family life. 'Waiting' seems to have consisted of a couple of weeks on duty, followed by a month or so off. While on duty, the ladies appear not to have left the queen's side either during the coronation, 'the most impressive ceremony possible', or in her subsequent life at Buckingham Palace and its schedule of balls, dinners and travels. Quotes in the text here are from 'The Coronet Pocket Book', 1838 (blue) and 'The Wreath' or 'Ladies Complete Pocket Book' for 1839 (red) (WAC HMC 110).

10 Blakiston, *Woburn and the Russells*, p. 196.

11 Repton's 'Minute for Mr Beauparke [?] respecting execution', signed H. Repton, 1809: a two-page letter, including three drawings, written it would seem in some haste, possibly as he was in his coach returning from a site visit. One drawing illustrates the arc of beds in front of the veranda, and specifies annual herbaceous plants, pots of geraniums, 'hedges of dwarf roses either with or without basket work', to be filled in with 'low plants, chiefly flowers and roses', while other beds should have 'taller shrubs – such as honeysuckles, lilacs, laburnums, portugal laurels, surrounded with dwarf roses'. A second drawing illustrates the small bridge constructed of 'one or two large flat stones to be laid on two upright stones' that is to carry to the path '3 feet wide as marked out by the stakes' that 'winds down to and across the Spring' and then follows the left bank of the brook. As to the entrance path, 'wherever the dug border can be of sufficient width to have flowers – it may be preserved – but where it is narrow as in the grass walk through the hollies, it will be better to carry the grass under the branches and leave no border' (private collection).

12 Although dated, this drawing – a plan and elevation of the structure – is unsigned. The dating, however, would suggest that it may be by Jeffry Wyatville, who was also busy at Woburn at this

time, and who went on to produce a design for alterations to the east front at Oakley in 1819 (WAC BE-P27, 'Design for Dairy', and WAC BE-P17–4, 'Elevation of East Front').

13 Blakiston, *Woburn and the Russells*, p. 196.

14 Quoted in Blakiston, *Woburn and the Russells*, p. 194.

15 Francis, 7th Duke of Bedford, *Plans and Elevations of Cottages for Agricultural Labourers, designed for and executed on the Duke of Bedford's Bedfordshire Estate: with Bills of Quantities of Materials Required in their Construction*, 2nd edn, 1860 (WAC WE – P829).

16 In Ridgemont, the school was added in 1854 by the 7th Duke, and the village itself was further expanded with new cottages built by the 11th Duke c.1910–11. These much severer red brick buildings, carrying the simple letter 'B', are easily distinguished from those built by Francis in the 1850s, since the front doors do not face the road, but rather are tucked round the side or at the back. This was because the 11th Duke did not wish to see families sitting around their front doors watching the world go by; this was, after all, the duke who gave strict orders that he was not to meet any of the indoor staff as he made his way along the corridors of the Abbey.

17 Tavistock estate cottages: the total of 300 included 170 built in five major terrace developments at Dolvin Road (1845), Westbridge (1850), Parkwood (1859), Fitzford (1862) and Trelawney Road (1866). Others were built at specific mine sites and at Morwellham Quay. For an overview of these cottages see the short film, 'Cornish Mining World Heritage Site – Tavistock and the Bedford Cottages', Cornish Mining, Youtube: https://www.youtube.com/watch?v=1qTr3XLq5Vc, accessed February 2015.

18 For her description of William Russell, Marquis of Tavistock and 8th Duke, and the quotation from his letter, see Blakiston, *Woburn and the Russells*, pp. 201–13.

19 The family photo albums start in the late 1850s (WAC), and it would seem that the two girls, particularly Ela, were both interested in this new medium. It is very possible that their interest was encouraged by their cousins at Weston Park, Lady Lucy and Lady Charlotte Bridgeman, who together became pioneering photographers. The family interest continued, particularly with Duchess Mary, wife of the 11th Duke, who filled a number of albums with shots of family life in India, Woburn, Scotland and Endsleigh.

20 Quoted in Blakiston, *Woburn and the Russells*, p. 211.

21 Elizabeth was 15 when she began keeping these diaries on 25 July 1834, and they run, with a few gaps, until 1876. The collection of volumes also includes her travel diary for a trip to Belgium, Germany and Holland in 1836–7 (WAC LOC31-8-5: 9th Duke of Bedford box containing '9th Duchess's Personal Diaries and Cash Account Books'). Elizabeth's father had been Lord of the Bedchamber to both George III and IV, and we are told in the diaries of her meetings with the 'princess'. In time she was to be a bridesmaid to Victoria when she married Prince Albert in 1840, before becoming the queen's Mistress of the Robes between 1880 and 1883.

22 Of this commission, Repton wrote: 'I have now the honour to deliver to your Lordship my opinion concerning the treatment of Stonelands, a Subject in which I have taken particular delight, from the beauty of the situation, from the style and character of the house which still bear the stamp of antiquity.'

23 Paris House was built for the Paris International Exhibition of 1878 by the architect Gilbert Redgrave; it was designed as an example of English vernacular architecture. Seen by the 9th Duke at the exhibition, he bought it and had it re-erected in the park at Woburn once the exhibition had ended. Used initially as staff quarters, it was converted during the First World War as part of the hospital facilities created at the Abbey by Mary, 11th Duchess, and leased to family friends after the war. During the Second World War it was requisitioned, along with the Abbey, by the secret services, as accommodation for a succession of staff members. Still standing today, it has been a restaurant since the 1980s, and the only reminders of its busy past are the intact air-raid shelter in the back garden and the Milton Gate behind it, which had provided access to the transmitter in Milton Bryan.

24 The conjoined estates of Buckhurst and Stonelands in East Sussex passed to Viscount Sackville, whose son's widow inherited the estates and married Lord Whitworth. Lord Whitworth engaged

Humphry Repton in 1805 to improve the landscape and house, and he produced the Red Book for 'Stonelands'. Lewis Kennedy was commissioned in 1819 to design new walks and a Swiss Bridge and improve the plantations. Following Lord Whitworth's death, Lady Whitworth amalgamated the two parks and called the new entity Buckhurst Park. When she died in 1826, the property passed to her daughter Elizabeth Sackville and Elizabeth's husband, George, 5th Earl de la Warr. Their eldest daughter, Elizabeth, was therefore 8 years old when her family took possession of the estate.

25 For further details and a list of site maps, see Bourn Hall, Cambridgeshire, Record Id: 493, parksandgardens.org, accessed 9 January 2015.
26 Christopher Trent, *The Russells*, London, Frederick Muller, 1966, p. 295.
27 John, Duke of Bedford, *A Silver-Plated Spoon* (1959), London, Sphere, 1967, p. 26. Other quotes pp. 14, 17 and 19.
28 Trent, *The Russells*, p. 291.
29 Richard Lydekker, FRS, FZS, 'The Duke of Bedford's Menagerie at Woburn Abbey', *The Zoologist*, no. 238, October 1896: archive.org/stream/zoologist1919lond/zoologist1919lond_djvu.txt (accessed December 2014).
30 Hastings, Duke of Bedford, *The Years of Transition*, London, Andrew Dakers, 1949, p. 241.
31 A vivid account of the hangar and airstrip at Woburn comes from Audrey Taylor in 'The Moth – Enterprise No. 108', *Quarterly Journal of the de Havilland Moth Club*, from www.airfieldinformationexchange.org/community/showthread.php?8088-Woburn-park, accessed July 2014.
32 Secret service staff at Woburn from 1940 eventually included staff from SIS (Secret Intelligence Services), SOE (Special Operations Executive), PWD (Psychological Warfare Division) and PID (Political Intelligence Department), but most were from PWE (Political Warfare Executive). For a detailed and personal account of the formation and work of PWE, see Dennis Sefton-Delmer, *Black Boomerang: An Autobiography*, vol. 2, London, Secker and Warburg, 1962. Sefton-Delmer was recruited in 1940 and ran the PWE operation at Woburn until, as he puts it, 'we just disappeared' in 1945. All quotations unless otherwise specified are from this source.
33 Information on the connections between Bletchley Park and Woburn Abbey and material from the Bletchley Park Oral History Project supplied in conversation with Jonathan Byrne, Bletchley Park Oral History Officer. Eyewitness accounts from Wrens billeted at Woburn Abbey are from the Bletchley Park Oral History Project unless credited otherwise (in order): Betty Warwick, née Boyd; Marigold Freeman-Attwood, née Philips; Margaret O'Connell, quoted by Joanne Riley in 'The Women Who Cracked Hitler's Code: Bletchley Park Wrens Reveal their Secrets', Express newspapers website (http://www.express.co.uk/news/uk/459896/The-women-who-cracked-Hitler-s-code-Bletchley-Park-Wrens-reveal-their-secrets, accessed 28 January 2015); Lorna Cockayne; Margaret Mortimer, née Broughton-Thompson; Jean Tocher; Joan Scoot, née Lawrence.
34 Chris Gravett, 'Woburn and D-Day: The Invasion of Normandy', Woburn Abbey website: www.woburnabbey.co.uk/abbey/abbey-today/blog/d-day/, accessed January 2015.
35 Lettice Curtis, 'The ATA Angle'. Lettice Curtis was one of the women pilots of the Air Transport Auxiliary (ATA) and remembers flying in and out of Woburn. Curtis is quoted in an exchange of postings on www.airfieldinformationexchange.org/community/showthread.php?8088-Woburn-Park. The full quote provides a useful account of these operations. She says that at Woburn 'aircraft were prepared for towing gliders for use in the invasion of France. Flights in and out of satellites were normally undertaken by MU pilots but in the run-up to D-Day, because of the pressure of work, ATA's No. 1 Ferry Pool at White Waltham (Maidenhead) were called in to help. The strip at Woburn ran slightly uphill ... during 1944 at Woburn, Stirlings were fitted with yokes and release gear for towing gliders ... Before D-Day some 200 Stirlings are said to have been stored there under the trees. 25 were on ½ hour alert and another 50 on 1 hour alert for delivery to operational squadrons.'
36 Hastings, Duke of Bedford, *The Years of Transition*, p. 196.
37 Louisa Crommelin Roberta Jowitt Whitwell (1893–1960). Hastings and Louisa married in 1914 and had three children: John (known as Ian), who became 13th Duke, Daphne (1920–1991) and Hugh (1923–2005). Louisa was the daughter of Robert Jowitt Whitwell, a medievalist at Oxford, which is where she met Hastings when he studied history there. Her life and interests are largely unrecorded, and after separation from the duke, she died a widow in Hastings in Sussex, never having lived in or had much to do with Woburn Abbey at all.
38 Hastings, Duke of Bedford, *The Years of Transition*, p. 198.
39 John, Duke of Bedford, *A Silver-Plated Spoon*, p. 137. A confirmed pacifist (one of the main reasons behind his estrangement from his father), Hastings had been heavily involved in politics and the appeasement movement in the 1930s. It did not help that he found allies in this cause in some of the more extreme right-wing parties, and attempted his own peace negotiations with the Germans in Dublin in 1940, by which time he was considered to be a considerable security risk. MI5 concluded that he held such pro-German views that, in the event of an invasion and his falling into enemy hands, he would be likely to accept a post as a gauleiter or even the head of a puppet government; certainly, he was never going to be allowed anywhere near the Abbey.
40 The demolition of the riding house and tennis court: it would appear that there may have been a fault in Holland's designs for these buildings, since the roofs had required extensive repairs in the 5th Duke's time and then had to be completely replaced by the 6th Duke. Continuing problems with the roofs, in addition to the cost of post-war refurbishment of the interiors (both buildings had been stripped out and divided up into offices), may well have sealed their fate.
41 Between 1945 and 1955, over 400 large country houses were demolished, their post-war owners either unable, or unwilling, to undertake the restoration of buildings that had been requisitioned during the war or left empty. Grants for restoration became available following the Gower Report, enabling a number of properties to make essential repairs, while the National Trust provided a means by which the families could remain in their homes as tenants and the house opened to the public. By 1960, by one of these means or another, nearly 600 houses and grounds were open to the public, with places like Chatsworth and Woburn receiving five to six hundred thousand visitors annually. Beyond this, during this period, as one commentator has put it, 'The reinvention of the purpose of the aristocracy was taking place, aristocrats as guardians of our national heritage.' Quotation and figures from 'The Aristocracy: Letting in the Hoi Polloi, 1945–70', TV documentary produced and directed by Rachel Bell, BBC Bristol, 1997. Focusing on the stories of Gosford in East Lothian and Ragley Hall, Worcs, this documentary has a short piece of footage of Woburn, the duke as main salesman and some of the attractions.
42 John, Duke of Bedford, *A Silver-Plated Spoon*, pp. 168, 164. John Ian Russell (1917–2002) worked as a rent collector in east London and a reporter for the Express newspapers. After his marriage to Lydia Yarde-Buller in 1947, the couple moved to South Africa. Here they ran a successful fruit farm, until his father's death caused his return to England in 1953. As Duke of Bedford he wrote four books: *A Silver-Plated Spoon* (1959), *The Duke of Bedford's Book of Snobs* (1965), *The Flying Duchess* (1968), and *How to Run a Stately Home* (1971). After retiring from Woburn in 1973, he and his third wife, Nicole, were based in Monaco and travelled widely.
43 Clare Holway (1903–1945) married Ian in 1939 and they had two children: Henry Robin Ian Russell, 14th Duke of Bedford (1940–2003), and Lord Rudolf Russell (b.1944).
44 Lydia Yarde-Buller, née Lyle (1917–2006), married 1947, divorced 1960, one son, Lord Francis Russell (b.1950).
45 John, Duke of Bedford, *A Silver-Plated Spoon*, pp. 161, 166.
46 Living at Woburn from 1954, Denise's children witnessed the whole process of the Abbey and attractions being opened, as well as having the run of the park and the Evergreens. The author would like to thank Hon. Richard Grosvenor and Lady Kiloran Grosvenor for answering questions and sharing their memories of those times.

47 John, Duke of Bedford, *A Silver-Plated Spoon*, p. 193.
48 John, Duke of Bedford, *A Silver-Plated Spoon*, pp. 188, 174.
49 John, Duke of Bedford, *A Silver-Plated Spoon*, p. 188.
50 Nicole Milinaire (1920–2012) was born in Paris and had four children by her previous marriage. With a background in film production, she proved the perfect match for Ian's flair for publicity, and between them Woburn became an international tourist destination.
51 Hosted by John Peel, the 'Festival of Flower Children' was one of the earliest festivals organized outside London and featured Jimi Hendrix, Tomorrow, Jeff Beck Group and the Small Faces. In keeping with the theme it opened with a balloon flying over from which flowers were scattered on to the park below.
52 Ray Barratt and the Woburn Park Zoo: the account given here and the quotations from Barratt are based on and taken from an undated interview with Barratt that features online at blooloop.com/features/ray-barratt (accessed July 2014). It has not been possible to ascertain any further information on the circumstances of this interview in order to provide further acknowledgement or accreditation.
53 Plan for 'Woburn Park Zoo', *c*.1968, Draft Map C (amended), Proposed Phases 1 and 2 (WAC WSP/P61).
54 From these first waterfalls at Woburn, Anthony Archer-Wills has gone on to work in the UK, Europe and USA. He lectures widely and is the author of a number of books on water and designing with it. More recently, he and his work have featured in 'The Pool Master' series for the Discovery Channel. This account of his work at Woburn was related in conversation with the author, May 2014. The main fall survived intact until 2014, when it was replaced by an arrangement of artificial rocks, but the watercourse down the hill survives, its intricate falls and pools providing a glimpse of how innovative this design was. No doubt its future depends as much on modern Health and Safety regulations as anything else. Barratt left Woburn when the duke and duchess decided to retire, and went to work for Wild Animal Kingdoms Ltd developing safari parks worldwide, before working with the Tussauds Group, Alton Towers and Chessington Zoo.

Anthony Archer-Wills joined Peter Barker in the Highlands where they helped build the Loch Lomond Bear Park between 1971 and 1972, and went on to work on East Midlands Safari Park at Bewdley, before concentrating on his private practice. Other parks that opened were Stapleford Lion Reserve, 1968, and Lowther Wildlife Park, 1969. It was a busy time for this first generation of managers, engineers and designers as this style of attraction caught on.
55 After living with his father in South Africa, Robin studied at Harvard University before becoming a stockbroker based in London. He married childhood friend Henrietta Tiarks in 1961, and was still working in the City when his father handed over management of Woburn and the Bedford estates to him in 1973.
56 Details of the dates and contents of the work carried out on the estate and at the Abbey during the period between 1978 and 2002, along with personal recollections, have been generously supplied by Harold Avis, Estate Property Manager, and Mike Cox, Head Gardener, both now retired.
57 Henrietta, Dowager Duchess, in conversation with the author, August 2014.
58 Andrew, Duke of Bedford, writing about his father in *Woburn Abbey* guidebook, Norwich, Jarrold Publishing, 2013, p. 65.
59 Of Mrs Moss's fifteen foals, 'twelve were winners, including Pushy (winner of the Queen Mary Stakes at Royal Ascot and the Cornwallis Stakes), Precocious (the unbeaten winner of five races, including the Gimcrack, Norfolk, Molecomb and National Stakes) and Jupiter Island (winner of fourteen races, including the Japan Cup).' See *Woburn Abbey* guidebook, p. 62.
60 Produced by Nigel Farrell for BBC2: twenty-nine episodes over three series 1999–2004.
61 'The Aristocracy: Letting in the Hoi Polloi, 1945–1970'.
62 For information on this period of activity at Woburn the author would like to thank Harold Avis, Estate Property Manager from 1985.
63 *Woburn Abbey: History and Treasures*, Norwich, Jarrold Publishing, 1967, Introduction (WAC WSP-20) .

SELECT BIBLIOGRAPHY

Andrews, C. Bruyn, ed., *The Torrington Diaries, 1781–94*, 4 vols, London, Methuen & Co. Ltd, 1970
Batchelor, T., *A General View of the Agriculture of Bedfordshire*, London, 1813
Bedford, Nicole, Duchess of, *Nicole Nobody: The Autobiography of the Duchess of Bedford*, London and New York, W. H. Allen, 1974
Beevers, David, ed., *Chinese Whispers: Chinoiserie in Britain, 1650–1930*, catalogue of exhibition held at Brighton Museum & Art Gallery and the Royal Pavilion, 2008
Blakiston, Georgiana, *Woburn and the Russells*, London, Constable, 1980
Bray, William, ed., *The Diary of John Evelyn*, London, Chandos Classics, Frederick Warne & Sons, n.d.
Brown, David, 'Reassessing the Influence of the Aristocratic Improver: The Example of the Fifth Duke of Bedford (1765–1802)', *Agricultural History Review*, 47: 2, 1999, pp. 182–95 (British Agricultural History Society, www.bahs.org.uk, accessed 7 November 2014)
Brown, Jane, *The Omnipotent Magician: Lancelot 'Capability' Brown, 1716–1783*, London, Chatto & Windus, 2011
Colvin, Howard, *A Biographical Dictionary of British Architects, 1600–1840*, 2nd edn, London, John Murray, 1978
Connor, Patrick, *Oriental Architecture in the West*, London, Thames & Hudson, 1979
Daniels, Stephen, *Humphrey Repton: Landscape Gardening and the Geography of Georgian England*, New Haven and London, Yale University Press, 1999
Delmer, Dennis Sefton, *Black Boomerang: An Autobiography*, vol. 2, London, Secker and Warburg, 1962
Draper, Marie, 'The Houses of the Russell Family', *Apollo*, CXXVII: 316 (new series), June 1988, pp. 387–92

Duggan, Dianne, '"London the Ring, Covent Garden the Jewel of that Ring": New Light on Covent Garden', *Architectural History*, 43, 2000, pp. 140–61
—, 'The Russells of Corney House', *Brentford & Chiswick Local History Journal*, 9, 2000
—, 'The Architectural Patronage of the 4th Earl of Bedford, 1587–1641', PhD thesis, University of London, 2001 (Woburn Abbey Archives)
—, 'The Fourth Side of Covent Garden Piazza: New Light on the History and Significance of Bedford House', *British Art Journal*, III: 3, 2002, pp. 53–65
—, 'Woburn Abbey: The First Episode of a Great Country House,' *Architectural History*, 46, 2003, pp. 57–80
—, 'Isaac de Caus: Surveyor, Grotto and Garden Designer', *Studies in the History of Gardens and Designed Landscapes*, 29: 3, 2009, pp. 152–68
Dunbar, John G., *Scottish Royal Palaces*, East Linton, Tuckwell Press, 1999
Fiennes, Celia, *The Journeys of Celia Fiennes*, ed. Christopher Morris, London, Cresset Press, 1947
Gotch, J. A., *Early Renaissance Architecture in England*, London, Batsford, 1901
Hadfield, Miles et al., *British Gardeners: A Biographical Dictionary*, London, A. Zwemmer in association with Condé Nast Publications, 1980
Harris, John, *The Artist and the Country House*, London, Philip Wilson Publishers for Sotheby Parke Bernet, 1979
—, *The Artist and the Country House from the Fifteenth Century to the Present Day*, exhibition catalogue, London, Sotheby's, 1995

Harris, John, Stephen Orgel, and Roy Strong, *The King's Arcadia: Inigo Jones and the Stuart Court*, exhibition catalogue, London, Arts Council of Great Britain, 1973

Harris, Oliver, 'Nyn Hall, Hertfordshire: An Alternative History', *Hertfordshire Archaeology*, 13, 1997–2003, pp. 99–100

Hastings, 12th Duke of Bedford, *The Years of Transition*, London, Andrew Dakers, 1949

Henderson, Paula, *The Tudor House and Garden*, New Haven and London, Yale University Press, 2005

Hunt, John Dixon, *Garden and Grove*, Princeton, N.J., Princeton University Press, 1986

—, ed., *The Dutch Garden in the Seventeenth Century*, Washington, D.C., Dumbarton Oaks, 1990

—, *The Picturesque Garden in Europe*, London, Thames & Hudson, 2002

Hunt, John Dixon, and Peter Willis, eds, *The Genius of the Place: The English Landscape Garden 1620–1820*, Cambridge, Mass., MIT Press, 1988

John, Duke of Bedford, *A Silver Plated Spoon*, London, Sphere, 1967

Lawson, Lesley, *Out of the Shadows: The Life of Lucy, Countess of Bedford*, London and New York, Hambledon Continuum, 2007

Lewalski, Barbara K., 'Lucy, Countess of Bedford: Images of a Jacobean Courtier and Patroness', in *Politics of Discourse: The Literature and History of Seventeenth-Century England*, ed. Kevin Sharpe and Stephen N. Zwicker, Berkeley, University of California Press, 1987

Linstrum, Derek, *Sir Jeffrey Wyattville: Architect to the King*, Oxford, Clarendon Press, 1972

Mowl, Timothy, *Gentlemen Gardeners: The Men Who Created the English Landscape Garden*, Stroud, History Press, 2010

Myers, Katherine, ed., *The Gardens of Wanstead*, London, London Parks and Gardens Trust, 2003

Scott Thomson, Gladys, *The Russells in Bloomsbury 1669–1771*, London, Jonathan Cape, 1940

—, ed., *Letters of a Grandmother 1732–35*, London, Jonathan Cape, 1943

—, *Family Background*, London, Jonathan Cape, 1949

—, *Life in a Noble Household*, London, Jonathan Cape, 1950.

Strong, Roy, *The Renaissance Garden in England*, London, Thames & Hudson, 1998

Stroud, Dorothy, *Humphry Repton*, London, Country Life, 1962

Trent, Christopher, *The Russells*, London, Frederick Muller, 1966

Webb, Rev. John, *Memorials of the History of the Civil War in Herefordshire*, 2 vols, London, Longmans, Green & Co., 1879

Wiffen, J. H., *Historical Memoirs of the House of Russell*, 2 vols, London, Longman, 1833

Winchester, Simon, *The Map that Changed the World*, Harmondsworth, Penguin, 2002

Wright, A. P. M., and Lewis C. P., eds, *A History of the County of Cambridgeshire and the Isle of Ely, Volume 9*, Oxford, Oxford University Press, 1989

INDEX

NOTE: Page numbers in **bold** refer to captions to illustrations

PHOTOGRAPHIC ACKNOWLEDGMENTS

With the exception of those listed below, all the photographs and illustrations in this book form part of the Woburn Abbey Collection and are reproduced by permission of His Grace, The Duke of Bedford and the Trustees of the Bedford Estates.

Author: 29, bottom; 92; 106, bottom right; 121, bottom; 126, top right; 131, bottom; 153; 162; 179; 184; 195; 209, bottom

For permission to reproduce the images listed below, the publishers wish to thank:

Anthony Archer-Wills: 209, top right & top far right

Peter Beadle ONZM: 214

Bedfordshire Archive Service (Russell Collection): 115; 117, top left; 118, left & right; 126, top left, top centre, bottom left & bottom centre

Beinecke Library, Yale University: 182, Pl. I, II; 183, PL. III, IVa, IVb

Berkeley Castle: 53, top

© The British Library Board, Add.MS.32467. fol.242: 28, above

Bridget Davey: jacket, front; 10; 48, top & bottom; 138; 150; 193; 212; 215; 216; 217; 218; 221; 222, top & bottom; 223, top & bottom; 225

© The Trustees of the British Museum: 36; 62; 131

Bodleian Library, University of Oxford (Gough Maps 30, fol. 63b): 53, bottom

By courtesy of Essex Record Office: 72

Hampshire Record Office, Ref: 92M95/F8/5/1: 70, top & bottom

Museum of London: 30

National Library of Scotland: 174, bottom right; 190

Northamptonshire Record Office: 29, top left

Private Collections: 82; 83; 107; 126; 149, top right

Private Collection/Bridgeman Images: 67

RIBA Collections: 33

Stapleton Collection: 174, bottom left

© Victoria & Albert Museum, London: 37

The publishers have made every effort to contact holders of copyright works. Any copyright holders we have been unable to reach are invited to contact the publishers so that a full acknowledgment may be given in subsequent editions.

AUTHOR'S ACKNOWLEDGMENTS

Thanks go out to the many people who have made working on this book such an interesting and enjoyable experience.

At Woburn, to Their Graces, the Duke and Duchess of Bedford, for their support and encouragement and to Her Grace, the Dowager Duchess of Bedford, for her help and memories. Particular thanks go to Robin Russell for first showing me the Repton Red Books, and for his enthusiasm and shared interest over the years of research that have followed.

In addition I would like to thank all those in the house and grounds of the Abbey and in the offices of the Bedford Estates who have helped in one way or another, and specifically those who have helped with their time and expertise to unravel the story of the landscapes at Woburn. These include Martin Towsey and Andrew Grout in the gardens, Nicola Allen and Andrew Mitchell in the archives, and Chris Gravett, Victoria Poulson and Dave Garrard in the curator's office. Thanks also to Ann Mitchell for her help and encouragement over the years while she was archivist, and for correcting those errors that have crept into the manuscript. Thank you too to Harold Avis and Mike Cox for vivid eyewitness accounts of their time at the Abbey, and Richard and Kiloran Grosvenor for their memories of

Woburn in the years it was first opened to the public. For all their help over the past few years, thanks also to Freya Whitney and Kim Wilkinson.

Beyond Woburn, thanks go to Helen Costello and Simon Woods, to David Stride and family, Martin Witherington, Beverley Murphy, and Susan Lousada for their time and interest, and to the staff at Bedford and Luton Records Office and Northamptonshire Records Office. Thanks also to Jonathan Byrne, Oral History Officer at Bletchley Park, for his expertise and help, and to all the former Wrens who have shared their memories with the Bletchley Park Oral History Project.

Thanks also to Jo Christian and everyone at Pimpernel Press, to Becky Clarke, Nancy Marten and Sue Gladstone, to Douglas Matthews for the index, to Bridget Davey for some wonderful photography, and to Jas Davidson for the maps, the Russell family tree and his help with many of the images.

Finally, many thanks to Jonathan and Sylvia Leiserach, Basil Postan and my wife, Linda Crockett, for helping make this book happen.